A VO.

TO THE
WEST COAST OF COREA,
AND
THE GREAT LOO-CHOO ISLAND

BY CAPTAIN BASIL HALL

PREFACE.

The following work contains a Narrative of the Voyage to the West Coast of Corea, and the Great Loo-choo Island; an Appendix, containing Nautical details; and a Vocabulary of the Language spoken at Loo-choo.

In drawing up the Narrative from journals written at the time, I have derived great assistance from notes made by Lieutenant H.J. Clifford, of the Navy. This officer obtained permission from the Admiralty to accompany me, though on half pay, and having no specific duty to perform, he was enabled to devote himself entirely to the acquisition of knowledge; and had it in his power to record many interesting occurrences of the voyage, which the numerous duties of my station left me but little leisure to observe or describe.

All the Charts, Tables, and Nautical Notices have been placed in an Appendix, in order to avoid the interruption which such details are apt to occasion when inserted in a journal; and the Nautical reader will perhaps consider it advantageous, to have this part of the subject set apart, and condensed, instead of being scattered over the pages of the narrative.

I am indebted to Mr. Clifford for very important assistance in collecting and arranging the materials which form this Appendix.

The northern part of the Chart of the Yellow Sea, given in the Appendix, was taken from a Chart by Captain Daniel Ross, of the Bombay marine, the scientific and able surveyor commanding the squadron which the Honourable East India Company, in the spirit of a liberal and enlarged policy, have employed for upwards of nine years, in surveying the China Seas.

The Vocabulary is exclusively compiled by Mr. Clifford, who took the greatest pains to collect words and sentences in common use; and though, from the shortness of our stay, this part of the work is necessarily incomplete, it is hoped that a future voyager will derive considerable assistance from it, in his intercourse with the natives.

The drawings of scenery and costume were made by Mr. William Havell, the eminent artist who accompanied the Embassy, from sketches taken on the spot, by Mr. C.W. Browne, midshipman of the Alceste, and myself.

Nothing respecting the west side of Corea has hitherto been accurately known to Europeans. The coast laid down in most Charts has been taken from the celebrated map of the Jesuits, which is very correct in what relates to China, but erroneous with respect to Corea. The Jesuits, indeed, did not survey this country, but have inserted it in their map, I believe, from Japanese authorities.

Captain Broughton in his voyage to the North Pacific Ocean visited the South Coast of Corea, and his account of the inhabitants agrees with ours in most particulars.

The same distinguished voyager visited the Great Loo-choo Island in 1797, after having been shipwrecked near Typinsan, one of its dependant islands. He was at Napakiang for a few days, and his account of the natives is highly interesting.

There is an article by Pere Gaubil, a missionary, on the subject of the Loo-choo Islands, in the 23d vol. of the "Lettres Edifiantes et Curieuses." It is a translation from the official report of a Chinese embassador sent to Loo-choo by the Emperor Kang Hi; our opportunities, however, were not sufficient to enable us to judge of the accuracy of this curious memoir.

CHAPTER I.

H.M.S. Alceste and Lyra leave the Yellow Sea on a Voyage of Discovery—Sir James Hall's Group on the Coast of Corea—Unsociable Character of the Natives—Hutton's Island—Interesting geological Structure—Anchor near the Main Land—Corean Chiefs Visit—Objections made to Strangers landing—Distress of the Chief—His Character—Departure from Basil's Bay—Clusters of Islands—Murray's Sound—Deserted Corean Village—View from the Summit of a high Peak—Interview with the Coreans—Peculiarities of their Character—Language—Erroneous geographical Position of this Coast—Leave Corea.

The embassy to China, under the Right Honourable Lord Amherst, left England in his Majesty's frigate Alceste, Captain Murray Maxwell, C.B., on the 9th of February, 1816, and landed near the mouth of the Pei-ho river, in the Yellow Sea, on the 9th of August. Shortly afterwards the Alceste and Lyra sloop of war, which had accompanied the embassy, proceeded to the coast of Corea, the eastern boundary of the Yellow Sea; for as these ships were not required in China before the return of the Embassador by land to Canton, it was determined to devote the interval to an examination of some places in those seas, of which little or no precise information then existed. The following pages give the details of this voyage.

1st of September.—This morning at daylight the land of Corea was seen in the eastern quarter. Having stood towards it, we were at nine o'clock near three high islands, differing in appearance from the country we had left, being wooded to the top, and cultivated in the lower parts, but not in horizontal terraces as at the places we had last visited in China. We proceeded to the southward of the group, and anchored in a fine bay at the distance of two or three miles from the southern island. Shortly after anchoring, a boat came from the shore with five or six natives, who stopped, when within fifty yards of the brig, and looking at us with an air of curiosity and distrust, paid no attention to the signs which were made to induce them to come alongside. They expressed no alarm when we went to them in our boat; and on our rowing towards the shore, followed us till we landed near a village. The inhabitants came in a body to meet us, forming an odd assemblage, different in many respects from any thing we had seen; their colour was a deep copper, and their appearance forbidding, and somewhat savage. Some men, who appeared to be superior to the rest, were distinguished by a hat, the brim of which was nearly three feet in diameter, and the crown, which was about nine inches high, and scarcely large enough to admit the top of the head, was shaped like a sugar-loaf with the end cut off. The texture of this strange hat is of a fine open work like the dragon-fly's wing; it appears to be made of horse-hair varnished over, and is fastened under the chin by a band strung with large beads, mostly black and white, but occasionally red or yellow. Some of the elderly men wore stiff gauze caps over their hair, which was formed into a high conical knot on the top of the head. Their dress consisted of loose wide trowsers, and a sort of frock reaching nearly to the knee, made of a coarse open grass cloth, and on their feet neat straw sandals. They were of the middle size, remarkably well made, and robust looking. At first they expressed some surprise on examining our clothes, but afterwards took very little interest in any thing belonging to us. Their chief anxiety was to get rid of us as soon as possible. This they expressed in a manner too obvious to be mistaken; for, on our wishing to enter the village, they first made motions for us to go the other way; and when we persevered, they took us kindly by the arms and pushed us off. Being very desirous to conciliate them, we shewed no impatience at this treatment; but our forbearance had no effect; and after a number of vain attempts to make ourselves understood, we went away not much pleased at their behaviour. A Chinese[1], who accompanied us, was of no use, for he could not read what the Coreans wrote for him, though in the Chinese character; and of their spoken language he did not understand a word.

On leaving these unsociable villagers, we went to the top of the highest peak on the island, the ascent being easy by a winding foot-path. From this elevation we saw a number of islands to the eastward, and the main land at a great distance beyond them. The top of the hill being covered with soft grass and sweet-smelling shrubs, and the air, which had been of a suffocating heat below, being here cool and refreshing, we were tempted to sit down to our pic-nic dinner. We returned by the other side of the hill; but there being no path, and the surface rocky and steep, and covered with a thick brushwood, we were not a little scratched and bruised before we reached a road which runs along the north face of the hill about midway. By following this, we came to a spot from whence we were enabled to look down upon the village, without being ourselves perceived by the natives. The women, who had deserted the village on our landing, had now returned; most of them were beating rice in wooden mortars, and they had all children tied on their backs. On a sudden they quitted their work and ran off to their huts, like rabbits in a warren; and in a few minutes we saw one of the ship's boats row round the point of land adjacent to the village, which explained the cause of their alarm. After remaining for some time in expectation of seeing the women again, we came down to the village, which the natives now permitted us to pass through. On this occasion one of the gentlemen of our party saw, for an instant, a woman at no great distance, whose feet he declared were of the natural size, and not cramped as in China. The village consists of forty houses rudely constructed of reeds plaistered with mud, the roofs are of all shapes, and badly thatched with reeds and straw, tied down by straw ropes. These huts are not disposed in streets, but are scattered about without order, and without any neatness, or cleanliness, and the spaces between them are occupied by piles of dirt and pools of muddy water. The valley in which this comfortless village is situated is, however, pretty enough, though not wooded; the hills forming it are of an irregular shape, and covered at top with grass and sweet-scented flowers; the lower parts are cultivated with millet, buckwheat, a kind of French bean, and tobacco, which last grows in great quantity; and here and there is a young oak-tree.

We saw bullocks and poultry, but the natives would not exchange them for our money, or for any thing we had to offer. They refused dollars when offered as a present, and, indeed, appeared to set no value upon any thing we shewed them, except wine glasses; but even these they were unwilling to receive. One of the head men appeared particularly pleased with a glass, which, after a good deal of persuasion, he accepted, but, in about five minutes after, he, and another man to whom a tumbler had been given, came back and insisted upon returning the presents; and then, without waiting for further persuasion, returned to the village, leaving with us only one man, who, as soon as all the rest were out of sight, accepted one of the glasses with much eagerness.

These people have a proud sort of carriage, with an air of composure and indifference about them, and an absence of curiosity which struck us as being very remarkable. Sometimes when we succeeded, by dint of signs and drawings, in expressing the nature of a question, they treated it with derision and insolence. On one occasion, being anxious to buy a clumsy sort of rake made of reeds, which appeared to me curious, I succeeded in explaining my wish to the owner, one of the lowest class of villagers; he laughed at first good humouredly, but immediately afterwards seized the rake which was in my hand, and gave it a rude push towards me with a disdainful fling of the arm, accompanying this gesticulation by words, which seemed to imply a desire to give any thing upon condition of our going away. One man expressed the general wish for our departure, by holding up a piece of paper like a sail, and then blowing upon it in the direction of the wind, at the same time pointing to the ships, thereby denoting that the wind was fair, and that we had only to set sail and leave the island. Several of the people were marked with the small-pox. The children kept out of our reach at first, but before we went away, their fears had, in some degree, subsided, for the boys, who, from their feminine appearance, were mistaken at first for girls, accompanied us to some distance from the village.

Captain Maxwell named these islands Sir James Hall's group, in compliment to the President of the Royal Society of Edinburgh. They lie in longitude 124° 46' E. and latitude 37° 50' N.

At eight o'clock in the evening we weighed and stood to the southward, but as the coast was quite unknown, we kept rather off shore during the night, and in the morning no land was in sight. On the 2d we stood to the eastward, but not having daylight enough to get in with the coast, it became necessary to anchor for the night, though in deep water.

3d of September.—Having reached nearly lat. 36-1/3 N. and long. 126 E. we sailed this morning amongst a range of islands extending as far as the eye could reach, both to the southward and northward, at the distance of six or seven leagues from the main land. By two o'clock we were close to the outer cluster of the islands, and the passages appearing clear between them, we sailed through and anchored inside. While passing one of these islands in the ships, at no great distance, it looked so curiously formed, that, on anchoring, we went in the boats to examine its structure more minutely[2]. While we were thus engaged, the natives had assembled in a crowd on the edge of the cliff above us; they did not seem pleased with our occupation of breaking their rocks, for, from the moment we landed, they never ceased to indicate by shouts, screams, and all kinds of gesticulations, that the sooner we quitted the island the better; the cliff being 200 feet high, and nearly perpendicular, it was fortunate for us that they confined themselves to signs and clamour, and did not think of enforcing their wishes by a shower of stones.

As soon as we had completed our investigation of this spot, we went round in the boats to a small bay where there was good landing. Here we were met by the natives, who addressed several long speeches to us in a very loud tone of voice; to which we replied in English, that our wish was merely to look at the island, without interfering with any body; at the same time we proceeded up a foot-path to the brow of a hill. This the natives did not seem at all to relish, and they made use of a sign which was sufficiently expressive of their anxiety, though we could not determine exactly to whom it referred. They drew their fans across their own throats, and sometimes across ours, as if to signify that our going on would lead to heads being cut off; but whether they or we were to be the sufferers was not apparent. It was suggested by one of our party that they dreaded being called to account by their own chiefs for permitting us to land. All these signs, however, did not prevent our advancing till we had reached the brow of the hill to which the path led; from this place we had a view of a village at the distance of half a mile, of a much better appearance than that above described. Trees were interspersed among the houses, which were pleasantly situated at the bottom of a little cove, with fishing-boats at anchor near it. We explained readily enough that our wish was to go to the village, but it was all in vain, for their anxiety increased every moment, and we desisted from any further attempts to advance.

The dress of these people is a loose white robe, cloth shoes, and a few wear the broad hats before described; by most the hair is tied in a high conical knot on the top of the head, but by others it is allowed to fly loose, so as to give them a wild appearance. Some confine the short hair by a small gauze band with a star on one side, forming, along with the top knot, rather a becoming head-dress. Their beards and whiskers which, apparently, had never been cut, and their fans and long tobacco-pipes, and their strange language and manners, gave a grotesque air to the whole group, which it is impossible to describe. They crowded about us, and, by repeated shouts, manifested their surprise at the form and texture of our clothes; but on a watch being shewn, they disregarded every thing else, and entreated to be allowed to examine it closely. It was evidently the first they had seen, and some of them while watching the second-hand, looked as if they thought it alive. From the watch they proceeded to examine the seals and keys; with the former they shewed themselves acquainted by pressing them on their hands, so as to cause an impression. Their attention was drawn away from the watch by our firing a musket, which made the whole party fall back several paces.

After amusing ourselves in this manner for some time, we walked back to the boats, to the great joy of the natives, who encouraged us by all means to hasten our departure. They took our hands and helped us over the slippery stones on the beach; and, on perceiving one of the boats aground, several of them stript and jumped into the water to push her off. This gave us an opportunity of observing their remarkable symmetry and firmness of limb; yet, as their long hair was allowed to flow about their neck and shoulders, their appearance was truly savage. During this visit we saw no women; but the children came round us without shewing any symptoms of fear. The people, upon the whole, are more free, and not so surly as our acquaintance on Sir James Hall's group. They have a singular custom of speaking with a loud tone, amounting almost to a shout. Captain Maxwell named this island after Dr. Hutton the geologist.

4th of September.—During all last night it remained perfectly calm. At nine o'clock in the morning we got under weigh with a fine sea breeze, and stood in for the land, leaving on either hand many well cultivated islands. The main land seems to be populous, from the number of large villages which we passed, and the cultivation which extends a considerable way up the mountains. Our object this morning was to discover some safe anchoring place in the main land, but we were obliged to coast along for a considerable distance before any opening appeared. About three o'clock we sailed round a point of land and discovered a bay, which, at first sight, promised shelter, but the water proved too shallow even for the Lyra, and we anchored far out in five fathoms. The natives who had assembled in crowds on the point shouted to us as we passed, in seeming anger at our approaching so near. This bay is about four miles in diameter, and is skirted by large villages built amongst trees, and surrounded by cultivated districts, forming altogether a scene of considerable beauty.

As soon as the Alceste had anchored, Captain Maxwell, Mr. Clifford, and I, went towards the nearest village in the bay. On approaching the shore we observed a great bustle among the inhabitants on the shore, as well as in the boats at anchor off the village. The people on the beach hastily jumped into canoes, whilst those in the large boats weighed the anchors, and pulled out with such expedition, as to meet us in a body before we were near the landing-place. Every boat was crowded with people, and ornamented with numerous flags and streamers; but one of them being distinguished by a large blue umbrella, we steered towards it, on the supposition that this was an emblem of rank; in which opinion we were soon confirmed by the sound of music, which played only on board this boat. On coming closer, we saw a fine patriarchal figure seated under the umbrella; his full white beard covered his breast, and reached below his middle; his robe or mantle, which was of blue silk, and of an immense size, flowed about him in a magnificent style. His sword was suspended from his waist by a small belt, but the insignia of his office appeared to be a slender black rod tipped with silver, about a foot and a half long, with a small leather thong at one end, and a piece of black crape tied to the other: this he held in his hand. His hat exceeded in breadth of brim any thing we had yet met with, being, as we supposed, nearly three feet across.

As this was evidently the chief of the party, we pulled alongside and got into his boat, where he received us with much politeness; but as he looked dissatisfied at this proceeding, we returned to our own boat, and there carried on the conference. While we were endeavouring to make ourselves understood, the other boats gradually separated, and began to form a circle round us. Apprehending treachery, we prepared our arms, and pushed off to a little distance. The old gentleman, perceiving this, looked about very innocently to discover the cause of our alarm; and at length being made aware by our signs of what was the matter, he commanded all the boats to go to the other side. We now remained a considerable time without being able to make ourselves understood; for the Chinese whom we had with us was quite ignorant of their language. We endeavoured, by pointing to the shore, to signify our desire to land, while the old Chief, by similar signs, expressed his wish to go to the ships. We accordingly rowed to the Lyra, which lay nearer to the shore than the Alceste. When the Chief's boat was within ten yards of the brig, they let go their anchor, and threw a rope on board her, by which they drew the boat alongside in a very seaman-like style. The old man did not find it an easy matter to get up the ship's side, encumbered as he was with his splendid robes; he was no sooner on board, however, than we were crowded with the natives, who boarded us on all sides. Some climbed up the rigging, so as to overlook the quarter-deck; others got on the poop, and a line was formed along the hammock netting from one end of the brig to the other. As the evening was fine, it was thought best to entertain the venerable Chief upon deck, rather than give him the trouble of going down to the cabin, which, indeed, we had reason to fear would prove too small for the party. Chairs were

4

accordingly placed upon the deck; but the Chief made signs that he could not sit on a chair, nor would he consent for a time to use his mat, which was brought on board by one of his attendants. He seemed embarrassed and displeased, which we could not at the moment account for, though it has since occurred to us that he objected to the publicity of the conference. At length, however, he sat down on his mat, and began talking with great gravity and composure, without appearing in the smallest degree sensible that we did not understand a single word that he said. We of course could not think of interrupting him, and allowed him to talk on at his leisure; but when his discourse was concluded, he paused for our reply, which we made with equal gravity in English; upon this he betrayed great impatience at his harangue having been lost upon us, and supposing that we could, at all events, read, he called to his secretary, and began to dictate a letter. The secretary sat down before him with all due formality, and having rubbed his cake of ink upon a stone, drawn forth his pen, and arranged a long roll of paper upon his knee, began the writing, which was at length completed, partly from the directions of the Chief, and partly from his own ideas, as well as the occasional suggestions of the bystanders. The written part was then torn off from the scroll and handed to the Chief, who delivered it to me with the utmost confidence of its being understood: but his mortification and disappointment were extreme on perceiving that he had overrated our acquirements[3].

[Illustration: *Drawn by Wm. Havell, Calcutta. Engraved by Robt Havell & Son.*

COREAN CHIEF and his SECRETARY.

Published Jany, 1, 1818, by John Murray, Albemarle Street, London.]

A debate now appeared to take place between the Chief and his followers, as to the mode of communicating with us; meanwhile, as we ourselves were equally at a loss, we became anxious to relieve the old man's embarrassment, by shewing him all the attention in our power, and completely succeeded in putting him into a good humour, by giving him some cherry brandy, and distributing rum to his people.

While these attempts at explanation were going on, the crowd of natives increased, and their curiosity became so great, that they pressed round us in a way nowise agreeable. Some of them roved about the ship, and appeared highly entertained with every thing they saw. The Chief himself, however, did not appear at ease, but continued giving directions to his officers and people about him with an air of impatience. He more than once ordered them all into their boats, but they always returned after a few minutes. One man persevered in climbing over the hammocks, close to the Chief, to see what was going on. The noise made to keep him back attracted the Chief's attention, who immediately gave orders to one of the attendants for his being taken away; it will be seen by and by what was his fate.

The persons forming the suite of the Chief were dressed nearly in the same manner as himself, excepting that their robes were white, and did not contain such a profusion of cloth. They wore the large hats and wide trowsers tied above the ancle, with cotton shoes turned up a little at the toe. The immediate attendants, who seemed also to be soldiers, are differently clothed: over a loose pink frock with wide sleeves, they have another which fits closer, and is without sleeves, the corners being tucked up, like the skirts of some military uniforms. Their hat is a broad flat cone made of thick grass, the under part being embossed with different coloured silks, and from a gilt ornament on the peak there hangs a tassel made of peacock's feathers, and another of hair dyed red: some are armed with bows and arrows, others with only a straight sword, having no guard for the hand. A coarse frock without sleeves, and trowsers, or rather drawers, covering the thigh, are worn by the lower orders.

It was nearly dark when the Chief gave directions for preparing the boats, at the same time calling to two of his attendants to assist him to get on his legs. Each took an arm, and in this way succeeded in raising him up, which was no sooner observed by the people, than they jumped into their boats with the utmost alacrity, and the Chief, after many bows and salams, walked into his boat. This did not give him so much trouble as he had experienced on coming on board, for a platform of gratings and planks had been prepared for his accommodation during his visit, an attention with which he seemed much pleased. So far all seemed well; but there was still something amiss, for the old man, seated in state under his umbrella, remained alongside with his attendants ranged on the deck about him, he and his people preserving the most perfect silence, and making no signs to explain his wishes. We were greatly puzzled to discover what the old gentleman wanted, till at length it was suggested, that having paid us a visit, he expected a similar compliment in return. This idea was no sooner started, than we proceeded to pay our respects to him in his boat. He made signs for us to sit down, honouring us at the same with a corner of his own mat. When we were seated, he looked about as if in distress at having nothing to entertain us with, upon which a bottle of wine was sent for and given to him. He ordered an attendant to pour it into several bowls, and putting the bottle away, made signs for us to drink, but would not taste it himself till all of us had been served. He was nowise discomposed at being obliged to entertain his company at their own expense; on the contrary, he carried off the whole affair with so much cheerfulness and ease, as to make us suspect sometimes that he saw and enjoyed the oddity of the scene and circumstances, as fully as we did ourselves.

After sitting about ten minutes, we left the Chief in great good humour, and returned on board, thinking, of course, that he would go straight to the shore; but in this we were much mistaken, for we had no sooner left him, than he pushed off to the distance of ten or twelve yards, and calling the other boats round him, gave orders for inflicting the discipline of the bamboo upon the unfortunate culprit, who had been ordered into confinement during the conference. This exhibition, which it was evidently intended we should witness, had a very ludicrous effect, for it followed so much in train with the rest of the ceremony, and was carried on with so much gravity and order, that it looked like an essential part of the etiquette. During the infliction of this punishment, a profound silence was observed by all the party, except by five or six persons immediately about the delinquent, whose cries they accompanied by a sort of song or yell at each blow of the bamboo. This speedy execution of justice was, no doubt, intended to impress us with high notions of Corean discipline.

As it was now quite dark, we did not expect the Chief to pay any more visits this evening; but we underrated his politeness, for the moment the above scene was concluded, he steered for the Alceste. Captain Maxwell, who during all the time had been on board the Lyra, hurried into his boat to be prepared to give him a proper reception in his ship, and had just time to change his jacket for a coat and epaulettes before the Chief arrived. After climbing up the ship's side with some difficulty, and being received in due form on the quarter-deck, which was lighted up, he was handed into the foremost cabin, where he was met by Captain Maxwell, and conducted to a seat in the after cabin. As he declined sitting on a chair, he was obliged to wait for his mat, and, in the meantime, looked round him in amaze at the magnificence of the apartments. The change of dress made him behave towards Captain Maxwell as to a perfect stranger; but the moment he recognised him, he appeared much amused with his mistake, and his manners became less reserved. He now turned about to see what was become of his mat, and was astonished to find himself alone with us in the cabin. It was then discovered that the sentry at the door, in repressing the crowd of his followers, had found it impossible to distinguish his more immediate attendants, and had therefore allowed nobody to pass.

The door being opened, the mat-bearer and four of the principal people were called in by the Chief; and when we were all fairly seated on the deck, the secretary was directed to prepare a writing, which was dictated and delivered much in the same manner as before. Whether the presentation of a written paper was considered by the Chief as a necessary piece of etiquette, or whether he really had more hopes of being understood on this occasion than before, was quite uncertain; but the mode adopted by Captain Maxwell to undeceive him was conclusive. He immediately called for paper, and wrote upon it in English, "I do not understand one word that you say," and presented this paper in return, with all the forms and ceremonies that had been adopted towards himself. The Chief, on receiving it, examined the characters with great attention, and then made signs that it was wholly unintelligible, alternately looking at the paper and at Captain Maxwell with an inquiring air, and was only made sensible of the awkward dilemma in which we were placed, by observing Captain Maxwell repeat all his looks and gestures as equally applicable to the Corean writing which he held in his hand[4].

The Chief had now recourse to signs, which he used ever afterwards. He was in great spirits, and seemed entertained with the efforts which were made to please him. He asked to look at a mirror which had caught his attention; when it was put into his hands, he seemed very well satisfied with the figure which it presented, and continued for some time pulling his beard from side to side with an air of perfect complacency. One of the attendants thought there could be no harm in looking at the mirror likewise, but the Chief was of a different opinion, and no sooner observed what he was doing, than he very angrily made him put down the glass and leave the cabin. The secretary too fell under his displeasure, and was reprimanded with much acrimony for overlooking our paper when we were writing. Scarcely five minutes elapsed, in short, during his stay, without his finding some cause of complaint against his people; but we could not determine whether this arose from mere captiousness, or was done to give us a higher notion of his consequence, because, in the intervals, he was all cheerfulness and good humour. He was offered tea and cherry brandy, which he took along with us, and appeared at his ease in every respect. We thought that he made signs, implying a wish for us to visit him on shore; to this we cheerfully assented, and an arrangement for landing in the morning was made accordingly by means of similar signs, with which the Chief appeared much pleased, and rose to go away.

He had not got much beyond the cabin-door, however, before the serenity of his temper was once more overturned. On passing the gun-room sky-light, he heard the voices of some of

6

his people whom the officers had taken below, and who were enjoying themselves very merrily amongst their new acquaintance. The old Chief looked down, and observing them drinking and making a noise, he called to them in a loud passionate voice, which made them leave their glasses, and run up the ladder in great terror. From thence the alarm spread along the lower deck, to the midshipmen's berth, where another party was carousing. The grog and wine with which they had been entertained was too potent for this party, as they did not seem to care much for the old Chief, who, posting himself at the hatchway, ascertained, by personal examination, who the offenders were. On this occasion, his little rod of office was of much use; he pushed the people about with it to make them speak, and used it to turn them round, in order to discover their faces. One man watching his opportunity when the Chief was punching away at somebody who had just come up, slipped past and ran off; but the quick eye of the old man was not so easily deceived, and he set off in chase of him round the quarter deck. The man had an apron full of biscuit, which had been given to him by the midshipmen; this impeded his running, so that the Chief, notwithstanding his robes, at last came up with him; but while he was stirring him up with his rod, the fellow slipped his cargo of bread into a coil of rope, and then went along with the Chief quietly enough. The old man came back afterwards, and found the biscuit, which he pointed out to us, to shew that it had not been taken away.

He continued for some time at the hatchway, expecting more people; but finding none come up, he went below himself, to the main deck, and rummaged under the guns and round the main-mast, to discover whether any one was concealed; but finding no person there, he came again upon deck, and shortly after went into his boat.

On returning to the Lyra, we found a number of boats anchored round her, which looked as if they meant to keep strict watch over us. We went in our boat to one of them, where we found the crew asleep. They seemed to have had orders not to follow the Chief to the frigate, and were here waiting his return. On our pointing to the shore, and making signs that the old man with the long beard and large hat had landed, they began immediately to get their anchor up, and called to the other boats to do the same. In a few minutes they were all at work, and every person in the boats joined in repeating the two words "ho ya, ho ya," the effect of which, from a great many voices, was not unpleasing.

The cable in these boats is wound round a large reel or barrel; to the ends of which two wheels with handles are fitted, which enables a considerable number to apply their strength at the same moment. The anchor is made of a dark coloured, heavy wood, with a long shank and flukes, and a short stock crossing the former, near the crown of the anchor, and not at the end of the shank, as with us in Europe. The mat sails are divided into horizontal divisions by slender pieces of bamboo. When not under sail, the boats are moved by oars having a circular piece of wood tied to the end, and are steered by a large scull over the stern. The bow is square above, but rises from the water in a slope, making a small angle with the water, like the end of a coal barge, but overhanging more. The planks are fastened together by means of square tree-nails, which pass in a slanting direction through the plank, and not straight, as with us.

5th of September.—A considerable bustle was observed on shore at daybreak this morning; and shortly afterwards, we saw the old Chief and his suite embark, and pull towards us, accompanied by a numerous fleet of smaller boats, all ornamented with showy flags, and crowded with people in gay and bright coloured garments, forming, upon the whole, a splendid and imposing scene. As the procession moved slowly along, the band in the Chief's boat struck up a lively, martial sort of air, on instruments similar to those we had heard last night; the tone of which is not unlike the drawling sound of the bagpipe, the bass or drone being produced by a long horn, and the squeaking sounds by four trumpets, two of which have stops in the middle, by which the notes are distinctly marked.

The Chief's visit was so unexpectedly early, that we had not put things in order for his reception, before he was alongside: he came on board, however, and seemed happy at being allowed to walk about the decks, and examine every thing at his leisure. When the cabin was ready, and the Chief seemed to have satisfied himself with looking round the upper deck, he was asked to walk down; which he complied with as soon as he understood what was meant. But he found it no easy matter to get down the narrow hatchway, in which there was barely room for his hat; but this he would by no means take off. As he entered the cabin, his robes and hat completely filled the door-way; and when seated at the table, (for he now made no objection to a chair) he occupied no inconsiderable portion of the whole apartment. He sat here for some time, and examined every thing in the cabin with great attention, pointing with the little stick whenever he saw any thing which he wanted to look at more closely. In this way, the books, globes, glasses, &c. were put into his hands; and it was not a little amusing to see the old gentleman wheeling the globes round, and hunting over the books for pictures, like a child. A person of rank who accompanied the Chief this morning, was asked to the cabin along with him; and was no sooner seated, than we observed that he had a very sickly look; which circumstance was the cause of a curious mistake. It had been supposed that the Chief, during last night's conference, made allusions to some friend of his who was unwell; and accordingly, in our arrangements for the morning, it was proposed to take the doctors of both ships on shore, to visit him. As the Chief had himself come on board, our plans for landing were interrupted, and we ascribed this early visit to his anxiety on account of his friend's health.

It was therefore taken for granted, that this sickly looking companion of the Chief, who, some how or other, got the title of the "Courtier," amongst us, was the patient alluded to last night; and no sooner were the first compliments over in the cabin, than the doctor was sent for to prescribe. On his being introduced, the Courtier was made to hold out his tongue, have his pulse felt, and submit to various interrogatories, the object of which the unfortunate man could not divine, particularly as there was nothing at all the matter with him. He submitted with so much patience to all these forms, and the Chief looked on with such grave propriety during all the examination, that they evidently considered the whole scene as a part of our ceremonial etiquette. When this gentleman was released from the doctor's hands, he began to examine the books with the air of a person who understands what he is about. He appeared desirous of passing for a literary character; and observing us hand the books about in a careless manner, ventured to ask for one, by drawing it towards himself with a begging look. As he happened to select a volume of the Encyclopædia Britannica, I was under the necessity of refusing; but offered in its stead a less valuable, though more showy book, which he accepted with much gratitude. No return, of course, had been looked for, and I was for a moment at a loss to understand what my friend meant, by slipping his fan into my hand, under the table. He did this in so mysterious a way, when the Chief was looking in another direction, that I saw it was his wish to conceal what he had done, and the fan was sent privately away. But unfortunately, my precaution was fruitless, for a few minutes afterwards, on finding the crowded cabin very hot, I called for a fan, and the servant, unconscious of the mischief he was doing, brought the Courtier's present; which no sooner met the old man's eye, than he rose half off his chair, and gave his unhappy companion such a look of furious anger, as made him tremble from top to toe: but he was soon pacified when he saw that we took an interest in the question, and the Courtier was allowed to keep his book.

After sitting half an hour, and drinking a glass of Constantia, the old man proposed to go upon deck. I accordingly led the way, and had gone some steps up the ladder, in advance, before I perceived that he had stopped at the door of the gun-room, where the officers mess, and was looking in, with his usual curiosity. I begged him to go in, which he accordingly did, and entertained himself for some time, with looking over the different cabins of the officers. From having observed the pleasure which he took in the sight of any thing new, I was induced to propose his going round the lower deck, and he looked quite pleased when I pointed along the passage. The state hat, which had been resolutely kept on during all this time, notwithstanding its perpetual inconvenience to himself and every one around him, was here destined to come off; for after making two or three attempts, he found it impossible to get along and wear the hat too; and being of a very inquisitive disposition, he chose the degrading alternative of being uncovered, and his researches proceeded without interruption. Nothing escaped the old man's observation; whatever was shut or tied up, he requested to have opened; and in this way he rummaged the midshipmen's chests, and the sailors' bags, all along the lower deck. He looked into the holds, took the lid off the boilers, and turned every thing topsy-turvy. Seeing a cutlass tied to the deck, overhead, he took it down, and on drawing it from the scabbard, its lustre, and the keenness of its edge, surprised and delighted him so much, that I asked him to accept it. At first he seemed willing enough, but after holding a consultation with the Courtier for five minutes, he reluctantly put it back again. As he went along, he took samples of every thing that he could easily put into his sleeve, which served him instead of a sack; so that when he came upon deck, he was pretty well loaded, and looked about with the satisfaction of a school-boy, on having visited a show for the first time in his life.

Whilst we were below, one of the natives had been busily employed in taking the dimensions of the ship with a string, and another person was engaged under him, taking an account of the guns, shot, and rigging, all which details he wrote down; but not being able to ascertain, himself, the exact number of people on board, he had recourse to me for the information; this I communicated by opening eight times the fingers of both hands. The only part of the ship to which he had not free access was the cabin under the poop, and from which he felt much annoyed at being excluded: but when told that a gentleman was shaving there, he shewed himself quite satisfied with the explanation, and waited patiently until the door was opened to him.

8

The old gentleman and his followers appearing anxious to see a shot fired, an eighteen pound carronade was loaded before them, and discharged with the muzzle so much depressed, that the shot struck the water close to us, and then rose and fell eight or ten times, to the great entertainment and surprise of the whole party. In the mean time, Captain Maxwell had come on board, and breakfast being ready, we prevailed upon the Chief to sit down with us. He ate heartily of our hashes, and of every thing else that was put before him, using a knife, fork, and spoon, which he now saw, probably, for the first time in his life, not only without awkwardness, but to such good purpose, that he declined exchanging them for Chinese chopsticks, which were provided for him. In fact, he was so determined to adopt our customs in every respect, that when the tea was offered to him in the Chinese way, he looked to the right and left, and seeing ours differently prepared, held up his cup to the servant, for milk and sugar, which being given to him, the old gentleman remained perfectly satisfied.

The politeness and ease with which he accommodated himself to the habits of people so different from himself, were truly admirable; and when it is considered, that hitherto, in all probability, he was ignorant even of our existence, his propriety of manners should seem to point, not only to high rank in society, but to imply also a degree of civilization in that society, not confirmed by other circumstances. Be this as it may, the incident is curious, as shewing, that however different the state of society may be in different countries, the forms of politeness are much alike in all. This polished character was very well sustained by the old Chief; as he was pleased with our attempts to oblige him, and whatever we seemed to care about, he immediately took an interest in. He was very inquisitive, and was always highly gratified when he discovered the use of any thing which had puzzled him at first. But there was no idle surprise, no extravagant bursts of admiration, and he certainly would be considered a man of good breeding, and keen observation, in any part of the world. Towards his own people, indeed, he was harsh and impatient at all times; but this may have arisen from his anxiety that no offence should be given to us by the other natives, whom he might know were less delicate and considerate than himself, and therefore required constant control.

When breakfast was over, and the old man once more upon deck, we endeavoured to signify to him that we meant to land, according to our engagement yesterday evening; but this he either did not, or would not comprehend; for whenever we pointed towards the shore, he directed our attention to the frigate. At length he got into his boat, pushed off, and was making for the Alceste, when Captain Maxwell followed in his boat, and drawing up alongside of him, tried to prevail upon him to accompany us to the village: the Chief shook his head by way of disapprobation, and turning towards his attendants, entered into a discussion with them, which terminated by the Courtier and himself stepping into Captain Maxwell's boat.

We ascribed this measure to a desire on the Chief's part to show publicly that he had not himself invited us on shore, and had only acceded to our request to land. We had not proceeded far before the Chief repented of his ready compliance, and tried to persuade us to return; but finding the ordinary signs of no avail, he held his head down and drew his hand across his throat, as if his head was to be cut off. It was now our turn not to comprehend signs, and thinking it would be idle to lose so favourable an opportunity, spared no pains to reconcile the old man to our landing. In this, however, we did not succeed, for, as we approached the shore, his anxiety increased, and he frequently drew his hand across his neck, as if to shew that he would lose his head if we persisted. We again tried to re-assure him, by explaining that we had no intention of going near the village, but merely desired to walk about for a short time, and then to go to the frigate to dine. He was of course included in this invitation; but his only answer consisted in pointing to us and making signs of eating, and then drawing his hand across his throat; by which he was understood to mean, that it might be very well for us to talk of eating, but, for his part, he was taken up with the danger of losing his head. We could not but laugh at this, as we had no notion of any such apprehension being well grounded; and, in a short time, landed at the distance of half a mile from the village.

The old man was lifted out of the boat by several of his people, and we were amazed to find, when they set him down, that he was in tears, and looking altogether very unhappy. In a few minutes a crowd, consisting of more than a hundred people, assembled round us, and we began to think we should pay dearly for our curiosity. But the poor old man had no thoughts of vengeance, and was no better pleased with the crowd than we were; for turning to his soldiers, he desired them to disperse the mob, which they did in a moment by pelting them with great stones. The Chief now began crying violently, and turning towards the village walked away, leaning his head on the shoulder of one of his people. As he went along, he not only sobbed and wept, but every now and then bellowed aloud. We had been nowise prepared for such a scene, and were extremely sorry for having pushed matters to this extremity. It had never occurred to us that the old Chief's head was really in danger; and even now we could not satisfy ourselves whether he was sincere, or merely acting in order to prevail on us to retire. The perfect tranquillity, nay even cheerfulness of the Courtier, who staid with us all this time, puzzled us extremely: nor could we account for the indifference of the other attendants, who looked on with as much composure as if such scenes were every day occurrences. But at all events, it was necessary before proceeding any further, that the old man should be pacified; and in order to effect this, we sat down on the beach, upon which he turned about and came crying back again. He seated himself by us, and waited very patiently whilst we remonstrated on the unreasonableness of his conduct, and contrasted the reception he had met with from us, with his present unaccountable behaviour. This was expressed by a dumb show acting of all that had taken place since we came to anchor in the bay; and these signs we thought might be intelligible to the Chief, because they were so to all of us, although no words were used. The signs used by different nations, however, are often dissimilar when the same thing is to be expressed: and it happened frequently with us that all attempts at explanation failed, on both sides, though the signs used appeared to be understood by all the people of the same nation with the person making the signs.

The old man made a long speech in reply; in the course which the beheading sign was frequently repeated. It is curious that he invariably held his hands towards his throat after he had gone through this motion, and appeared to wash his hands in his blood: probably he did this in imitation of some ceremony used at executions.

Upon one occasion the Chief endeavoured to explain something to us which had a reference to a period of two days; this he did by pointing to the sun, making a motion twice from east to west, and, at the end of each time, closing his eyes as if asleep. This sign was variously interpreted: some believed it to mean that in two days his head would be taken off: others imagined that in two days a communication might be made to his government, and that orders for our reception would be transmitted. Whatever might have been meant by this particular sign, it seems very probable that some general instructions were in force along the whole of this coast by which the treatment of strangers is regulated. The promptitude with which we were met at this place, where, perhaps, no ship ever was before, and the pertinacity with which our landing was opposed, seem to imply an extraordinary degree of vigilance and jealousy on the part of the government.

We expressed a desire to eat and drink, in the hopes of working on the old man's hospitality, and, perhaps, inducing him to entertain us in his house; but he made no motion towards the village, and merely sent off a servant for some water and a few small cockles. When this sorry fare was laid on the beach, the old gentleman made signs for us to begin; but we did not choose to be pleased either with the entertainment itself, or with the place and manner in which it had been served. We explained to him that the proper place to eat was in a house, and not on a wet dirty beach; he made no offer, however, of any other; but leaning his head pensively on his hands, seemed entirely resigned to his fate.

The case was now utterly hopeless; and after an ineffectual attempt to cheer him up, we went on board, as the last, and indeed only favour we could grant him. Thus we quitted this inhospitable shore, after a stay of not quite an hour, in which time we had never been twenty yards from our own boats. We saw the village, however, to some advantage; it is neatly built, and very pleasantly situated under fine trees, in a valley cultivated like a garden, in small square patches.

It was now determined to prosecute the voyage to the southward, and the Lyra was accordingly ordered to proceed as usual to sound the passages a-head of the frigate, but had not gone far before the Alceste, still at anchor, was observed to be surrounded with boats. In about an hour she weighed and stood to sea. Captain Maxwell had received another visit from the old Chief, whose appearance was described as being quite altered; his sprightliness and curiosity all gone, and his easy unceremonious manner exchanged for cold and stately civility: he looked embarrassed and unhappy, as it appeared, from an apprehension of having offended Captain Maxwell. When this was discovered, no pains were spared to convince him that, in this respect, there was not the slightest cause for uneasiness. He would not accept any presents, but appeared much relieved by the unexpected kindness with which he was received, and before he went away, was restored, in some degree, to his wonted spirits. When looking over the books in the cabin, he was a good deal taken with the appearance of a Bible, but when offered to him he declined it, though with such evident reluctance, that it was again shewn to him just as he was pushing off in his boat, and he now received it with every appearance of gratitude, and took his leave in a manner quite friendly.

We quitted this bay without much regret. The old Chief, indeed, with his flowing beard, and pompous array, and engaging manners, had made a strong impression upon us all; but his pitiable and childish distress, whatever might have been the cause, took away from the respect with which we were otherwise disposed to regard him: yet this circumstance, though it makes the picture less finished, serves to give it additional interest; whilst every thing ridiculous in the old man's character is lost in the painful uncertainty which hangs over his fate.

From this bay we steered amongst the islands, during all the 6th and 7th, to the S.W. before the natives were met with again; we saw them indeed, but never got near enough to converse with them. They were frequently observed seated in groups watching us on the islands which we passed. We saw several fishing-boats, with a crew of about a dozen men, crowded on a sort of poop. At a little distance these boats appeared to be formed of two vessels lashed together. This appearance we believe to be caused by their having an outrigger on one side, on which their oars, sails, and masts are piled, in order probably to keep the boat clear when they are at anchor fishing. Their mast is lowered down and hoisted up by means of a strong tackle from the mast-head to the stern, as in the barges on the Thames.

We threaded our way for upwards of a hundred miles amongst islands which lie in immense clusters in every direction. At first we thought of counting them, and even attempted to note their places on the charts which we were making of this coast, but their great number completely baffled these endeavours. They vary in size, from a few hundred yards in length to five or six miles, and are of all shapes. From the mast-head other groups were perceived lying one behind the other to the east and south as far as the eye could reach. Frequently above a hundred islands were in sight from deck at one moment. The sea being quite smooth, the weather fine, and many of the islands wooded and cultivated in the valleys, the scene was at all times lively, and was rendered still more interesting by our rapid passage along the coast, by which the appearances about us were perpetually changing. Of this coast we had no charts possessing the slightest pretensions to accuracy, none of the places at which we touched being laid down within sixty miles of their proper places. Only a few islands are noticed in any map; whereas the coast, for near two hundred miles, is completely studded with them, to the distance of fifteen or twenty leagues from the main land. These inaccuracies in the charts naturally gave a very high degree of interest to this part of the voyage; yet the navigation being at all times uncertain, and often dangerous, considerable anxiety necessarily mingled itself with the satisfaction produced by so new and splendid a scene. We always anchored during the night, or when the tides, which were very rapid, prevented our proceeding in the deliberate manner absolutely required by the nature of the circumstances. An instance of the necessity of these precautions occurred on the 7th of September, at four o'clock in the afternoon, when, it being quite calm, we were drifting along with the tide, which suddenly shifted and carried us rapidly towards a reef of rocks, which was invisible till the strong rippling of the water shewed us our danger: we let go the anchor immediately, but the jerk was so great, as to break the Lyra's cable. A second anchor, however, brought her up at a sufficient distance from the reef.

As soon as the tide slacked, a boat was dispatched to examine the anchorage on the other side of an island near us. The officer landed about sunset, and from the top of the island could discover a village on the other side, on the shores of a fine large bay. He afterwards sounded the anchorage, and found it of a convenient depth. On his way back he landed near the village, but though it was bright moonlight he saw none of the inhabitants.

8th of September.—About noon we weighed and sailed round the north end of the island, which had been visited last night. The Alceste anchored nearly in the middle between the two islands which form the anchorage; but as the Lyra draws less water, she was placed as close off the village as was safe, being then about a quarter of a mile from the beach. At this distance, by means of a telescope fixed on a table on the poop, we were enabled to see what was going on in the village, while the people were unconscious of being observed. Mr. Clifford, who was too unwell to land with Captain Maxwell and myself, placed himself at the glass, and made many observations which must otherwise have escaped notice.

At first the only inhabitants visible were seated on the top of the hill watching us, the village itself being quite deserted; but shortly after our anchoring, the inhabitants began to assemble from different parts of the island. Of these several were women, some of whom had children on their backs, and others carried them in their arms. They looked stout, were fairer in complexion than the men, and were dressed in a long white robe, loose and open in front, with a petticoat of the same colour reaching a little below the knees; their hair was tied in a large knot behind; a small piece of white cloth was thrown loosely over the head to protect them from the rays of the sun. Some women were engaged in husking rice in a mortar with a wooden beater; these had no dress above the waist. The men and boys were seen carrying loads on a wooden frame hooked to the shoulders.

In a square flat place near the village a number of women and children were employed winnowing corn by pouring it from a height, so that the husks blew away. Fishing-nets were spread to dry on most of the houses. We landed about five o'clock, and found in the village only two men, who obstinately remained at one place without speaking, and looking anxious that we should go away; they refused the buttons which we offered them, and resisted our persuasions to accompany us to the upper part of the village, which we were anxious they should do, to shew that we had no intention of hurting any thing, but merely to look about us. We went on alone, and on reaching a deserted house thought it a good opportunity to examine it. Before the door, on a neat clean level space, enclosed by a hedge covered with a sweet-scented white flower, we found several heaps of corn and straw, and several of the wooden mortars in which the rice is pounded, also a number of vessels, some filled with water and others with rice. Cooking utensils were lying about, and a number of fishing lines coiled neatly in baskets, and split fish spread out to dry on the top of little corn ricks on one side of the court. The inside was dark and uncomfortable; the mud floor was full of hollow places; the walls were black with soot, and every thing looked dirty. On the left of the entrance two large metal boilers, twenty inches deep, were sunk in the brickwork, the upper part being about a foot above the floor. The fire-place was between the boilers, and on the hot embers lay three split fish. On the wall opposite to the fire were shelves, having a number of cups, basons, and cooking utensils, principally of coarse stone ware, and some few of a sort of bell-metal. The number of inhabitants in one house must be considerable, if we can form an estimate from the quantity of their dishes and vessels. There were three neat small pieces of furniture on one of the shelves, the use of which we could not discover; they were made of wood, elegantly carved and varnished, with a round top about a foot in diameter, and four legs a foot and a half long. The roof was well constructed, the rafters being mortised into the ends of the horizontal beams, and tied to the middle by a perpendicular beam or King-Post. Over the rafters is laid a net-work of rods, to which the thatch is tied. There was no chimney to this house, and only one window made of slender bars of wood, forming square spaces three inches by two, covered by a thin semi-transparent paper defended by the roof, which extends so far beyond the wall as to shelter it not only from the rain but from the sun. Most of the houses had a sort of raised verandah under the eaves, about a foot or more above the ground, extending from the door on either hand to the end of the house; these places were neatly levelled, and must afford a cool seat. The walls of the houses are from six to eight feet high, and from fourteen to twenty feet long; the top of the roof being about fourteen. The walls are of stone and mud, the door moves on the bar, which forms one of its sides; this bar is prolonged, and works in holes in the beam above, and a stone below. There was a back door to the house which we examined. On opening this we found a bare bank of earth as high as the house, at the distance of three feet from the walls, and a hedge rising still higher on the top; this effectually excluded all light.

This minute survey of the house being completed, we returned to our friends, who seemed in some measure re-assured. We tried to prevail upon them to accompany us in our walk, in hopes that the rest of the cottagers might be induced to return when they saw how peaceably we were disposed. Captain Maxwell used every sign he could think of to no purpose, and tired at length of these attempts, took hold of the oldest man's hand, drew it through his arm, and walked off with him. I followed his example with the other; and this familiarity amused the natives, who now accompanied us in perfect good humour. The ease and apparent indifference with which they walked along with us was curious, and had so little of awkwardness in it, that one might have supposed it to be the fashion of Corea to walk arm in arm. Having reached the house which we had before examined, we sat down in the verandah, and made signs that we wished to smoke a pipe with them. In the meantime a boat was observed to come to the landing-place; the crew quitted her and came towards us at a rapid pace. The quick manner of these people, so different from the ordinary behaviour of the Coreans we had seen, made us apprehend that some violence was meditated; but in this we were mistaken, for they sat down with us, gave us their pipes to smoke, and laughed immoderately at some of our words: we took the hint from them, and laughed heartily whenever we observed that any thing good had been said amongst them; this was well received, and proved afterwards a good mode of introduction.

Their curiosity was strongly excited by our clothing, which they examined minutely; they wished to see some parts of our dress taken off, and in order to gratify them they were allowed to have our coats, shoes, stockings, hats, &c. They were more struck with the stockings than with any thing else, frequently shouting "Hota! Hota!" This word, which is pronounced with a strong aspiration, was noted down in our list as the Corean word for stockings; but it was found afterwards to be an expression of approbation, applied indiscriminately to whatever they consider remarkably good. After sitting some time with these people, and smoking several pipes with them, we gave up all hopes of seeing the villagers return while we were there, and as the night was falling we proposed taking a short walk with our friends, and then going on board. But as soon as they saw us go up the hill instead of returning to the boat, they became very uneasy, and wanted us to turn back. As we had reason, however, to conjecture that the women and children were on the other side of the hill, we went on in the expectation of getting a sight of them before dark. This the Coreans prevented by following us with shouts wherever we went, so as to give warning of our approach. The women and children probably retreated before us to a ravine on the north side of the island, for when we approached it the Coreans became more anxious than ever for our return; and one man seeing us still advance, took hold of my arm and gave it a sharp pinch. I turned round and exclaimed, "Patience, Sir!" He drew back on observing my displeasure, and a moment after called out himself, "Patience, Sir!" The others hearing this caught the words too, and nothing was heard for some time amongst them but "Patience, Sir," pronounced in every instance with perfect propriety. They seemed surprised themselves on discovering powers of imitation hitherto in all probability unexercised. This incident brought us better acquainted, and we remained on the top of the hill teaching them English words till it was dark. They were certainly entertained with our instructions, but nevertheless shewed much more satisfaction in attending us down hill again to our boats. Before going on board we invited them to come to the ship next day, which one of the party was supposed to comprehend: he first made preparations for going to bed, then closed his eyes, hung his head on his hand, and snored very properly; after a time he opened his eyes, started and looked about him, then laid his hands on Captain Maxwell's shoulders with an air of welcome. This was interpreted by some into a wish for our departure till the morning, and by others that he himself would visit us at daylight. As he never came on board, and received us on landing next day with any thing but welcome, probably both guesses were wrong: of one thing there was no doubt, his anxiety to get rid of us; and his signs may have meant that it was time for all honest people to be in bed.

9th of September.—At sunrise we landed at the same village, and found it deserted as before. We left it and made for the highest peak on the island, accompanied by a few of the Coreans, who did not interfere with us till about halfway up, when on our entering a grove of fir trees, with the appearance of which we had been struck, one of the Coreans objected; we went on, however, and upon reaching the stump of an old tree the Corean fell on his knees, bowed his head to the ground, and as he raised it again held his hands closed and pressed together towards the stump. This had very much the air of a stratagem to dissuade us from going further in that direction, where the women probably were concealed. Admitting this to have been the motive, it is curious that he should have supposed such a shew of religious form calculated to restrain us. It is further remarkable as being the only circumstance which we have seen on this coast implying a knowledge of religion or religious ceremony. There are here no temples, idols, nor tombs, whereas in China, villages much smaller than these of Corea have them in every corner. The other Coreans took no notice of the stump, and the man who was prostrating himself before it finding that his behaviour produced nothing but a number of questions from us concerning the nature of the tree, got on his legs and walked sulkily away. In the course of our walk we saw six bullocks of a small breed and very fat, but which the Coreans were not to be tempted to sell by any thing which we had to give them. Dogs were the only quadrupeds besides that we saw. There were pigeons, hawks, and eagles, but few small birds. Crows were as numerous here as in every other part of the world. We returned on board to breakfast, and afterwards set out on an excursion to the top of a high island lying some leagues to the south-east of us. On our way we landed, and observed the sun's meridian altitude with an artificial horizon, by which we ascertained the latitude to be 34° 22' 39" north, the longitude by the mean of two chronometers is 126° 2' 45" east.

We passed, for the distance of five miles, amongst islands, all, except the very smallest, inhabited. The villages are built in the valleys, where the houses are nearly hid by trees and hedges. The sides of the hills are cultivated with millet and a species of bean; and in the numerous small gardens near the villages, we saw a great variety of plants.

As the peaked island which we had undertaken to climb was steep, and covered with a long coarse grass, it cost us a tiresome scramble to gain the top, which is about six hundred feet above the level of the sea. The main land of Corea is just discernible in the north-east and east, from this elevation; but it commands a splendid view of the islands, lying in thick clusters, as far as the eye can reach, from north-west quite round by east to south. We endeavoured to count them. One person, by reckoning only such as were obviously separate islands, made their number one hundred and twenty. Two other gentlemen, by estimating the numbers in each connected cluster, made severally, one hundred and thirty-six, and one hundred and seventy; a difference, which at once shews the difficulty of speaking with precision on this subject. But when it is considered, that from one spot, which though considerably elevated, was not centrical, one hundred and twenty islands could be counted, and that our course for upwards of one hundred miles had been amongst islands no less crowded than these, some idea may be formed of this great Archipelago.

After enjoying this scene for some time, we went down on the other side of the peak, which is much less steep. We found the boat's crew preparing dinner for us, under some trees,

13

close to a well of cool water. The village to which the well belonged not being many yards off, we proceeded to explore it, and found it deserted by all except an old woman and a man. The woman, seated on a pile of stones, in the middle of the village, took no notice of us as we passed; and indeed, she was herself so very homely, as to occupy but little of our attention. The man was seated at the door of a cottage, making a straw sandal: on our entering his inclosure, he looked up for an instant, and immediately resumed his work, with as much composure as if we had been a party of the villagers. A button was offered to him, which he accepted without scruple: he agreed, with equal readiness, to exchange his unfinished sandal for another button, which having carelessly put away, in a bag lying near him, he took some straw and re-commenced his business, without seeming to notice that we were rummaging his house. He is the only Corean we have met with, who has not shewn some slight symptoms of curiosity: indeed, he seemed totally indifferent about our staying or going, or about what we were doing in his house; and we left him without knowing whether to ascribe his apathy to fear, or to absolute stupidity.

On returning from the village, we saw a party of the natives assembled on a rising ground near us; they were invited, by signs, to join us at dinner, but they kept their places unmoved. While we were at dinner, the sailors, who had been rambling about, joined the natives, and in a few minutes became very good friends with them; the natives giving up their pipes, and the sailors in return supplying them with tobacco. We have frequently remarked during this voyage, that the sailors make acquaintance with the natives much sooner than the officers. This seems the natural effect of the difference in our manners. On meeting with natives, we feel so anxious to conciliate, and to avoid giving offence, that our behaviour, thus guarded and circumspect, has an air of restraint about it, which may produce distrust and apprehension on their part; whilst, on the other hand, Jack, who is not only unreflecting and inoffensive himself, but never suspects that others can possibly misconstrue his perfect good-will and unaffected frankness, has an easy, disengaged manner, which at once invites confidence and familiarity.

In about an hour after we had sat down, one of the natives hastily rose, and without appearing to deliberate, but as if actuated by a sudden impulse, strode rapidly down to us, and in the most unceremonious way possible, presented his lighted pipe for us to smoke. We received him as kindly as we could, and prevailed upon him to take a glass of wine; which he had no sooner drank off, than he roared out, "Hota! Hota!"

This exclamation brought the rest down, who seating themselves by us, drank freely, and became very cheerful and communicative, telling us the Corean names of every thing we pointed to, and asking, in return, the English names for our clothes.[5] But though the wine made these people far more sociable than any we had yet seen, they never forgot the principal object of their thoughts, and suggested, every now and then, by pointing to our boats, the propriety of our going away. After sunset, they became very impatient and uneasy at our stay; but when at length we yielded to their entreaties, the whole party accompanied us to the water's side, and took leave with the most lively marks of satisfaction at our departure.

10th of September.—This morning, about ten o'clock, we got under weigh, and stood to the southward. By sunset we were clear of all the islands, and could just distinguish the island of Quelpaert in the south-east quarter.

The shortness of our stay on this coast, and the difficulty we experienced in communicating with the inhabitants, will account for the scanty and disjointed nature of the information obtained. A future voyager would do well to be accompanied by a person who can write the Chinese character, and should have full leisure to overcome, by patient management, the distrust of strangers evinced by this unsociable people.

A chart of our track along this coast is subjoined to this work, in the hope that it may prove useful to a future voyager. As it was constructed under circumstances of great haste, it is necessarily incomplete; yet it will probably be found more accurate than any maps or charts hitherto published.

FOOTNOTES:

[Footnote 1: A servant of the embassy, left behind by accident at the Pei-ho river.]

[Footnote 2: We found the north-east end composed of a fine-grained granite; the middle of the island of a brittle micaceous schistus of a deep blue colour; the strata are nearly horizontal, but dip a little to the S.W. This body of strata is cut across by a granite dyke, at some places forty feet wide, at others not above ten; the strata in the vicinity of the dyke are broken and bent in a remarkable manner; this dislocation and contortion does not extend far from the walls of the dyke, but veins of granite branch out from it to a great distance, varying in width from three feet to the hundredth part of an inch: the dyke is visible from the top of the cliff to the water's edge, but does not re-appear on the corresponding cliff of an island opposite to it, though distant only thirty yards. This island is composed of the same schistus, and is cut in a vertical direction by a whin dyke, four feet wide, the planes of whose sides lie N.E. and S.W., being at right angles to those of the great granite dyke in the neighbourhood, which run S.E. and N.W. The strata contiguous to the whin dyke are a good deal twisted and broken, but not in the same degree as at their contact with the granite dyke.

The whin dyke is formed of five layers or sets of prisms laid across in the usual way. Beyond the small island cut by the whin dyke, at the distance of only forty or fifty feet, we came to an island rising abruptly out of the sea, and presenting a high rugged cliff of breccia, fronting that on which the granite dyke is so conspicuous: the junction of this rock with the schistus cut by the granite and the whin would have been interesting; but although we must have been at times within a few yards of it, the actual contact was every where hid by the sea.

The whole of the S.W. end of this island is formed of breccia, being an assemblage of angular and water-worn pieces of schistus, quartz, and some other rocks, the whole having the appearance of a great shingle beach. The fragments of the schistus in this rock are similar to that which forms the cliff first spoken of.

The theory which presented itself to us on the spot was, that the great mass of strata which forms the centre of the island was formerly at the bottom of the ocean; and that the western part, which is now a firm breccia, had been a beach shingle produced by the action of the waves on the strata: the granite which forms the eastern end of the island had been forced into its present situation from beneath the strata, with sufficient violence to dislocate and contort the beds nearest to it, and to inject the liquid granite into the rents formed by the heaving action of the strata as they were raised up. It is natural to suppose that the ragged edges of the strata forming the sides of these cracks would be subjected to a grinding action, from which the strata more remote might be exempted; and in this way we may account for the extraordinary twisting, and separation of masses along the whole course of the granite dyke. In the dyke, as well as in the veins which branch from it, there are numerous islands of schistus. That this last was softened, seems to follow from the frequent instances which occur of its being bent back upon itself without producing cracks. The same heat, propagated by the melted granite in the neighbourhood, may also be supposed to have reduced the shingle beach to a state of semifusion by the aid of some flux contained in the sand scattered amongst it. We could not discover any circumstance by which the relative antiquity of the two dykes mentioned above, could be ascertained.]

[Footnote 3: *Note on the peculiar character of the written language in that quarter of the globe.*

In China, Japan, Corea, and the islands in the adjacent seas, the spoken languages are different from one another; the written language, on the contrary, is the same in all. Thus a native of China is unintelligible to a Corean or Japanese, while he is speaking, but they mutually understand one another when their thoughts are expressed in writing. The cause of this may be thus explained. We in Europe form an idea in the mind, and this we express by certain sounds, which differ in different countries; these sounds are committed to writing by means of the letters of the alphabet, which are only symbols of sounds, and, consequently, a writing in Europe is unintelligible to every one who is ignorant of the spoken language in which it happens to be written. The Chinese and the other natives in these seas have, on the contrary, no alphabet; no symbols of sounds; their ideas are committed to writing at once without the intervention of sound, and their characters may therefore be called symbols of ideas. Now, as the same characters are adopted in all these countries to express the same ideas, it is clear that their writings will be perfectly intelligible to each other, although their spoken languages may be quite incomprehensible.

The case of the Roman numerals in Europe furnishes a ready illustration of this symbolical language. There is nothing in the symbols 1, 2, 3, &c. by which their pronunciation can be ascertained when presented to the eye, yet they communicate meaning independent of sound, and are respectively intelligible to the inhabitants of the different countries of Europe; while, at the same time, the sounds by which a native of one country distinguishes the written symbols 1, 2, 3, &c. are unintelligible to all the rest.

The knowledge of writing is supposed to be very generally diffused over the countries using what is called the Chinese character, and, as probably none but the lowest vulgar are ignorant of it, the surprise of these people on discovering our inability to read their papers is very natural. The case, we may imagine, had never occurred to them before, and it was highly interesting to watch the effect which so novel an incident produced. At first they appeared to doubt the fact of our ignorance, and shewed some symptoms of impatience; but this opinion did not last long, and they remained completely puzzled, looking at each other with an odd expression of surprise.]

[Footnote 4: This paper, presented by the Corean Chief, has been translated by Mr. Morrison at Canton, and is as follows: "Persons, of what land—of what nation (are you)? On account of what business do you come hither? In the ship are there any literary men who thoroughly understand, and can explain what is written?"]

[Footnote 5: See note at the end of the Loo-choo vocabulary.]

CHAPTER II.

Enter the Japan Sea—Sulphur Island—Volcano—See the Great Loo-Choo Island—Lyra nearly wrecked—First Interview with the Natives—Anchor at Napakiang—Natives crowd on Board—Their interesting Appearance and Manners—Several Chiefs visit the Alceste—Land to make Observations—Astonishment of the Natives—Six Chiefs visit the Ships—Alceste and Lyra proceed farther in Shore—A Chief of high Rank waits upon Captain Maxwell—Return his Visit—Feast—Projected Survey of the Anchorage—Visit Reef Island—The Lyra sent to look for another Harbour—Arrangements for landing the Alceste's Stores—Description of the Temple and Garden—First Acquaintance with Mádera—Study of the Language.

After leaving Corea, we stood to the southward and eastward, with a strong breeze from the north, and a mountainous swell from the north-east. Shortly after daybreak on the 13th of September, we saw Sulphur Island, in the south-west quarter, and by eleven in the forenoon were close up to it. We intended to land, but were prevented by the high wind, which caused so great a surf all round the island, as to render this impracticable. The sulphuric volcano from which the island takes its name is on the north-west side; it emits white smoke, and the smell of sulphur is very strong on the lee side of the crater. The cliffs near the volcano are of a pale yellow colour, interspersed with brown streaks: the ground at this place is very rugged, as the strata lie in all directions, and are much broken; on the top is a thin coat of brown grass. The south end of the island is of considerable height, of a deep blood red colour, with here and there a spot of bright green: the strata, which are here nearly horizontal, are cut by a whin dyke running from the top to the bottom of the cliff, projecting from its face like a wall. As the weather still looked threatening, we gave up the intention of examining this spot, and proceeded to the southward till four o'clock, at which time land was seen in the south-west quarter; but as there was not sufficient daylight to close with it, we hauled off to the westward for the night. Shortly after sunset the sky became overcast, the wind veered about from one point to another, the air became suddenly quite chill, the sea rose high, and every thing, in short, seemed to indicate an approaching tyfoong or hurricane. All our preparations were made to encounter a violent tempest; but we were much pleased at finding it turn out nothing more than an ordinary gale of wind.

14th of September.—The weather was still stormy, but being anxious to close with the land, we bore up, and steered in the supposed direction of the Great Lieou Kieou, or Loo-choo Island. At eight o'clock we saw the Sugar Loaf of Captain Broughton, which is a small green island, having a high remarkable cone in the middle. We left this to the eastward, and continued steering to the south south-west, hoping to get to leeward of the great island before night, where we might remain in smooth water till the weather became fine. While going along at a quick rate, we suddenly saw breakers close to us; we instantly hauled to the wind, and made all the sail we could carry. Our situation was now very critical, for the swell caused by the recent gale checked our way considerably, and a lee current drifted us gradually towards the reef. From the mast head we could look down upon the reef, which was of a circular form, with a low island on its southern side; the surf broke all round, but in the inside the water was quite smooth, and being only a few feet deep, the coral, which was of a bright green, appeared distinctly through it. At the distance of one-third of a mile from where we were, no bottom was to be found with our lead lines, so that anchoring was out of the question. After being in this unpleasant predicament for some time, we succeeded in weathering the western end of the reef, which we had no sooner done, than we saw a passage four or five miles wide, by which we proceeded to leeward of the reef island, where we found the water perfectly smooth. The Alceste rounded the reef without difficulty, being half a league farther off than the Lyra, which, as usual, had been stationed a-head to look out, but had not perceived the danger sooner, owing to the extreme haziness of the weather.

15th of September.—In the morning, it was arranged that the Lyra should proceed in shore in search of a harbour, while the frigate remained in deep water. At ten o'clock I thought we had discovered a place of security, and having anchored the Lyra, sent three boats to examine it. A sort of harbour was found, formed by coral reefs; but the passages being all intricate for large ships, and the water shallow inside, it is by no means safe. We fell in with several people in canoes; one man, who seemed to know what we were searching for, directed us to a point of land to the northward, and waved for us to go round it. While the boats were away, several natives came off to the Lyra. No people that we have yet met with have been so friendly; for the moment they came alongside, one handed a jar of water up to us, and another a basket of boiled sweet potatoes, without asking or seeming to wish for any recompense. Their manners were gentle and respectful; they uncovered their heads when in our presence, bowed whenever they spoke to us; and when we gave them some rum, they did not drink it till they had bowed to every person round. Another canoe went near the Alceste, and a rope being thrown to them, they tied a fish to it, and then paddled away. All this seemed to promise well, and was particularly grateful after the cold repulsive manners of the Coreans.

The day was spent in trying to beat round the point to windward, but the tide was too strong against us, and when it became dark, we found ourselves awkwardly situated. To the east and west of us there were islands at the distance of a few miles. To leeward was a circular coral reef, just appearing above the surface at low water; and to windward were seen the reefs upon which we were so nearly wrecked on Saturday. As the exact position of these numerous dangers was unknown to us, we were determined to anchor for the night, though in eighty fathoms water.

16th of September.—At daylight we weighed, and beat to windward all the morning; but owing to the tide being contrary, it was two o'clock before we passed the point mentioned above; which we had no sooner done, than we came in sight of an extensive town, having a harbour filled with vessels at anchor. On steering towards the town, we had to sound our way cautiously amongst coral reefs, which were tolerably well defined by the surf breaking upon them[6]. The Alceste followed as soon as we had ascertained that the passage was clear, and both ships anchored at the distance of half a mile from the town.

In a short time we were surrounded by canoes, full of the natives, who, with their children, flocked on board. They wear a loose dress, tied with a belt round their waist; their hair is brought tight up from all sides, and formed into a knot on the top of the head, with two metal pins stuck in it. In the course of an hour, a native came on board who appeared to be somewhat higher in rank than the rest; and we now discovered, to our great satisfaction, that this man understood our Chinese servant, who had been of no use to us at Corea. As it was found that there were other chiefs on shore superior in rank to this man, Captain Maxwell declined receiving his visit; as well with the view of inducing the principal people to come on board, as of maintaining an appearance of dignity, a point of great importance in all transactions with the Chinese and their dependents, who invariably repay condescension with presumption. As we had heard of these people being tributary to China, it was natural to conclude that there might be some similarity in manners. At all events, it was evidently much easier at any future time to be free and cordial with them, after having assumed a distance and reserve in the first instance, than it would be to repress insolence, if at first encouraged by too hasty familiarity.

Before this man went on shore, he requested to know the reason of our coming into this port; the interpreter was instructed to acquaint him that the ships had experienced very bad weather, and had been a long time at sea; that the large ship had sprung a leak, and required repairs which could only be done in a secure harbour: further explanations, it was observed, would be given to the superior chiefs when they came on board. We had been prepared for these inquiries, not only from the reception we had met with at Corea, but from the well-known character of the nations in this quarter of the globe; and it was so far fortunate, that the Alceste was actually in want of repairs; because to have assigned curiosity, and a desire of gaining information as our object, to people wholly unconscious of such feelings, would naturally have led them to ascribe our actions to some more interested, and consequently more dangerous motive.

The canoes which we have seen to-day are mostly made of one piece of wood; they have two sails, and are moved with considerable velocity, by two or more paddles, assisted by an oar over the stern, which acts both as a scull and a rudder. There is a neat low seat, made of rattans, for each person in the canoe. As the day closed, the fishing canoes came in great numbers from sea, and all came on board the ships on their way; some of the fishermen pulled up our lines and baited the hooks. The whole shore abreast of the ships was covered with people, but the crowd was greatest on two pier-heads, forming the entrance to the harbour; and the variety of colour in their dresses made this a very lively exhibition. In the evening, Captain Maxwell and I rowed round to examine the anchorage, which we found tolerably clear of rocks. An officer was at the same time sent to examine the inner harbour, but he did not go far within the entrance, which was much too shallow for the frigate.

On returning to the Lyra, I found that Mr. Clifford had been entertaining several respectable looking natives who had paid him a visit. As they readily comprehended his desire to know their words for various things, he has succeeded in collecting a considerable number, among which we are surprised to find their name for tobacco the same as ours; all the others are quite new to us.

17th of September.—I carried the interpreter to the Alceste, after breakfast, where I found two chiefs, who had been on board some time, and had been taken care of by the officers, as Captain Maxwell was not prepared to receive them. A message was then sent to intimate that the Ta-yin (a Chinese title, used also by these people to persons of rank) was desirous of seeing the chiefs, and they were introduced into the after-cabin, where they were received in form. They objected to sitting down, making at the same time many low obeisances, which they did by stooping the body, and raising the hands, closed one over the other, to their face. Their scruples about being seated were at length overcome, and the first chief took his place on Captain Maxwell's left hand, the next on my left, and a third, who was evidently of a lower rank, sat beyond the second. The chiefs sat respectfully silent, and Captain Maxwell finding that he was expected to speak first, communicated to them that the ships under his command belonged to the King of England; that they had gone to China with an Embassador, carrying presents to the Emperor, at Pekin; that on their way back to Canton, they had experienced very bad weather, and had been obliged to put in here to refit, and to procure supplies.

In reply, they expressed their willingness to assist us as much as lay in their power, but said that the harbour was too shallow for so large a ship, and recommended our proceeding to another harbour called Kinching, which they described as being secure and commodious, and only a few hours sail from this anchorage: they offered to furnish pilots and a boat to conduct us. Captain Maxwell, however, was unwilling to quit this anchorage unless certain of finding a better; he therefore proposed to send the Lyra to examine and report upon the harbour alluded to. The chiefs paused upon this, and said they could not take upon them to send pilots to the Brig without consulting the Great Man on shore. We were very curious to know who this great personage might be, but they evaded all our inquiries. Captain Maxwell asked where the king resided, and intimated his intention of waiting upon him; to this they strongly objected, declaring moreover, that it was impossible, as his majesty lived a thousand miles off. They did not seem aware of their inconsistency, when they undertook, immediately afterwards, to get an answer from court about pilots for the Lyra, in a few hours.

We had been led to hope, from the frankness and kindness of these people, that no restraint would be imposed on us; and we were the more disappointed at observing, that whenever we spoke of landing, or asked any questions about the king, the chiefs became uneasy, and replied in a mysterious manner. We consoled ourselves, however, with the supposition, that upon further acquaintance their apprehension would wear off.

Business being over, the chiefs were asked to walk round the cabin, an invitation which they accepted with manifest satisfaction. During the conference they had preserved a gravity suited to an important ceremony, and, though surrounded by new and curious objects, had never expressed the least curiosity. They were now no longer formal, and looked over the various articles with attention, taking particular notice of the globes, books, and mirrors. Their manners are remarkably gentle and unassuming. They are observant, and not without curiosity, but they require encouragement to induce them to come forward, being restrained, it would seem, by a genteel self-denial, from gratifying curiosity, lest it might be thought obtrusive. Their dress is singularly graceful; it consists of a loose flowing robe, with very wide sleeves, tied round the middle by a broad rich belt or girdle of wrought silk, a yellow cylindrical cap, and a neat straw sandal, over a short cotton boot or stocking. Two of the chiefs wore light yellow robes, the other dark blue streaked with white, all of cotton. The cap is flat at top, and appears to be formed by winding a broad band diagonally round a frame, in such a manner, that at each turn a small portion of the last fold shall be visible above in front, and below at the hinder part. The sandal is kept on by a stiff straw band passing over the instep, and joining the sandal near the heel; this band is tied to the forepart by a slight string, drawn between the great toe and the next, the stocking having a division like the finger of a glove for the great toe. They all carry fans, which they stick in their girdles when not in use, and each person has a short tobacco pipe in a small bag, hanging, along with the pouch, at the girdle. When they had satisfied themselves with looking over the cabin, they went away, with a promise of returning in the evening as soon as the answer from the Great Man should arrive.

During all this morning, the whole space between the ships and the shore has been covered with canoes, each containing about ten persons. The scene was very lively, for few of the parties which came to visit the ships remained long on board, so that the canoes were continually passing backwards and forwards, and the number which came in this way must have been immense. They all seemed highly gratified at being allowed to go wherever they liked over the ships, nor was this liberty ever abused. The manners even of the lowest classes are genteel and becoming; their curiosity is great, but it never makes them rudely inquisitive: their language is musical, and in most cases easy of pronunciation. We heard a boat song to-day, the air of which was sweet and plaintive; we tried in vain to catch the words, and unfortunately, none of us had skill enough to note down the air. We observed several people in canoes, making drawings of the ships, but they hid their work when they were observed. In consequence of what had been said last night of our wanting repairs, a party of shipwrights and caulkers was sent on board the Alceste this morning, but their tools were of a Lilliputian order, and quite unsuited to the rough work required.

The variety of colour and pattern in the dresses of the people to-day, is remarkable. Many wear printed cottons, others have cotton dresses with the pattern drawn on it by hand, instead of being stamped; but blue, in all its shades, is the prevalent colour, though there were many dresses resembling in every respect Highland tartans. The children, in general, wear more shewy dresses than the men, and of the dress of the women we can say nothing, as none have yet been seen. Every person has one of the girdles before described, which is always of a different colour from the dress, and is, in general, richly ornamented with flowers in embossed silk, and sometimes with gold and silver threads. This dress is naturally so graceful, that even the lowest boatmen have a picturesque appearance. Their hair, which is of a glossy black, is shaved off the crown, but the bare place is concealed by their mode of dressing the hair in a close knot over it. Their beards and mustachios are allowed to grow, and are kept neat and smooth. They are rather low in stature, but are well formed, and have an easy graceful carriage, which suits well with their flowing dress. Their colour is not good, some being very dark and others nearly white, but in most instances they are of a deep copper. This is fully compensated for by the sweetness and intelligence of their countenance. Their eyes, which are black, have a placid expression, and their teeth are regular and beautifully white. In deportment they are modest, polite, timid, and respectful, and in short, appear to be a most interesting and amiable people.

Two of our friends who had visited us in the morning, and whose names we have discovered to be Ookooma and Jeema, came on board again about half past five, and staid an hour; they had not received any answer, they said, from the Great Man, and therefore could not send pilots to the "hoonee gua," or little ship. They were accompanied by a chief whom we took to be a Chinese from his looks, and his appearing to understand the interpreter better than the others. His formal and suspicious manner did not promise so well as that of the others. They came to say that a present of stock and vegetables had been sent to the ships. It was intimated to them that we intended to land the next day, and upon their objecting to this, we said that our wish was to wait upon the Great Man; to which they replied, that no person answering to this description resided here. We then said, that it was right we should return their visit. This argument they combated by saying that they were men of unequal rank to us, and therefore nowise entitled to such an honour; and that we, at the same time, would be degrading ourselves by such undue condescension. This having failed, Captain Maxwell told them of his illness; upon which, our new acquaintance, who seemed more earnestly bent against our landing than the others, offered to send a physician on board to see him. Captain Maxwell replied, that his own doctor had recommended a ride on shore; upon which they laughed, and turned the discourse to something else.

In this way every proposal to land, or even allusion to the shore, was industriously put aside; and as it was our wish to gain their good will, the matter was dropped for the present. Before they went away, Captain Maxwell, pointing to their pipes, begged them to smoke if they wished it; they were grateful for this considerate attention, but would not on any account begin till we shewed them the example, by smoking with pipes which they prepared for us. They appeared more at their ease after this incident, and after sitting for some time, took leave for the night on the most friendly terms.

18th of September.—Captain Maxwell sent to me to say that he meant to land on a point at some distance from the town, in order to observe the sun's meridian altitude with an artificial horizon. Just as I was setting out to accompany him, I was taken by surprise by two well-dressed natives, who were halfway down the cabin ladder before I knew of their approach. One came to superintend the measurement of the Lyra, and the other, who seemed of inferior rank, to explain why some poultry, only then sent, had not come on the preceding night, along with the other presents. I forgot to mention, that a bullock, two hogs, two goats, a dozen and a half of fowls, some candles, wood, and water, were sent to each of the ships. I asked them to sit down, and they were so well satisfied with the Constantia which I gave them, that they remained for some time; owing to which delay, I did not reach the shore till the time for observing the sun had gone by. I found Captain Maxwell with Ookooma and several of the chiefs, and an immense crowd of the natives, all of whom had left the town on seeing the boat put off, and had hastened to this spot, either out of curiosity or respect, or more probably to watch our proceedings. At our request, Ookooma, who appears to possess considerable authority, made the whole crowd, chiefs and all, sit down on the grass in a circle round us. Their astonishment at our operations was strongly expressed in their countenances, and, indeed, our apparatus and behaviour must have looked, to perfect strangers, somewhat magical.

In the first place the quicksilver, which to them would appear like melted metal, was poured into a trough, in a fine stream from a wooden bottle; while it was running out the people repeated in an under tone "yi, yi, yi, yi!" but were silent when the glass roof was placed over the trough. The circular instrument and sextant, fixed on stands, next attracted their notice, and they looked on in profound silence while we were taking the sun's altitude. As we were too late for the desired observation, we amused the natives by letting them look at the two reflected images of the sun through the telescope of the instruments. Ookooma was the first who looked, and being quite unprepared for what he saw, started back in astonishment, as if he had unconsciously beheld something supernatural and forbidden. The other chiefs, in their turn, placed themselves at the instrument, as well as several old men who stepped forward from the crowd. Some testified their surprise by a sudden exclamation; others were perfectly calm, so that we could not guess what they thought; and some held up their hands, and looked as if the whole matter was totally beyond the reach of their comprehension. When this was over, and there was no longer any necessity for the crowd being seated, they closed round and watched us while we were putting the instruments up. Some of the boys held out their hands for quicksilver, with which they ran off, quite happy.

During this time we were about fifty yards from the foot of a cliff, on the brow of which was posted a group of women with baskets on their heads; we were unfortunately not near enough to discern their features, nor to make out their dress distinctly; it appeared, however, to be like that of the men, though somewhat shorter, and without any girdle round the waist.

The rock here rises in perpendicular rugged cliffs of coral, with a number of rude square excavations on its face, which, at first sight, appear to have been worn by the elements, but on examination shew evident traces of art. Most of these caves are closed up by a wall of loose stones, but in one, of which the mouth was open, several human bones were found lying amongst the sand. On removing a stone from a closed cave, a vase was observed in the inside, of an elegant shape; the people signified to us that these were the remains of the dead, but we did not make out distinctly whether the bones or the ashes only were thus preserved. They made no objections to our examining these caves, though they certainly were not pleased with it. No notice was taken of what Captain Maxwell and I did; but Mr. Clifford, who had remained below collecting words from some intelligent natives, was strongly recommended by Ookooma to go back to the boat; he walked up, however, without opposition, to the cave which we had been examining, and they ceased to importune him. A number of little boys who had observed us occasionally pulling flowers and plants, ran about collecting for us, and after presenting what they had gathered, with much politeness, ran away laughing with an arch expression of ridicule at our curiosity.

On our way back, instead of going directly off to the ships, we coasted along shore in our boats, which gave us a new view of a stone bridge, of one arch, connecting two parts of the town. On the south side of the bridge we passed a space of considerable extent, probably set apart as a burying ground. We saw here a number of large horse-shoe tombs like those used in China, whitewashed, and apparently kept in good repair. Most of the tombs, however, are in the form of small square houses, with low pyramidal roofs; some of these were tiled, others thatched. It is evident that, in what relates to the dead, they follow, in some respects, the Chinese customs.

[Illustration: NAPAKIANG.]

The whole coast at this place is of coral cliffs, the base of which appears to have been scooped out by the action of the sea. As this excavation is at some places higher than the waves of the sea can be supposed to have ever reached, there is difficulty in assigning the sea as the cause; yet the roof of the excavation is horizontal for a great extent, and its appearance, in every other respect, suggests that it has been formed by the dashing of the waves. There is, moreover, some difficulty in accounting for coral cliffs being so much above the level of the sea, in which, according to every supposition, they must have been formed.

The scenery here, as in most countries in these climates, does not admit of a satisfactory description. It may be said, however, that it is more pleasing to the eye than that of islands near the equator, where the vegetation is so profusely luxuriant, as to overload the picture with foliage to the exclusion of every thing else. Here there is much variety; the numerous groves of pine-trees give some parts of it an English air, but the style of landscape is what is called tropical. The general character of the scenery at this spot is faithfully preserved in the drawing of Napakiang.

19th of September.—No answer having yet come from the Great Man, we begin to apprehend that they are going to treat us in Chinese style, and exclude us from their country altogether. We have tried in vain to discover whether the King is at this place, or a hundred, or as some maintain, a thousand miles off; in the mean time, as we know the island to be not more than sixty miles long, it is fair to suppose that they wish to deceive us.

We conjecture that a large building on a rising ground, three or four miles from us in an eastern direction, with two flag-staffs near it, is the palace mentioned in the account quoted by Pere Gaubil, Lettres Edifiantes et Curieuses, Tom. XXIII. The natives always refuse to give any information when asked about this building.

Whenever the natives come on board, if at all well dressed, they are asked into the cabin, where we treat them with cherry brandy and Constantia. In the course of conversation they contribute a number of new words, and, in general, when they see what the object is, are very willing to lend their assistance, and take much pains to teach us the true pronunciation of their words. One man, however, who was not so quick as they generally are, was in the cabin to-day for some time; Mr. Clifford was getting from him the Loo-choo words for sour, sweet, salt, &c.; and in order to make him comprehend the questions, made him taste different things that were sour, sweet, and so on: the poor fellow stood this very well, till some quassia was given to him to get the word "bitter;" he had no sooner tasted it, than he ran off quite astonished at the manner in which he had been entertained.

It blew hard this morning, so that there was little intercourse with the shore; but towards sunset it moderated, and Ookooma, Jeema, and four other Chiefs, came on board, bringing with them a present of a bullock, two hogs, goats, and vegetables. The Chief whose name is Shayoon is the most clever of them all; he is next in rank to Ookooma, but he generally takes the lead in discussion; he has a quick intelligent look, with more determination in his manner than any of the others. They were very particular on all these state occasions to observe the order of precedence, and no one sat down till his superior was seated. When any subject was discussed, one at a time rose to speak, but not in order of rank, and they never attempted to interrupt one another.

The weather at this moment looked so stormy, that I went on board the Lyra to prepare for a gale; by which I lost a very interesting conference with the chiefs. I learnt from Captain Maxwell afterwards, that he had remonstrated with them on their inconsistency and the pretended difficulty of getting answers from court; he gave them to understand, that he did not conceive it was treating the King of England with due respect to deny his officers permission to walk on shore. Again, that they had promised to send pilots, but that none had come; and that many other promises had not been performed. He desired the interpreter to say, that he was not pleased with their telling him so many different stories, all of which could not be true; first they said that the bullocks, hogs, &c. were gifts from themselves; then, that they were sent by the Great Man; then, that there was no Great Man here: in fine, he urged them strongly to tell him the truth on all points. They made the interpreter repeat six times over what Captain Maxwell had desired him to say; they then consulted amongst themselves a long time, and at last assured Captain Maxwell, that a reply to the communications made by them to government would reach this place next day.

As the stock and vegetables received by the ships had, by this time, amounted to a considerable quantity, a bag of dollars was offered to them, and they were urged to take payment for what had been sent on board; this offer, which had been made more than once before, was still declined; upon which they were informed, that we considered it improper, as servants of government, to receive presents to such an extent from individuals. Upon this they gave their assurance, that the stock had been sent on board by order of the Loo-choo government, on their being informed that the King of another country's ships had arrived. No payment they said could therefore be taken. With this Captain Maxwell was satisfied. Their wish seems to be, to prevent our opening any communication with their government, and they appear so decided upon these matters, that they will probably succeed, notwithstanding all our efforts.

The chiefs have dresses adapted to the state of the weather; yesterday being cold and threatening, they all came on board with a sort of cloak or great coat made of a thick blue stuff like woollen cloth, buttoned in front. It is tighter than the ordinary dress, and is worn over it. It is only in fine weather, and on state occasions, that they wear the band turban, called by them "hatchee matchee;" at all other times they go uncovered, having their hair dressed like the rest of the people.

20th of September.—The mercury in the barometer fell last night from 29. 72, to 29. 51, and the sky assumed a yellow appearance. We expected a heavy gale, more particularly as it was so near the equinox, but we were so sheltered by the land, that though it appeared to blow hard at sea, we felt nothing of it where we lay.

Three or four canoes came round the south-west point of land this forenoon; the people in them were supposed to have come from the other side of the island, for they did not appear to have seen the ships before. One of these people was much delighted with a looking-glass which was shewn to him; he took it in his hands, and calling his companions about him, shewed them in turn its effect. Having done so several times, he held it opposite to his own face for four or five minutes without altering his countenance in the least; at last he smiled, and immediately and involuntarily nodded assent to the image in the glass, which had so exactly expressed what he felt himself; he seemed, however, aware, that it was a reflection of his own countenance, as he pointed to himself, yet he could not restrain his curiosity from looking behind, but instantly turned it round again. While the glass was in his hands, he made us several long speeches, in which he frequently repeated the word "Kagung," the Loo-choo name for mirror; but, from his behaviour, it is probable he knew it only by name. One of this party sold his "Jeewa" or head ornaments for a wine glass. Sometime afterwards, the others saw a bottle, which they wished to purchase in the same way; it was, however, given to them as a present, and they went away very well satisfied. These canoes were of pine, from twelve to twenty feet long, and from two to four wide; their anchor is made of wood loaded with stones.

As no answer came this morning from the Great Man, Captain Maxwell took the ships into a more secure anchorage at the north-east corner of the bay; our first anchorage being too close to a reef, and moreover open to the south-west winds. The place we had now shifted to, though apparently exposed, is, in fact, sheltered by a chain of reefs under water outside of us to the westward. By this change, we have been brought close to the bridge spoken of before, and are now abreast the east end of the town: the Lyra not being more than a quarter of a mile from the shore. A strict watch is kept on shore, so that no boat leaves the ships without being observed. Orders have been given for the whole anchorage to be carefully sounded; in doing this, the boats often approach the shore, and whenever this happens, a crowd of the natives, headed by one or other of the chiefs, repair to the spot, and wave them to keep farther off.

21st of September.—There appears to be some embargo upon the canoes, for there has not been one near us this morning, and only one on board the Alceste. It was found necessary to-day to move the frigate still farther in, and four or five hawsers were laid out for the purpose of warping her a-head. While this was going on, the beach, and all the heights near us, were crowded with people, wondering, no doubt, how the ship was made to move without sails, for the hawsers were low down, and might have escaped their observation. In the canoe which visited the Alceste, there came two men, who had not been seen before; they remained but a short time, which was spent in examining the hawsers and the mode of warping the ship. As soon as they had made themselves master of this subject, they went on shore, as if to make a report. During their visit they said little, being intent upon what was going on; but the interpreter learnt from one of them, that a Great Man had actually come, or was expected in the town to-day. A report prevails, that the King of the island has lately been on board in disguise. We cannot trace the report to any good foundation, and it is probably false. At the same time, if his Majesty has any curiosity, it is not unlikely that he may have come near enough to see such a strange sight as we must be.

It is possible that our moving up so close to the town has alarmed the people, and may have prevented their visiting us as heretofore; at all events, it is very unfair in our friends, the Chiefs, neither to let the people come on board, nor to allow us to go on shore to look at them.

Our occupation in the mean time is to observe the natives through the telescope placed on a table on the Lyra's poop. The stone bridge appears to be a great thoroughfare, several roads from the country leading to it; it seems also to be the only entrance to the town on this side. Nobody crosses it without stopping to look at us, and a crowd of idle people have taken post on and about it. We see a number of women coming from the country with baskets on their heads. Their outer dress differs from that of the men, it is open in front, and they have no girdle; they have an under dress, or sack, which is also loose, but not open; in some we can see that this comes nearly to the feet, in others just to the knee, and we imagine that those who work in the fields have the short dress: most of them allow their upper garment to flow out with the wind behind them. We observe a woman carrying a child across the hip as in India, with its hands on its mother's shoulder, while her arm is round the child's waist. One young lady has been seen for some time amusing herself by making a dog bark at the ships. We see women beating rice in wooden mortars. On the banks of the stream which the bridge crosses, there are a number of people washing clothes, which they perform in the Indian way, by dipping the clothes in water and beating them on stones. From one end of the beach to the other there is a range of people watching us, they are formed here and there into groups; one of which, on a craggy knoll abreast of the ships, has struck us as being particularly interesting. A fine majestic looking man, whose full beard and flowing garments remind us of a figure in the Cartoons of Raphael, is standing in the middle of a circle of old men, who are lying on the grass, and appear to be listening to him.

22nd of September.—This morning brings us no news, no permission to land! A number of flags and streamers are displayed on the masts of the vessels in the inner harbour, and there seems to be something going on on shore; no boats have come to us, and we have no occupation but looking through the glass, which, however, affords a good deal of entertainment, particularly as the people whom we see with it act in the usual way, being unconscious of our scrutiny.

In the afternoon a number of boats left the shore and proceeded to the Alceste in procession. In the foremost boat there seemed to be a person of consequence, whom we immediately conjectured to be the Great Man alluded to by the people yesterday. He got on board the Alceste before us, and the natives also had left their canoes, so that we found the ship's decks crowded with people. The Chief, whom we found seated in the cabin, was clothed in purple silk, with a light purple hatchee matchee. An official communication of our history was now repeated at the old man's request. He listened with great attention till Captain Maxwell concluded his statement, by informing him that the ship was leaky and required frequent pumping. He then begged permission to see this operation, if it would not give too much trouble. As this was exactly what we wished, the chain pumps were ordered to be got ready, and the conference went on, consisting principally of compliments. Observing that we took notice of his being a little deaf, he seemed anxious to explain that this was the effect of age. He made us feel his pulse, and look at the withered state of his hand, then taking ours and feeling the pulse, held them up along with his own, and laughed with great good humour at the contrast which age had produced. He was about sixty years old, and his beard of thin hair was as white as snow: he had a cheerfulness of expression, and a liveliness of manner, which are remarkable for a man of his years. His manners were graceful and elegant, and from the first moment he seemed quite at his ease. Every thing about him, in short, indicated good-breeding, and a familiarity with good society; and we could not help remarking his decided superiority in appearance over the other chiefs.

When the pumps were ready, he was escorted to the main deck, where he sat for some time in great admiration of the machinery; and seeing the labour required to work it, he seemed really affected at our situation, which he naturally thought must be very bad, from the immense quantity of water thrown out by the pumps. The ship being upright, the water did not run off freely from the deck, and in a short time it flowed round the chair in which the old man was seated. Three or four of the sailors seeing him somewhat uneasy at this inundation, took him up chair and all, and placed him on a dry spot. The old gentleman was surprised, not displeased, and very graciously replied to the low bows which the sailors made him. On returning to the cabin, they were all entertained as usual with sweet wine, cherry brandy, and pipes. The old man filled pipes for us, and as soon as this part of the ceremonial had been gone through, a formal request was made for permission to land the Alceste's casks and stores, in order to stop the leak and make other repairs. This produced a long discussion amongst the chiefs, in which the old man joined but little; he spoke, however, now and then, and whatever he said, appeared to be to the purpose. Whenever the chiefs spoke, they rose and addressed themselves to him in a most respectful manner. At length, having agreed about an answer, they communicated to Captain Maxwell that there was no good place here for the purposes he wanted, and that as our present anchorage was unsafe, they recommended our going round to the harbour alluded to on a former occasion. At this place, which they call Winching or Oonching, he said we might put on shore whatever we chose. On our asking if in Winching the water was deep enough to admit a large ship, a long discussion arose, during which they appeared to be considering the merits of the harbour. They seemed apprehensive of giving it too high a character, and that on our reaching it we should be disappointed. The old man at length suggested sending the "little ship" to see whether it would answer. To this Captain Maxwell agreed, only requesting that a person might accompany us, in order to save time in the search. Simple as this appears, they took a long time to consider it, and ended by saying that no reply could be given till the next day.

While the subject of this harbour was under discussion, the old man drew on a sheet of paper, a chart of the island, and pointed out the place where the harbour lay. It proved afterwards, when we had surveyed the island, that this sketch possessed considerable accuracy, as the situation of the harbour of which they spoke corresponds exactly with that of Port Melville, discovered in the Lyra. It is much to be regretted that this curious sketch is lost.

The Chief now walked about the cabin, examined the globes, books, and pictures, with great attention. The wainscot struck him particularly, as well as the machinery and finish of the windows and sliding shutters. Captain Maxwell tried to make him comprehend our track on the globe. He had felt it becoming to preserve some state while business was going on, but he now became quite chatty and familiar. He went all over the ship, accompanied by the other chiefs and his own personal suite, consisting of a pipe bearer, a man who carried his large camp chair, another with a cover of red cloth for the chair, and a man who carried a round Japan box for the hatchee-matchee. Two others took it in turn to fan him, and to hold his arm by the elbow and wrist whenever he walked about; probably as a piece of state, for the ship had very little motion: these fanners were very expert at their business, for not content with cooling his face and neck, they lifted up his large sleeves and fanned his arms. On returning to the cabin, he saw Mr. Clifford using gloves, and begged leave to try them on; with the right one he succeeded very well, but the nails of his left hand being about an inch long, he found it not so easy a matter: he seemed to think them the oddest things he had met with, and laughing much, held them up repeatedly to the other chiefs.

The old man brought a present for Captain Maxwell, and sent another to the Lyra, consisting of a hog, a kid, two bags of potatoes, a basket of charcoal, thirty bundles of eggs (five in each), a bundle of vermicelli, and a jar of an ardent spirit called samchew. All the chiefs, who were in their best attire, were severally accompanied by a man carrying a box for the hatchee-matchee; their dresses were of various colours, and their sandals and stockings all alike. On rising to go away, the old man bowed to me, and said that he meant to visit my ship; but this being evidently complimentary, I begged him not to take so much trouble: he, in return, expressed himself obliged to me for being satisfied with the politeness intended. The Embassador's barge was manned to take him on shore, but as soon as he saw what was intended, he drew back, and declared that he could not land in any boat but his own. As it was supposed that his modesty prevented his accepting this offer, he was urged to overcome his scruples, and land in the manner proposed; he still, however, declined the honour, but at last went down the ladder, and having stepped into the barge, made a bow to Captain Maxwell, as if in acknowledgment of the attention, but immediately afterwards went into his own boat and pushed off, under a salute of three guns from each ship.

Our intention of returning this visit the next day was not mentioned during the discussions in the cabin, from the certainty of its being combated, and perhaps overruled: but when the last of the chiefs was getting into the boat, the interpreter was desired to tell him, in a careless way, as a matter of course, that next morning this visit would be returned on shore. As had been foreseen, this did not receive their approbation; the interpreter went into the boat, where every persuasion was used to convince him of the impropriety of our intention: they could not succeed, however, in making him yield this point, and at length went away. This interpreter is called "John" by all parties, and though merely an under servant of the factory at Canton, he is a very shrewd fellow. His English is certainly not the best, and probably the Chinese he speaks is the base provincial language of Canton; so that misunderstandings are no doubt often caused by his erroneous interpretation.

John's report after the boat had put off, and from which we gather that we shall be expected, was as follows: "They ax me, 'what for my Ta-yin come sho?' I say, 'to make chin-chin[7] they Ta-yin;' they tell me, 'You Ta-yin too much great mandarine, no can come sho;' I say, 'What for my Ta-yin no come sho? He great man; he[8] Ta-wang-tee too much great man; he let you Ta-yin come board ship, and you no let him come sho, chin-chin you Ta-yin; what for this?' Then they speak long time together; and by and by ax me, 'how many people bring sho you Ta-yin?' So I shake my head, I no like give answer long time, (they always take long time answer me). When they ax me again, I say, 'Ta-yin bring five people mo besides me.' They say, 'too much men come;' I say, 'No, no too much.' They ax, 'What time come?' I give no answer."

23d September.—As we had not contemplated such adventures as these, we had made no preparations for them; and now that it was necessary to make some return to the chief whom we were going to visit, we found great difficulty in preparing a suitable present. Captain Maxwell took with him several dozens of wine, some books, glasses, various trinkets, and a large piece of blue broad cloth. I took half the quantity of Captain Maxwell's other presents, and a table cloth in place of the broad cloth. Smaller presents were also made up for each of the chiefs. At one o'clock we set out in the barge, with a large union jack flying, and as it blew fresh, we soon reached the harbour. As we rowed past the shore, the people were seen running along all the roads leading to the town, so that by the time we reached the harbour, the crowd on both sides was immense: the trees, walls, and house tops, and in short every spot from which we could be seen, was literally covered with people, forming a sight as striking and animated as can well be conceived. As we entered the harbour several of the chiefs were observed to come down to a point, and wave for us to go round the end of a pier or mole, forming the inner harbour, where there was a good landing-place.

The chiefs helped us out, and then led us along, Ookooma taking Captain Maxwell's hand, Shayoon mine, and Jeema Mr. Clifford's; the others, according to their rank, conducted Mr. M'Leod of the Alceste, Mr. Maxwell, and another midshipman, Mr. Browne. They held our hands nearly as high as the shoulder, while a lane was formed for us through the crowd of people, who were perfectly silent. The children were placed in front, and the next rank sat down, so that those behind could see us in passing. At about a hundred and fifty yards from the landing-place, we came to the gate of a temple, where we were met by the Chief, who stood just on the outside of the threshold, on a small raised pavement: he took Ookooma's place, and conducted Captain

Maxwell up a few steps into the temple, which was partly open on two sides, with deep verandahs, which made the interior shady and cool. A large table, finely japanned, was spread, and two ornamented chairs were placed for us. The Chief seated himself at one end of the table, and placed Captain Maxwell on his left.

He expressed himself much gratified and honoured by the visit, asked our ages, and if we were married. He was greatly pleased with Captain Maxwell's account of his family, which nearly corresponded with his own. He guessed Mr. Maxwell's age to be twenty-seven, and was with difficulty persuaded to believe that a person six feet high could be only sixteen. The same mistake was made by all the natives, who invariably judged of the age of our young men by their height alone. An entertainment was now served, beginning with a light kind of wine, called sackee, which was handed round in very diminutive cups, filled by Issacha, from a small high pot in which the sackee was kept hot. They insisted on our emptying the cup every time, shewing us a fair example themselves. During the whole feast the sackee never left the table, being considered apropos to all the strange dishes which we partook of. The first of these consisted of hard boiled eggs, cut into slices, the outside of the white being coloured red. A pair of chopsticks[9] was now given to each person, and these were not changed during the feast. Next came fish fried in batter, which we found an excellent dish; then sliced smoked pork, next pig's liver sliced. After this, tea was handed round in cups of a moderate size; the tea was quite new, resembling, as was observed, an infusion of hay. Pipes and tobacco served to fill up the short intervals between the courses. A man attended behind each of our chairs, whose sole business it was to fill and light the pipes. The next dish was the strangest of any, and disgusted most of the party; it consisted of a mass of coarse, soft, black sugar, wrapped up in unbaked dough, powdered over with rice flour, dyed yellow. After this we had dishes of round cakes, like gingerbread nuts; then cakes made in the form of wreaths, and in a variety of other shapes. There was something like cheese given us after the cakes, but we cannot form a probable conjecture of what it was made. Most of the dishes were so good that we soon made a hearty dinner, but the attendants still brought in more, till the Chief seeing that we did not eat, recommended the sackee to us. The old gentleman's eyes at length began to glisten, and observing that we felt it hot, he requested us to uncover, shewing the example himself. He seized the doctor's cocked hat and put it on, while the doctor did the same with his hatchee-matchee. The oddity of the Chief's appearance produced by this change overcame the gravity of the attendants, and the mirth became general; nor was the joke relished by any body more than the Chief's two sons, who stood by his chair during all the entertainment: they were pretty little boys, with gaudy dresses, and their hair dressed in high shewy top-knots.

[Illustration: LOO-CHOO CHIEF and his TWO SONS.]

During the early part of the feast, our presents were brought in on trays, and laid at the feet of the Chief: the old man rose and saw them arranged, he then made a graceful bow, and acknowledged his satisfaction, observing that we had sent him too much, and had done him more honour than he was entitled to, and that he could not think of accepting the whole. This we considered matter of form, and in reply lamented our inability to make suitable presents; upon which he sat down and said no more. The other chiefs ran about shewing the list of their presents to their friends among the crowd.

The room in which this entertainment was given was open at first on two sides only, but afterwards the partitions on the other two sides were taken down, being contrived to slide in grooves; thus the rooms are enlarged or diminished at pleasure. When the partition behind us was removed, several strange looking figures made their appearance, who we found were Bodezes or priests. Their heads and faces were shaved, their feet bare, and their dress different from that worn by the rest of the people, being somewhat shorter, and much less free and flowing, without any belt round the waist, the robe being merely tightened a little by a drawing string tied at the side; over the shoulders hangs an embroidered band or belt, like that used by drummers: the colour of their dress is not uniform, some wearing black, others yellow, and some deep purple. They have a timorous, patient, subdued sort of look, with a languid smile, and ghastly expression of countenance. They are low in stature, and generally look unhealthy; they all stoop more or less, and their manners are without grace, so that a more contemptible class of people cannot easily be imagined. Along with the Bodezes were several boys, whom we took to be their children from the resemblance they bore to them; but this mistake must have arisen from these boys being dressed like the priests, for the Bodezes are strictly confined to a life of celibacy. From the circumstance of our being in a temple, as well as from our general habits of respect to persons filling sacred stations, we felt at first disposed to treat these Bodezes with attention, but this was looked upon as ridiculous by the chiefs, who seeing us bowing to them, begged we would take no further notice of them. Instead of being the class most respected, they are considered the lowest, and if not held in contempt, are at least neglected by all other ranks.

During all the time we were at table, the crowd pressed round the verandahs, and perched themselves upon the walls and house-tops in the vicinity, or wherever they could get a peep at us. The satisfaction here was mutual, as we were anxious to make the most of the opportunity, not knowing if we should ever be allowed to land again. After sitting two hours we rose, and were escorted to the boats in the same order as when we landed. An attempt had been made during the feast, when the whole party were in good humour, to prevail upon the old gentleman to sanction our taking a walk into the town; but the bare mention of such a thing sobered the whole party in an instant, and the subject was accordingly dropped. The sailors, who had been kept in the boats for fear of their doing mischief, had not been neglected by the Chief, who had sent them part of the feast, nor did it seem that they had any objection to the sackee. We looked anxiously on the right and left as we passed through the crowd, in hopes of seeing some of the women, but in this expectation we were disappointed. At a considerable distance indeed, on the opposite side of the harbour, we saw a group of women, several of whom came down to the causeway to obtain a better view of the boats as they passed. Six or eight young girls ran to the pier head, round some rocks near the end; they reached this spot just as we rowed past, but looked quite frightened at finding themselves so near us, and immediately drew back out of our sight. We fancied that we could discover a good deal of beauty in some of their faces, and that their figures were handsome; but as we had not seen a fair lady's face for nearly half a year before, our judgment in this case is not perhaps to be depended on. Ookooma and his associates put off to accompany us in one of their own boats, but as it blew hard, they came no farther than the pier head: Jeeroo, however, was sent along with us, to see that there were no stray sheep.

What is to follow is uncertain, but it is clear that we have made little progress of late, while fresh obstacles have been hourly rising against our landing; in the meantime, the Loo-chooans shew no little sagacity and kindness of disposition in supplying us liberally with all kinds of stock.

24th of September.—Last night and to-day it has blown a hard gale of wind, beginning at north north-east, and shifting to north-west, but the reefs and the land break its force, and enable us to ride in perfect security: in all probability it blew severely in the open sea. The barometer fell from 29.62, to 29.50, yesterday; in the evening it had reached 29.48, and this morning stood at 29.40. About four in the morning it began to rise rapidly, and the severity of the gale did not come on till it had risen a good deal. The thermometer both in the day and night stands at 82°, with very little variation, but the sky being constantly clouded, no observations could be made.

25th of September.—Jeeroo came on board this morning with a present of vegetables and fruit, and afterwards went on board the Alceste to join Ookooma and Jeema. They had preceded him with a present from the Chief, by whose desire they made a number of kind inquiries, and repeatedly expressed, in his name, surprise and satisfaction at our having been able to ride out the gale. They also apologized for not visiting us yesterday, which the gale had rendered impossible. It was represented in the conference to-day, that our limbs were getting quite stiff for want of exercise, and that it became absolutely necessary for us to land, on account of our health: they debated amongst themselves for some time, and then said that a final answer would be given to-morrow. They have quite forgotten their promise to send a pilot for the harbour to the northward: they wish also that we should forget it, since they change the subject whenever it is spoken of, and affect total ignorance of our meaning. The government probably think it best to keep us where we are, and therefore discourage our investigating the island any further.

Jeeroo, who begins to get quite familiar with us all, is a laughing good-humoured man, about thirty: he shakes every one cordially by the hand when he comes on board, and engages in all our amusements with great cheerfulness. He is very useful to us, because the anxiety he has to learn English makes him communicate freely the knowledge of his own language: thus there is little difficulty in fixing him over a glass of Constantia, upon which occasions he contributes largely to Mr. Clifford's vocabulary. Some of our words the Loo-chooans cannot pronounce; the letter *l* preceded by *c* appears the most difficult; they call Clifford "Criffar," and even this requires many efforts: not one of the natives has yet been able to make any thing of child; they call it shoidah, choiah, and chyad.

26th of September.—No boats have been near us to-day, and we might readily land if we chose it; but Captain Maxwell is resolved not to do so till he gets the consent of the natives.

27th of September.—As we were still prevented from going on shore, we amused ourselves by examining a reef which forms the north side of the anchorage. We found a field of coral about half a mile square, dry at low water, with the surf breaking very high on the outer edge, which lies exposed to the waves from the north. The surface of the rock is every where worn into small holes, which being left full of water as the tide goes out, are occupied by a number of beautiful blue fish. The coral is exceedingly hard, and though at many places it sticks up in sharp points, it requires a hammer of considerable weight to break it, and emits sparks like flint when struck; in a short time it entirely defaces the hammer. This extent of level space has suggested the idea of measuring a base on it in order to survey the anchorage, since there appears so little chance of our being allowed to land for this purpose on the beach.

While we were deliberating on this matter, we had a striking proof of the inconvenience to which we were likely to be exposed during this survey, by the tide rising and fairly washing us off. Notwithstanding this, we determined to commence next morning, and returned to make preparations, in high spirits at the prospect of an occupation, if not on terra firma, at least out of the ship, within whose sides we had been confined so long. On returning, we found that Captain Maxwell had arranged a party to visit the small island and reef which we were so close to on the 14th instant; the survey was therefore postponed.

Jeeroo sent us off some fresh fish to-day; some were red, and one or two blue: he came himself afterwards, and was happy to find us much gratified by his present. A formal message was sent to-day to the chiefs in attendance, stating that both ships were in want of fresh water, and that the boats must go on shore with casks to bring some off. In a short time after this message had been delivered, a number of canoes came alongside with large tubs of water; a strong proof of their alertness in getting rid of all our excuses for landing, and at the same time, it must be owned, of their readiness to supply our wants. An elderly gentleman, not a chief, visited us to-day, accompanied by his secretary. His appearance and manners being greatly in his favour, we paid him all the attention in our power. His wish was to be permitted to go all over the ship at his leisure; and in this way he examined every thing on board with far more attention than any body had done before him. His secretary, who was equally inquisitive, accompanied him in order to take notes. He employed himself for about six hours in examining the upper deck, and never quitted any thing till he understood its use. While he was thus occupied, he was attended by the sailors, who were pleased with his reverend appearance, and very readily assisted the old man in his enquiries.

It was interesting to observe, indeed, how early the gentle and engaging manners of all classes here won upon the sailors, no less than upon the officers. The natives from the first were treated with entire confidence; no watch was ever kept over them, nor were they excluded from any part of the ships; and not only was nothing stolen, but when any thing was lost, nobody even suspected for an instant, that it had been taken by them.

The old man next came down to the cabin, where he remained a long time examining the books and furniture, and occasionally engaging in conversation with Mr. Clifford, for whose Vocabulary he supplied many new words, and corrected others which had been written down erroneously. He would not accept any thing valuable, but was grateful for samples of rope, canvas, and cloth. This old gentleman renewed his examination of the brig next day; nor was it till the third day that he completed his survey.

28th of September.—At sunrise we set out for Reef Island, which lies about six miles from the anchorage: we reached it in about an hour, but as it was low water, the coral was left almost bare for a considerable way out, and our large boat could not get near the beach. In this dilemma we took possession of a canoe which was at anchor, and in several trips all the party landed. Near a hut we saw about a dozen people who stood looking at us till we landed, and then ran away, leaving their tobacco-pipes, pouches, and various other things on the ground about the hut, in which we found a pot of boiled sweet potatoes and several jars of water. Having, in vain, tried to allay the apprehensions of the natives by waving to them, to induce them to approach us, we sat down to breakfast; which we had hardly done, when two of them, an old man and a boy, came to the door of our tent and prostrated themselves before us, apparently in great alarm, for they answered incoherently, "ooa" (yes) to every question we asked them. At last we raised the old man on his knees, but he would not quit this posture till we gave him a glass of rum, which re-assured him a little, and shortly afterwards he consented to stand on his legs. Having thus gradually gained confidence, he made signs that we had taken his canoe: upon which an order was given to the coxswain to restore it. He guessed immediately what was said, and in the joy of his heart was proceeding to prostrate himself again, but was stopped by our holding out buttons and some pieces of meat and bread to him, which he received in both hands, and touching his head each time with the presents, made three low obeisances and retired.

On rising from breakfast we found, near the tent, about a dozen natives, who, in most respects, resembled our friends at Napakiang, but were not so neatly dressed; and their hair, instead of being formed into a knot, was allowed to fly loose. During the morning the party amused themselves in various ways. Some took their guns and went in search of curlews and sea-snipes: others set out to explore the reefs; and two or three remained near the tent, for the purpose of making observations on the sun at noon; but as it became cloudy about this time, the latter party failed in their object. The rest were more successful; the sportsmen having shot some game for dinner; and the other party having found all things favourable for inspecting the reef.

The examination of a coral reef during the different stages of one tide, is particularly interesting. When the tide has left it for some time it becomes dry, and appears to be a compact rock, exceedingly hard and ragged; but as the tide rises, and the waves begin to wash over it, the coral worms protrude themselves from holes which were before invisible. These animals are of a great variety of shapes and sizes, and in such prodigious numbers, that, in a short time, the whole surface of the rock appears to be alive and in motion. The most common worm is in the form of a star, with arms from four to six inches long, which are moved about with a rapid motion in all directions, probably to catch food. Others are so sluggish, that they may be mistaken for pieces of the rock, and are generally of a dark colour, and from four to five inches long, and two or three round. When the coral is broken, about high water mark, it is a solid hard stone, but if any part of it be detached at a spot which the tide reaches every day, it is found to be full of worms of different lengths and colours, some being as fine as a thread and several feet long, of a bright yellow, and sometimes of a blue colour: others resemble snails, and some are not unlike lobsters in shape, but soft, and not above two inches long[10].

The growth of coral appears to cease when the worm is no longer exposed to the washing of the sea. Thus, a reef rises in the form of a cauliflower, till its top has gained the level of the highest tides, above which the worm has no power to advance, and the reef of course no longer extends itself upwards. The other parts, in succession, reach the surface, and there stop, forming in time a level field with steep sides all round. The reef, however, continually increases, and being prevented from going higher, extends itself laterally in all directions. But this growth being as rapid at the upper edge as it is lower down, the steepness of the face of the reef is still preserved. These are the circumstances which render coral reefs so dangerous in navigation; for, in the first place, they are seldom seen above the water; and, in the next, their sides are so steep, that a ship's bows may strike against the rock before any change of soundings has given warning of the danger.

The island at high water is formed into three parts, which at low water are joined by reefs; the whole being about two and a half or three miles from east to west, and tolerably clear of rocks on the south side; but on the north it is guarded by a semicircle of coral extending upwards of a mile from the shore. On the centre island is only one hut, which, as there was reason to believe it to be the actual abode of the inhabitants, it may be allowable to describe. The walls were sunk under ground, so that only the roof appeared from without, the inside was fifteen feet by six: the walls of neatly squared stones, being two feet high, and the roof in the middle about six or seven high, formed of a ridge pole supported in the centre by a forked stick; the rafters of rough branches were covered with reeds, and thatched over with the leaf of the wild pine, which grows on all the coral islands. The fire-place was at one end on a raised part of the floor, and the other end appeared to be the sleeping place. It was conjectured, that this wretched place could only be meant as a temporary residence of fishermen, whose nets we saw lying about; but the number of water jars and cooking utensils which we found in and about it, gave it the appearance of a fixed habitation.

It was almost dark when we quitted the island, and the tide carrying us out of our proper course, we missed the ships and grounded on the reefs near the town; but as the tide was flowing, we easily got off, and by coasting along, soon gained the anchorage.

Sunday, 29th of September.—This day is memorable, on account of its being the first on which we were permitted to land.

Yesterday, when we were absent at Reef Island, the chiefs had come on board to say that we might land, but that our walk must be confined to the beach, and that we were neither to enter the town, nor to go into the country. At one o'clock several of the chiefs came on board and accompanied us to the beach, where we landed amidst an immense crowd, and were handed along by Ookooma and the rest, who, in their desire to be civil, held us by the arms. The day, however, being excessively hot, and the sand deep, we found this troublesome, and begged leave to walk alone, to which they reluctantly consented, and we proceeded along the beach for a quarter of a mile.

Beginning to get tired of our walk, we stopped and expressed some surprise at such a reception, and told them how disagreeable it was to us to be in the sun at such an hour. But our remonstrances did not produce much effect, for, on our objecting particularly to the heat, they shewed us to a sort of cave in a rock on the beach, where they put down a mat and wished us to drink tea in the shade, since we disliked the sun. This could not be submitted to, however, and we told them that our object in landing was not to sit down on the beach to drink tea, but to walk about under the trees in order to recover our health, impaired by a long stay on board ship. They tried all their eloquence to persuade us that our walk, thus limited, was perfectly pleasant; till at length Captain Maxwell gave them to understand, that he wished to go to the top of the hills under the trees; but that, as he did not mean to advance a single step beyond what was approved of, he would return instantly to the ship if they persisted in confining him to the beach. A consultation was held upon this, during which, frequent reference was made to several elderly men, whose opinions appeared to have great weight. They did not wear the dress of chiefs, but, from all that passed, we suspected them to be persons about court, who had been sent to assist the councils of the local commission, without superseding its authority. They at last agreed to our going to the top of the hill, taking the precaution before we set out, of sending on a couple of runners, probably to give warning to the women who might be in that direction. About half way up the road, which winds along a steep face, there is a neatly-built well, supplied by a stream which runs along a carved water-course, and near it were three or four rudely carved stones about a foot long and four inches across, with slow matches and a small quantity of rice laid upon each. Mr. Clifford distinctly made out that this was meant as a religious offering, but its precise object could not be discovered, though it was conjectured that the guardian deity of the well might have some title to the honour. The side of the hill is cut into horizontal irregular terraces, which are cultivated with apparent care, and irrigated by means of ditches leading from the well. On gaining the brow of the hill which overlooks the anchorage, the chiefs stopped, but as we were within a few yards of the summit, where we saw a shady grove, we begged them to proceed, to which, after a short deliberation, they consented. By gaining this eminence, we commanded a view of an extensive valley more beautiful than any thing we had ever seen; and on the side opposite to us we saw the large building spoken of before, generally suspected to be the King's palace: our questions, however, on this subject were always answered in so evasive a manner, and with such apparent distress, that we seldom made any allusion either to it or to the King.

Here we remained under the trees for an hour, drinking tea and smoking pipes in company with all the chiefs, besides four or five of the old men mentioned before. We amused them by lighting their pipes with a burning glass; but one old gentleman, who suspected some trick, and did not join in the surprise shewn by the rest, held out his hand that it might be exposed to the focus; and he was soon undeceived, to the great amusement of the circle. The magnifying power of the glass engaged the attention of them all, but they were differently affected by it: a start and an exclamation of pleased surprise was the most usual effect; some laughed immoderately at every experiment, while others were made very grave by it, who had not been particularly serious before. Advantage was taken of the moment when their admiration of the glass was at the highest, to present it to Jeeroo, whose good-will it was thought expedient to conciliate: he had not expected this, and felt obliged to us for so public a mark of our esteem.

A man on horseback happening to ride by, it was gravely suggested to the chiefs that nothing would so materially contribute to the establishment of our health as this species of exercise; but they insisted upon treating our request as a mere joke. On the way back an attempt was made to vary the walk by turning to the left on reaching the brow of the hill, and so walking along the edge of the cliff to another road; the chiefs observed upon this that we should infallibly tumble down and kill ourselves; affecting, notwithstanding the absurdity of any such apprehensions, to be greatly distressed at our danger: so we turned back, after having had a short interview with an old man seated in a shed on the edge of the precipice. His white beard, which covered his breast, suited well with his sedate and contemplative air, and gave him much the aspect of a hermit. Our appearance did not in the least discompose him, nor did he take any notice of us till desired to do so by Ookooma; he then bowed slightly, but immediately resumed his fixed look, as if he had been quite alone.

As we drew near to the place where we had landed, our companions surprised us by an invitation to a feast, prepared, they said, on our account in a temple close to the shore. Here they gave us painted eggs, smoked salt pork, and various preparations of eggs and fish, with sweet cakes in numberless forms, besides tea, pipes, and sackee, a light kind of wine made hot. Nothing could be more cheerful than they all were to-day: they placed us on the floor at the upper end of the room, and, for some time, they would not allow us to move; but Mr. Clifford, who, from the progress he has made in their language, has become a great favourite, was invited to join a merry party in the verandah, to which they brought flowers, fruits, and every thing they could think of, in order to learn their English names, and give in return those of Loo-choo.

On reaching the boats, Jeeroo and two of his friends seemed disposed to go on board; they were accordingly invited to do so, which made him so happy, that he took a rudely-carved ivory ornament, in the shape of a monkey, from his tobacco-pouch, and gave it to me. Dinner was on table when they came on board, but there was time before taking my friends below, to intimate to the servants, that these gentlemen were going to dine with me, so that when we reached the cabin, three plates were laid in addition. They had probably not expected to find dinner ready for them on board, for they expressed surprise at these preparations having been made, and would not sit down for some time. When the covers were removed, they became silent, and looked on either hand for directions how to proceed. On being helped to soup, they did not stir till they saw us take spoons, in the management of which they shewed but little awkwardness. The knife and fork gave them more trouble, but they set seriously about acquiring a knowledge of their use, and, in a short time, found no difficulty.

Their grave propriety on this occasion is the more worthy of remark, from its standing in some measure opposed to our own behaviour under similar circumstances: for instance, when we first tried to eat with their chopsticks: on that occasion there was a sort of giggling embarrassment shewn by some of us, a contempt as it were of ourselves, for condescending to employ an effort to acquire the use of a thing apparently so unimportant. Their diminutive cups and odd dishes, too, sometimes excited mirth amongst us. Our Loo-choo friends, however, never committed themselves in this way; a difference of manners, which may arise from their looking upon us as their superiors, and vice versâ; but even admitting this, which we were sufficiently disposed to do, it is certainly no excuse for us.

On this occasion Jeeroo and his friends had evidently made up their minds to find every thing quite new, for all three made a slight involuntary exclamation when one of the covers was lifted up, and shewed a dish of their own sweet potatoes. They ate of every thing, using a great deal of salt, with the fineness and whiteness of which they were much pleased. A tart, however, being put on the table, they all objected at first to touching it; they would not say why: they were at length prevailed upon to taste it, which they had no sooner done, than they exclaimed that it was "masa! masa!" (good! good!) It was made of Scotch marmalade, and Jeeroo, in recommending it to his friends, told them it was "injássa, amása," (bitter, sweet), a union which they appeared not to have met with before. They drank wine with us, but said they feared it would make them tipsy; upon which we shewed them our mode of mixing it with water, which was evidently new to them, for they relished it so much in this form, that they were in a fair way of running unconsciously into the very excess which they dreaded. As soon as the cloth was removed, they rose, and went to walk about the ship: on our shewing a wish to accompany them, they intreated us to keep our seats.

During dinner, though it was the first they had ever seen in the European style, these people not only betrayed no awkwardness, but adopted our customs, such as drinking wine with each other, so readily, that we were frequently at a loss to determine whether they had but just learned these customs, or whether their own usages in these cases were similar to ours. As they pushed off in their boat they were asked to sing, which they did at once, and by their manner we suspected that the song had some allusion to us, but we could not make out the words.

30th of September.—During the whole of this morning we were engaged in the survey, accompanied by several of the midshipmen of both ships. We measured a base, and continued taking angles till the tide rose and drove us off.

1st of October.—As a free intercourse was now established with the natives at this place, and little doubt remained of our being able to gain their permission in a day or two for landing the Alceste's stores, it became an object to ascertain, without further delay, whether or not this anchorage was better than the harbour described by the natives as being a few miles only to the northward. While any apprehensions existed of our not being able to land here, it was not thought prudent to send the Lyra to look for that harbour, lest the chiefs should become still more suspicious of our intentions. At this moment, however, there was reason to believe that the chiefs wished the Alceste to remain where she was, and it was expected that any show of moving to another harbour would stimulate their exertions to render our present situation agreeable.

The Lyra was accordingly ordered to weigh this morning at daylight, for the purpose of examining the coast for ten or twelve leagues to the northward. We went out by a narrow passage through the reefs, and in the course of the morning beat up to Sugar Loaf Island. We did not land upon it, but passed near enough to see that it is richly cultivated on the lower parts, and that all the houses are collected into villages, shaded as usual by large trees round the bottom, and for one-third of the way up the sides of the peak. As this was our furthest point in the present survey, we tacked on reaching the Sugar Loaf, and coasted round the shores of a large square bay on the west side of the great island. The wind shifted gradually as we sailed along, blowing directly off the shore at every place, by which means we were enabled to complete the circuit of the bay before dark, after which we anchored in sixty-five fathoms water. Next morning we resumed our examination of the coast, but as the weather was fine, we hoisted out a boat and pulled close along the shore, while the brig kept her course at the distance of several miles. In this manner we traced the whole shore, till we came close to Napakiang, without seeing any port. We tried to land at several places, but were every where kept off by coral reefs stretching along the coast, at the distance of two or three hundred yards, and forming, to strangers at least, an impenetrable barrier. The canoes of the natives paddled away from us, and passed through the surf by passages which we were afraid to approach. We returned to the brig about two o'clock, and at three anchored in our former place at Napakiang.

The departure of the Lyra had excited a great sensation on shore; the chiefs came off to inquire of Captain Maxwell where the "honee gua" (little ship) was; but he did not choose to satisfy them, except by saying that they had trifled with him so long, and refused to let him land his casks and stores with such obstinacy, that he must endeavour to find some more favourable place at which to refit his ship. The effect was exactly what he wished; they intreated him not to think of moving from Napakiang; offered him not only large boats to put his stores in, but said he should have store-rooms on shore for whatever he desired, while his ship was refitting. They moreover granted him permission to land with his officers, and to go to the top of the hill without being guarded as formerly.

On the Lyra's anchoring, the chiefs came on board in great agitation, desiring to know what we had discovered. As we had actually nothing to relate, there was little difficulty in keeping our secret. They accompanied me on board the Alceste when I went to make my report, but Captain Maxwell, having found the advantage he had already gained by keeping them in ignorance of his intentions, was nowise communicative. They now offered to allow his people to land for the purpose of washing their clothes, which they had before refused to do, and in short, were in a mood to grant any thing, provided we were willing to remain at this part of the island. They did not pretend that this was out of regard for us, and it was easy to see that they apprehended more trouble in managing us any where else than at this place. Amongst the arguments used by them to dissuade us from going to the other end of the island, they said it was inhabited by savages. It came out accidentally too, that in the event of the ship's actually proceeding to other parts of the island, the six chiefs were to accompany us: so that they were probably influenced by considerations of personal convenience to make every exertion to prevent our moving.

3d of October.—The Lyra's crew were allowed to go on shore to-day to wash their clothes, and amuse themselves by running about on the side of the hill. Two of the sailors of this party, who happened to be singing near the well, drew a number of natives round them, who expressed great pleasure at hearing their songs. At first the crowd consisted entirely of the peasantry, who listened with great attention, and never interrupted the sailors; but in about half an hour, a person of some rank, with a number of attendants, came up, and begged them to sing several of their songs over again: we could not find out who this person was, but it was probably one of the chiefs, some of whom are remarkably fond of our music.

4th of October.—The survey on the reef was completed to-day: the only inconvenience we had experienced here, was the limited time which the tide allowed us each day, otherwise the situation was well adapted for a base, from its commanding a view of all parts of the anchorage. During the progress of the principal survey, the young gentlemen sent by Captain Maxwell, in conjunction with the midshipmen of the Lyra, completed a survey of the reef itself. A native of a genteel appearance, but not in the dress of a chief, visited the Lyra to-day, and gave me a present of two pipes and two bags of sweet potatoes.

5th of October.—Captain Maxwell called for me this morning at sunrise, on his way to the shore. The chiefs had not expected us so early, and our only companion for some time was an old peasant, who now and then ran on before to give notice of our approach. Two well dressed people shortly afterwards came up, and continued with us during our walk, which at first lay along the beach, but afterwards led into the country; some exception was taken to this by our companions, but as no attention was paid to them, they desisted.

After walking about a mile, we passed through a grove of young trees, and found ourselves close to a village, which lies in the bottom of a glen highly cultivated, the houses being almost entirely hid by trees, of which the bamboo is the most conspicuous.

This village is surrounded by a close hedge, and every separate house also has an inclosure: some of the houses have attached to them neat arbours, formed of a light frame of bamboo covered with a variety of creepers. The rice fields are divided by small banks of earth, made to retain the water, and along the top of each bank there is a foot-path; the whole valley having much the air of a scene in India. A number of the villagers, accompanied by their children, came out to meet us, but there were no women amongst them: we passed on, as they were evidently averse to our entering the village.

On our way across the valley we were attracted by the appearance of a cottage, so buried in foliage as to be completely hid from our view till we were within a few paces of the door. It was surrounded by a slight fence of rods, about an inch apart, with a line of creepers along the top, and hanging down on both sides: a wicker gate admitted us, and we entered the house, which we found divided into two apartments, eight feet square, besides a small verandah at one end. The floors, which were made of slips of bamboo, were raised about six inches from the

31

ground, and covered with a straw mat. The walls were five feet high, being neatly wattled with split bamboo, above which rose a pointed thatched roof. It was occupied by an old man, whom we appeared to have disturbed at breakfast, for cups and tea-things were arranged on the floor; he asked us to sit down, and gave us pipes and tea. The little apartment we were in was as neat as any thing we had ever seen: on one side there was a set of shelves, with cups, bowls, and cooking utensils; on the others were hung various implements of husbandry, with hats and various dresses, all clean and in order. Higher up was a sort of loft or garret, formed by bamboo poles, laid horizontally from the top of the walls; on this were placed various tools, nets, and baskets. The fire-place was in the middle of one side, and sunk below the level. On the outside, in the space between the house and the fence, there was a pigeon house and a poultry yard, and close to the little verandah spoken of before, there stood two spinning-wheels of a light and ingenious construction. All round on the outside of the fence, the trees were high and thick; and though the sun was above the hills, the house was completely shaded except at the end, where a small opening admitted the rays into the verandah. We staid some time with the old farmer, trying to express our admiration of the simplicity and beauty of his cottage, and then went up the opposite side of the valley.

Here we found a road like a dressed walk in a garden: following this, we passed through a series of beautiful groves of bamboo and other trees, till at length, after winding about a good deal, we came to a double row of tall pine trees, interspersed with many others whose names we did not know, so as to form a walk which must be shady at all hours of the day. This road we knew would lead to the town, and therefore when we had reached the highest point we turned to the right, and after a short walk reached the grove of trees which had been made the limit to our first walk on the 29th ultimo. At this place Captain Maxwell surprised the natives a good deal by shooting several birds on the wing, but they could not be prevailed upon to fire themselves, nor even to pull the trigger when no powder was in the pan.

6th of October.—After divine service to-day on board the Alceste, a long conference was held between Captain Maxwell and the five chiefs, when, after a good deal of discussion, it was agreed on their part to allow the Alceste's stores to be landed, for the purpose of getting at the leak. Our means of interpreting on these occasions are not the best that could be wished; but John, our Chinese, is nevertheless a keen fellow, and very ready with answers when pressed. We generally explain as fully as possible to John what our wishes are, and then leave him to communicate them the best way he can. An instance of his quickness occurred to-day, which seems worth mentioning. John had communicated to them, by Captain Maxwell's desire, that as the leak complained of was in the magazine, it would be necessary to land the powder: they debated a long time upon this, and then asked John "Why the powder was not put on board the little ship?" John, who was not aware of any good reason, affected to be surprised at this question, which he refused to interpret, saying that if Captain Maxwell thought such a measure right, he would surely not have waited till they suggested it. The light in which he had thus put the question, made them earnestly desire him not to mention any thing about it, declaring at the same time, that they would willingly give a place for the powder, and for any other stores which Captain Maxwell might wish to land.

To-day for the first time they talked unreservedly of the king, whose name even they had hitherto studiously avoided: they spoke freely of his majesty's having sent all the stock and vegetables with which we were daily supplied. Captain Maxwell, who of course was very desirous of opening a communication with the court, intimated his wish to pay his respects as soon as might be convenient. They heard this with apparent satisfaction, and signified that his request should be made known to the king. We are at a loss to discover what can have caused this change of manner. We can only conjecture, that perhaps the king, on hearing so many reports about us, may have become desirous of seeing us himself. At all events it is clear that some alteration in the instructions to the chiefs must have been made, otherwise they would have shewn their usual reserve when the king's name was mentioned, and would on no account have allowed us to talk of visiting him.

At one o'clock we went on shore to look at the place assigned by the chiefs for the reception of the Alceste's stores. It is an oblong inclosure, sixty yards by forty, surrounded by a wall twelve feet high, rather well built with squared coral: the entrance is by a large gate on the south side, from which there extends raised gravel walks, with clipped hedges, the intermediate spaces being laid out in beds, like a garden. The temple in which we were feasted on the day of our first visit, occupies one corner of the inclosure; it is completely shaded by a grove of trees, which also overhang the wall. In that part of the garden directly opposite to the gate, at the upper end of the walk there is a smaller temple, nearly hid by the branches of several large banyan trees; and before it, at the distance of ten or twelve paces, a square awkward looking building, with a raised terrace round it. The temple first spoken of is divided by means of shifting partitions into four apartments, and a verandah running all round, having a row of carved wooden pillars on its outer edge to support the roof, which extends considerably beyond it. The floor of the verandah is two feet from the ground, the roof is sloping and covered with handsome tiles, those forming the eaves being ornamented with flowers and various figures in relief; there are also several out-houses, and a kitchen communicating with them by covered passages. In one of the inner apartments, at the upper end, there is a small recess containing a green shrub, in a high narrow flower-pot, having a Chinese inscription on a tablet hanging above it on the wall. On another side of the same room, there hangs the picture of a man rescuing a bird from the paws of a cat; the bird seems to have been just taken from a cage, which is tumbling over, with two other birds fluttering about in the inside: it is merely a sketch, but is executed in a spirited manner. In one of the back apartments we find three gilt images, eighteen inches high, with a flower in a vase before them. The roof of the temple within is ten feet high, and all the cornices, pillars, &c. are neatly carved into flowers and the figures of various animals. The ground immediately round it is divided into a number of small beds, planted with different shrubs and flowers; and on a pedestal of artificial rock, in one of the walks close to it, is placed a clay vessel of an elegant form, full of water, with a wooden ladle swimming on the top. On a frame near one of the out-houses, hangs a large bell, three feet high, of an inelegant shape, resembling a long bee-hive; the sides are two inches thick, and richly ornamented: its tone is uncommonly fine.

It was determined to appropriate part of the large temple to the use of the sick and their attendants; the assistant surgeon of the Alceste taking one room, and the gunner, who was to have the whole inclosure in his charge, another. The small temple at the upper end, being a retired spot, was fixed upon for the Lyra's observatory; the square building in the centre seemed well adapted for a magazine. At the gate a notice was hung up, both in English and Loo-choo, signifying that no person was to enter without a written pass from Captain Maxwell, or from one of the chiefs.

7th and 8th of October.—These days have been occupied in carrying the arrangements of Sunday into effect. It was very interesting to observe the care which the natives took of the sick, whom they assisted all the way from the beach to the temple; a number of people attended to support such of them as had barely strength enough to walk. When they were safely lodged, eggs, milk, fowls, and vegetables, were brought to them; and whenever any of them were tempted by the beauty of the scenery to walk out, several of the natives were ready to accompany them.

The powder was landed, and Mr. Holman, the gunner of the frigate, began the operation of drying it on hides spread in the sun round the magazine. The cows and other stock were also landed. One of the cows calved that night, to the surprise of every body, and the great joy of the natives, who took a great fancy to the little bull born amongst them. Mr. Mayne, the master of the Alceste, took up his quarters in the temple, in order to be near his observatory, which was in the centre of the garden. The stores of all kinds were sent on shore from the Alceste, which produced an apparent confusion, and the chiefs, seeing so many valuable things lying about, began to fear that they would be taken away; at least, it was supposed that they had such an apprehension, for the wall of the temple was immediately fenced in by a sort of net-work of long bamboo poles, the ends of which were fixed in the ground at the foot of the wall on the outside, and the tops made to cross one another four or five feet above the wall. This contrivance, instead of rendering the place more secure, made it more accessible; but as our opinion was not asked, and we had no apprehensions of theft, we let them proceed in their own way.

Mrs. Loy, wife of the boatswain of the Alceste, was the only female in our squadron, and as such excited no small interest at this place. She was a perfectly well behaved person, and sufficiently neat in her dress, but without great pretensions to good looks. The natives, who from the first paid her much attention, shewed at all times their desire of granting her every indulgence. They even went so far as to say she might go into the city; but, upon consulting with her husband, who was apprehensive of some accident, she declined it. When this circumstance became known to us, we easily convinced the boatswain that no mischief could possibly arise from trusting his wife amongst such kind people; but Mrs. Loy could not be persuaded of this; and thus was lost the only opportunity of seeing the town which occurred during all our stay.

Two of the natives have been studying English with great assiduity, and with considerable success. One is called Mádera, the other Anya. They carry note books in imitation of Mr. Clifford, in which they record in their own characters every word they learn. They are both keen fellows, and are always amongst the strangers. From the respect occasionally paid to them, it is suspected that their rank is higher than they give out, and that their object in pretending to be people of ordinary rank, is to obtain a more free intercourse with all classes on board the ships. Mádera, by his liveliness and his propriety of manners, has made himself a great favourite; he adopts our customs with a sort of intuitive readiness, sits down to table, uses a knife and fork, converses, and walks with us, in short, does every thing that we do, quite as a matter of course, without any apparent effort or study. He is further recommended to us by the free way in which he communicates every thing relating to his country; so that as he advances in English, and we in Loo-choo, he may be the means of giving us much information. As an instance of his progress in English, it may be mentioned, that one day he came on board the Lyra, and said, "The Ta-yin speak me, 'you go ship, John come shore;'" by which we understood that Captain Maxwell had sent him on board the brig for the interpreter. This was about three weeks after our arrival.

[Illustration: PRIEST and GENTLEMAN of LOO-CHOO.]

Most of the natives have acquired a little English, so that Mr. Clifford has now no difficulty in finding people willing to instruct him, and to take pains in correcting his pronunciation. One of his teachers, called Yáckabee Oomeejeéro, will not permit him to write down a single word till he has acquired the exact Loo-choo sound: but he is like the rest in shewing an invincible objection to giving any information about the women. He admits that he is married, and gives the names of his sons: but when his wife or daughters are alluded to, he becomes uneasy, and changes the subject. On Mr. Clifford's gravely telling him that he believed there were no women on the island, he was thrown off his guard, and answered hastily, that he had both a wife and daughter, but instantly checking himself, turned the conversation another way. On the picture of an English lady being shewn to him, he commended it highly, saying, at the same time, "Doochoo innágo whoóco oorung" (Loo-choo women are not handsome.) This old gentleman is a better teacher than scholar; he calls the letter L "airoo;" veal, "bairoo;" flail, "frayroo;" in which instances of mispronunciation, we may recognize a difficulty not uncommon amongst English children.

FOOTNOTES:

[Footnote 6: This circumstance is by no means common, and therefore cannot be depended on. In fine weather these reefs give no warning whatever, and a ship on approaching them ought invariably to have a boat a-head.]

[Footnote 7: Chin-chin in the corrupt dialect of Canton, means the ceremony of salutation, which consists in the action of holding up the closed hands, pressed together before the face, and bowing at the same time.]

[Footnote 8: Ta-whang-tee is Chinese for Emperor, King.]

[Footnote 9: Chopsticks are two pieces of ivory or wood, about a foot in length, of the thickness of a quill; they serve in China instead of a knife and fork, and are held in the right hand. Until the difficult art of holding them is attained, they are perfectly useless. The Chief at this feast, seeing that we made little progress, ordered sharp pointed sticks to be brought, which he good humouredly recommended our using instead of the chopsticks.]

[Footnote 10: A large collection, which was at this time made of these Zoophites, was unfortunately lost in the Alceste.]

CHAPTER III.

The Lyra sent to survey the Island of Loo-choo—Discovery of Port Melville—Description of that Harbour, and the Villages on its Banks—Lyra nearly wrecked—Interview with Natives at the South Point—Return to Napakiang—Behaviour of the Natives at a Seaman's Funeral—Mádera's Character and Conduct—Sociable Habits of the Natives—Dinner given to the Chiefs of the Island by Captain Maxwell—Mádera's Behaviour on this Occasion—Two Women seen—A Lady of Rank visits the Boatswain's Wife—Captain Maxwell fractures his Finger—Loo-choo Surgeon—Concern of the Natives—Visit of the Prince—Discussion about the King of Loo-choo's Letter—Mádera appears in a new Character—Feast given by the Prince—List of Supplies given to the Ships—Behaviour of the Prince on taking Leave—Preparations for Departure—Mádera's Distress—Last Interview with the Chiefs—Brief Memorandums upon the Religion, Manners, and Customs of Loo-choo—Advice to a Stranger visiting this Island.

As soon as the survey of Napakiang anchorage was completed, and a perfectly good understanding established with the natives, it was determined to make a survey of the whole island, and the Lyra was ordered upon this service. She were absent about a week, during which period the general chart of the island was constructed. It will be obvious to every one acquainted with the subject, that, in so short a time, a very exact survey of the coast of an island nearly sixty miles long could not have been made: yet, as the weather was in general fine, and other circumstances favourable, the chart will be found sufficiently correct for most practical purposes. As the chart and the nautical and hydrographical details are given in the Appendix, I propose at present to relate only such particulars of the cruise as seem likely to interest the general reader.

9th of October.—At daybreak we got under weigh and stood to sea through a passage discovered by the boats; it was so extremely narrow, that the least deviation from the course brought us close to the rocks. We were regulated in steering by two marks on the land, which lie in the same straight line with the centre of the passage; these it is necessary to keep always together: but not conceiving that such nicety was required while sailing out, the marks were allowed to separate, by which we found ourselves in a minute or two within a few yards of a coral reef, the ragged tops of which were distinctly seen two or three feet below the surface, whilst, at the same time, the leadsman on the opposite side sounded in nine fathoms. This early proof of the danger of navigating amongst coral, by teaching us the necessity of extreme caution, was of great importance to us in our future operations.

As the coast lying between Napakiang and the Sugar Loaf had already been examined, we proceeded at once round that island, which, from its having the same aspect on every bearing, and being quite different in shape from any land in this quarter, is an excellent land-mark for navigators. The natives call it Eegooshcoond, or castle[11]. The English name was given, I believe, by Captain Broughton.

Having rounded this peak and stood in for the north-west side of the Great Loo-choo, where there is a deep bight, a small island was observed close in shore, behind which it was thought there might be shelter for ships; the coast, however, being unknown to us, it was not thought safe to carry the brig very close in, and a boat was therefore dispatched with an officer to reconnoitre: he returned at eight o'clock to say that there was a harbour in the main land, the entrance to which lay on the inside of the small island mentioned before; but that the passages were narrow and winding, and that a more careful examination was necessary before the brig could venture in.

11th of October.—In the morning we again stood in, using the precaution of sending a boat a-head to sound the way; when we had nearly reached the entrance we anchored, and proceeded in three boats to examine the harbour discovered last night. As it was near noon when we passed the small island, we landed and observed the meridian altitude of the sun; after which we entered the harbour in the main island, by an intricate passage of about a quarter of a mile in length, and at one place not two hundred yards wide. Here we found ourselves in a circular bason upwards of half a mile across, with deep water, and completely sheltered from all winds. On its western shore we saw a large and beautiful village almost hid amongst trees, with a high wooded range behind it stretching to the south. The eastern shore was low and laid out in salt fields, with a few huts here and there. At first sight this bason did not appear to have any outlet except by the one we had examined; but on rowing to its upper or southern side, we found that it joined by a narrow channel with another harbour still larger, and if possible more beautiful than the first, for here the land was high on both sides, and richly wooded from top to bottom. Proceeding onwards through this bason, which had all the appearance of an inland lake, we came to another outlet, not above a hundred yards wide, formed by cliffs rising abruptly out of the water to the height of a hundred feet. Both sides being covered with trees, which almost met overhead, the space below was rendered cool and pleasant, and the water, thus sheltered from every wind, was as smooth as glass. We rowed along for some time by various windings through this fairy scene in total uncertainty of what was to come next, and at last, after advancing about three miles, it opened into an extensive lake several miles in length, studded with numerous small islands.

The depth of water in the lake varied from four to six fathoms; but in the narrow neck which connects it with the sea the depth is from ten to twenty fathoms, being deepest at the narrowest parts. Ships might ride in any part of this extraordinary harbour, in perfect safety during the most violent tempests: and the shores are so varied, that every purpose of re-equipment might be served. At some places natural wharfs are formed by the rocks, and eight and ten fathoms water close to them. Ships might lie alongside these places, or might heave down by them: there are also shallow spots on which ships might be careened. Many of the cliffs are hollowed into caves, which would answer for storehouses; and in the numerous lawns on both sides encampments might be formed of any number of people.

We rowed directly across, and landed at the southern side at the foot of a wooded range of hills, which forms the southern boundary of the lake. As no road was observed, it was resolved to go directly up the hill, and, in about an hour, after a good deal of scrambling amongst the bushes and long grass, we gained the top, where we found a neat pathway with a ditch on each side, and a hedge growing on the top of the mound, formed of the earth from the ditch; it resembled not a little an English lane. Without knowing where this might take us to, we followed it, in the hope of meeting some of the people, but in this we were disappointed. Yet this place must, at times, be frequented, as we observed a number of similar paths leading to the right and left.

The trees on this range of hills are low, and of no great beauty; the fir is the most common, but we did not know the names of the rest. After walking about a mile, our path took an abrupt turn down the brow of the hill, and appeared to lead to a large village at some distance. The view from this elevation was very satisfactory, as it enabled us to check our rough eye draught of the harbour and coast. The road down the hill was so steep that it was just possible to stand upon it, being inclined, as was conjectured on the spot, at an angle of 45°. At the foot of the hill there was a little cottage, consisting of two parts, made of wattled rattans, connected by a light open bamboo roof, so covered with a large leaved creeper as to afford a complete shelter from the sun. The cottage, which was thatched, was enveloped in creepers, encircled by the usual rattan fence at two or three yards distance. One of the wings was occupied by goats; the other, which was dark, seemed to belong to the people, who had deserted it on our approach. There being only a small hole in the wall to admit light and air, and to allow the smoke to escape, every thing inside was black and dirty. Two spears hung on one side, which, upon enquiry afterwards, we were told were for striking fish.

On coming to our boats, we found them surrounded by a party of the natives, smaller in stature than our friends at Napakiang, and shewing less curiosity: probably their surprise at our sudden appearance had not subsided sufficiently to allow of their indulging curiosity in detail. A large party of them watched attentively while a musket was loaded, and when pointed over their heads in the air, they seemed aware that something was going to happen, but from their not shrinking or removing out of the way, it seemed they knew not what. When it was fired, the whole party fell as if they had been shot, but rose instantly again, and looking to the right and left of each other, indulged in a timorous laugh. A cartridge was given to one man, with which he was nearly blowing himself up by placing it on his lighted pipe. The officer of the boat informed us that a gentleman had come to him and offered his horse to ride; he had dismounted for that purpose, but the horse was frightened, and would not suffer the officer to get upon him. We saw this person riding along when we were at the top of the hill; he called out to us repeatedly, probably to offer his horse, but we thought he wished to dissuade us from walking over the hill, and accordingly took no notice of him.

In the meantime Mr. Clifford, who had been unwell, and felt unequal to the labour of climbing the hill, proceeded in one of the boats towards a large village on the eastern side of the lake. He was met by a number of the inhabitants, whose dress and appearance were inferior to what we had been accustomed to see at Napakiang; on his asking them in Loo-choo for some water, they gave it cheerfully; but they shewed little curiosity, and the party which followed wherever he went, seemed to have no other object than to prevent disturbance. They made no objection to his going into the village, where he saw in one inclosure a complete farm-yard. The principal house was closed, but to the offices there was free access. In the stable were two handsome bay ponies; there was also a well stocked pig-sty, and a poultry-house. In another quarter stood a mill for husking corn, consisting of a grooved solid cylinder of wood, fitting neatly into a hollow cylinder, the sides of which were also grooved; near this lay a hand flour-mill and several baskets of cotton. In another part of the court was a granary erected on posts about six feet above the ground, having billets of fire-wood piled below it. At another place, under a tree in the village, he saw a blacksmith's anvil fixed in a block; the forge was of masonry, having an air hole, but the bellows was wanting.

In the centre of the village stood a building like a temple, surrounded by a stone wall. It was filled with elegant vases of different shapes and sizes, closed up and ranged in rows on the floor; the verandah encircling the building was also covered with vases. According to the account of the natives, the remains of the dead are deposited in these jars. Round the building bamboo poles were placed so as to lean against the thatched roof, having notches cut in them, to which bundles of flowers were hung, some fresh, others decayed, apparently funereal offerings; but their exact import Mr. Clifford was not able to learn. The elegant shape of the vases, and the tasteful way in which they were arranged, with the flowers hanging all round, gave to this cemetery an air of cheerfulness, which we are in the habit of thinking unsuitable to a depository of the dead.

This village, which is at the head of a bay, is sheltered from the north wind by a row of trees between it and the beach; behind it is sheltered by a range of hills. A broad road runs between it and the water; trees are planted among the houses, so as nearly to conceal them. In the middle of the village near the cemetery, in an open square, there is a cluster of granaries like the one described above; the walls are made of wattled rattan, and overhang the lower part.

Mr. Clifford tried in vain to see the Chief of the village; but either there was no such person, or he was out of the way: the inhabitants pointed out a man on horseback as a Chief, who passed on to another village; this was probably the same man who offered his horse to Mr.

Hall, the officer of the boat. Mr. Clifford went to the top of the range behind the village, and afterwards into the valley on the other side, which he found highly cultivated.

From the heights we saw that the large space which was at first considered a lake, communicates with the sea to the north-eastward, as well as by the narrow passage through which we had come, but there was not time to allow of its being fully examined. As we returned by the narrow straits, we called at some of the small villages on the eastern side. At one of these, the people of the village, headed by a man who appeared to be superior to the rest, came towards the boat, and stopped for some minutes at the distance of fifty yards; after which, appearing to have gained confidence, they came on, with the old man in front, carrying a green bough in his hand. He would not come close, however, till invited by Mr. Clifford in Loo-choo to look at the boat; he then advanced and presented his bough, in return for which we broke a branch from a tree, and gave it to him with the same formality he had used towards us. Soon after this exchange was made, they left us, and went to examine the boat, to fishermen always an object of great interest.

On our entering the village we were met by a man who appeared to be the principal person of the place; he was very polite, shewed us through the village, and took us over his garden, where he had some sugar-cane growing; this we admired very much, upon which he ordered one of the finest of the canes to be taken up by the roots and presented to us; we immediately gave him a few buttons off our jackets, with which he was quite pleased. On its beginning to rain while we were in the garden, he invited us into his house, which, from the walls being of wattled cane, looked like a large basket. Rude pictures and carved wood-work figures were hanging on the walls, together with some inscriptions in Chinese characters.

On returning to the lower harbour of all, we went to the large village before spoken of, which is by far the most finished of any that we have seen on this island. The streets are regular and clean swept; each house has a neat cane wall, as well as a screen before the door; plantain and other trees are growing so thickly in the inside of the fence, that they completely shade the house. Near the beach were several large houses, in which a number of people were seated writing: on going up to them they gave us tea and cakes, and afterwards allowed us to go over the village without restraint; they were curious to know whether the brig was coming into the harbour or not, and if so, how many days we meant to stay; they expressed neither pleasure nor regret when we said that we were not coming in. In front of the village, and parallel with the beach, there is a splendid avenue thirty feet wide, formed by two rows of large trees, whose branches join overhead, and effectually screen the walk from the sun; here and there are placed wooden benches, and at some places stone seats are fixed near the trees: this space, which is about a quarter of a mile long, is probably used as a public walk.

A range of hills of a semicircular form embraces the village, and limits its extent: at most places it is steep, but at the point where the north end joins the harbour, there is an overhanging cliff about eighty feet high, the upper part of which extends considerably beyond the base; at eight or ten yards from the ground on this inclined face, a long horizontal gallery has been hewn out of the solid rock: it communicates with a number of small square excavations still deeper in the rock, for the reception of the vases containing the bones of the dead.

The trees and creepers on the edge of the precipice hung down so as to meet the tops of those which grew below, and thus a screen was formed which threw the gallery into deep shade: every thing here being perfectly still, the scene was very solemn and imposing. It took us somewhat by surprise, for nothing in its external appearance indicated the purpose to which the place was appropriated: happening to discover an opening amongst the trees and brushwood, and resolving to see what it led to, we entered by a narrow path winding through the grove. The liveliness of the scenery without, and the various amusements of the day, had put us all into high spirits, but the unexpected and sacred gloom of the scene in which we suddenly found ourselves had an instantaneous effect in repressing the mirth of the whole party.

This village is called Oonting, and is certainly the same that is alluded to by the chiefs, and which we formerly wrote down Winching and Oonching.

This excellent harbour, which we discovered, has been named Port Melville, in honour of Lord Viscount Melville, First Lord of the Admiralty.

It was quite dark when we reached the brig. As a heavy swell was rolling in, no time was lost in getting under weigh, but before we could succeed in running well off the reefs, the wind suddenly changed, and the weather, which before had been fine, became so dark and squally, that we almost lost sight of the shore. Our situation was now very critical, for we had just sufficient knowledge of the coast, to be sensible how extremely dangerous it was; and the wind, which blew directly on the shore, came in such violent gusts, that there was every reason to apprehend the loss of our topmasts; to reef the sails was impossible, as the delay which this operation must have caused would have been fatal. While things were in this state, it became necessary to tack, but owing to the heavy and irregular swell, the brig came round again against our will, and before the sails could be properly trimmed, she had gone stern foremost almost to the verge of the reef, on which the sea was breaking to a great height. Had this occurred a second time, nothing could have prevented our being wrecked. After beating about in this awkward predicament for two hours, the wind shifted a little, and enabled us to stretch off clear of all danger.

12th of October.—It blew so hard that we kept out at sea clear of the shore.

13th of October.—As the weather had become moderate, we stood in, and determined the position of five islands which lie to the northward of Port Melville.

14th of October.—During this day the whole of the east side of the great island was explored. The north and north-east sides are high, and destitute of cultivation; nearly in the middle, on this side, there is a deep indenture on the coast, and the wind being such as to admit of sailing out again, we ran in under low sail with the usual precautions; notwithstanding which we were very nearly on the reefs, for the water shoaled suddenly from twenty-four to eight fathoms; and although the brig was instantly tacked, the soundings as she came round were only five fathoms, and to leeward of us the ragged tops of a rock just level with the surface were discovered at the distance of only fifty yards. In exploring such places there ought to be a boat on each bow, as well as one a-head. The coast from this bay to the south point of the island has a belt of coral reefs at the distance of ten and fifteen miles from the shore, and therefore cannot be approached by a ship without great danger. The extreme south point is comparatively clear of coral; we therefore anchored off it at sunset, proposing to land next day to determine its position. We found the iron cables of great use when anchoring amongst coral reefs.

15th of October.—It blew hard last night, but in the forenoon it moderated sufficiently to allow of our landing. We ascertained the latitude of the extreme south point with precision, and made several other observations, all circumstances being favourable.

We had scarcely landed when the natives began to assemble in groups on the top of the cliffs, and in a short time they came down to us, most of them carrying long poles in their hands; we were sufficiently aware of their inoffensive character to have no apprehension of their intentions, otherwise their appearance would have been somewhat formidable. There was no person of rank among them; they were communicative and full of curiosity, which difference in manner from the inhabitants on the shores of Port Melville may have arisen from these people knowing something of us by reports from Napakiang, which is not above ten miles distant. It was to be expected that we should have become a topic of discourse at so short a distance, and probably what was said of us would be favourable, or at all events such as would excite curiosity rather than fear. Most of these people had fish spears tatooed on their arms in the form of a trident, with rude barbs. When drawn on the right arm it is called "Oódeemaw;" when on the left, "Toóga." This is the only instance we have met with of this practice. Our curiosity was farther excited by the appearance of these spears, from the circumstance of our never having seen any warlike weapon on this island; but the people invariably called them "Eéo stitchee" (fish spear). Several of the tallest of these people were measured, but none were above five feet six inches; they are, however, strong limbed and well proportioned. One of them wore a ring on his finger, which is the only instance we have met with of any ornament being worn at Loo-Choo. The ring finger is called in the Loo-choo language, "Eébee gánnee," finger of the ring; and it seems a fair inference from this, that amongst some part of the community rings are habitually worn; probably by the women. The coast here is formed of cliffs, about seventy or eighty feet high, with numerous caverns hollowed out by the waves. The pools of water left by the tide were full of beautiful fish of a great variety of colours.

16th of October.—In the morning we weighed and stood to the westward, among the group of islands called Amakírrima by the natives. At one of these there seemed at first sight to be a harbour for ships; but on sending the boats to explore, it proved only safe for small vessels being filled in every part with coral. On our way across from the south point of the great island to the Amakírrimas, we passed near a coral reef exactly circular, and half a mile in diameter; it is just level with the water's edge at half ebb, so that in fine weather the sea does not break upon any part of it. As it is upwards of seven miles from any land, and lies directly in the passage towards Napakiang, it is exceedingly dangerous, and ought not to be approached in the night by a stranger.

At four o'clock we anchored in our old place in-shore of the Alceste. As we stood towards the anchorage we could see the coral from the mast-head so distinctly as to be able to trace the forms of all the reefs as we passed among them. This can rarely be done, although the water is always clear, because an unusual degree of smoothness in the surface is requisite to make the rocks visible; and the sun must also shine upon the water at a particular angle. A stranger cannot therefore calculate upon having the danger pointed out in this way; but when such circumstances do occur they may be taken advantage of to check the surveys of reefs made in boats.

We find things at Napakiang nearly as we left them; the best understanding seems to exist between Captain Maxwell and the chiefs. Every body is allowed to walk about and do as he likes. The frigate has been bountifully supplied with stock and vegetables; and the sick on shore are rapidly recovering under the kind care of the natives, who take a peculiar interest in their comfort.

A young man belonging to the Alceste had died during our absence. When the natives were informed of this circumstance, they requested permission to make the grave, and begged Captain Maxwell to point out a place for this purpose. Captain Maxwell said that no situation could be more appropriate than under the grove of trees near the temple, a spot already rendered sacred by many Loo-choo tombs.

Next day the body was carried to the grave with all the formalities usual on such occasions, Captain Maxwell, according to custom, walking last, with the officers and crew before him. The ready politeness of the natives was never more strikingly displayed than now; for perceiving that those who were of the highest rank walked in the rear, they considered that their station must of course be in front; and they accordingly placed themselves at the head of the procession, and preserved throughout the ceremony the most profound silence. They were all dressed in white robes, which we have reason to believe is their mourning.

On the next day the natives requested leave to raise a tomb over the grave; this was of course agreed to, and when it was completed, they performed their own funeral service over it, by sacrificing a large hog, and burning a quantity of spirits. Jeeroo officiated on this occasion, and when he had done, he carried the hog to the sick in the hospital.

The chiefs also gave directions for a small square stone to be smoothed and prepared for an epitaph; which being traced upon the stone by Mr. Taylor, the clergyman of the Alceste, was carved very neatly by the natives. The epitaph, after mentioning the name and age of the deceased, stated briefly, that he and his companions in his Britannic majesty's ships Alceste and Lyra, had been kindly treated by the inhabitants of this island. When the purport of the writing was interpreted to the chiefs, they appeared very much gratified at our acknowledging their attentions.

18th of October.—Our friends expressed much pleasure on meeting us again, particularly Jeeroo, who seems to take great interest in our concerns: he carried us up to the sailor's tomb, where we were joined by Ookooma, Jeema, and some of the others, who unaffectedly expressed their sorrow for this man's untimely fate. I found my people who had been landed previous to our sailing on the survey, much recovered, and very grateful for the kindness of the natives. Milk, eggs, meat, and vegetables, had been brought to them every day, and whenever they felt disposed to walk they were accompanied by one or two of the natives, who took their arms on coming to rough ground, and often helped them up the steep side of the hill behind the hospital, to a pleasant grassy spot on the summit, where the natives lighted pipes for them: in short, I suppose sailors were never so caressed before.

The chiefs were anxious to know what we had been doing during the week in which we had been absent. From an apprehension that they might be displeased at our having instituted a regular examination of the whole island, we said we had been looking at the harbour they had spoken of; they immediately mentioned the village of Oonting, and asked how we liked it. But they guessed that we had been round the island, from seeing that we returned by the south, though we had sailed to the north; they said repeatedly, that the island was very small, appearing to be anxious to depreciate it; our reply of course was, that it was very large and beautiful.

Mádera has made great improvement in English, and his character is altogether more developed. He is quite at his ease in our company, and seems to take the most extraordinary interest in every thing belonging to us; but his ardent desire to inform himself on all subjects sometimes distresses him a good deal; he observes the facility with which we do some things, and his enterprising mind suggests to him the possibility of his imitating us; but when he is made sensible of the number of steps by which alone the knowledge he admires is to be attained, his despair is strongly marked. He sometimes asks us to read English aloud to him, to which he always listens with the deepest attention. One day, on shore, he saw me with a book in my hand: he begged me to sit down under a tree, and read: Jeeroo was the only chief present, but there were several of the peasants in attendance upon him; they all lay down on the grass, and listened with an attention and interest which are natural enough: every one expressed himself pleased and satisfied except Mádera, whose anxiety was to read in the same manner himself. From the earnest way in which he inquired into every subject, we were sometimes inclined to think that he must have been directed by the government to inform himself on these topics; and certainly a fitter person could not have been selected; for he adapted himself so readily to all ranks, that he became at once a favourite, and every person took pleasure in obliging him.

Jeeroo is esteemed in another way; he is uniformly good humoured and obliging, and not without curiosity; but he is not clever, and has none of the fire and enthusiasm of Mádera. We all think kindly of Jeeroo, and shake him cordially by the hand when we meet him; but Mádera is admired and respected, as well as esteemed, and his society is courted for his own sake.

Mádera is about twenty-eight years of age, of a slender figure, and very active; his upper teeth project in front over the lower ones, giving his face a remarkable, but not a disagreeable expression. He is always cheerful, and often lively and playful, but his good sense prevents his ever going beyond the line of strict propriety. When required by etiquette to be grave, no one is so immoveably serious as Mádera, and when mirth rules the hour, he is the gayest of the gay: such indeed is his taste on these occasions, that he not only catches the outward tone of his company, but really appears to think and feel as they do. His enterprising spirit and versatility of talent have led him to engage in a number of pursuits; his success, however, is the most remarkable in his acquisition of English. About a month after our arrival, he was asked what had become of his companion Anya; he replied, "Anya, him mother sick, he go him mother house;" and when asked if he would return, he said, "Two, three day time, him mother no sick, he come ship." With all these endowments and attainments he is unaffectedly modest, and never seems aware of his being superior to the rest of his countrymen. We were a long time in doubt what was his real rank; for at first he kept himself back, so that he was well known to the midshipmen, before the officers were at all acquainted with him: he gradually came forward, and though he always wore the dress of the ordinary respectable natives, his manners evidently belonged, to a higher rank, but he never associated with the chiefs, and disclaimed having any pretensions to an equality with them. Notwithstanding all this, there were occasional circumstances, which, by shewing his authority, almost betrayed his secret. One morning a difficulty arose about some supplies which the chiefs had engaged to procure, but which they had neglected to send; as soon as Mádera was told of the circumstance, he went to Captain Maxwell, and undertook to arrange it to his satisfaction, at the same time begging that if any difficulty occurred in future, he might be applied to. Whatever may be Mádera's rank in his own society, it is highly curious to discover in a country so circumstanced, the same politeness, self-denial, and gracefulness of behaviour which the experience of civilized nations has pointed out as constituting the most pleasing and advantageous form of intercourse.

The great interest which Mádera took in the English, and the curiosity he always expressed about our customs at home, suggested the idea of taking him with us to England, where he would have been an interesting specimen of a people so little known; and he also might have carried back knowledge of the greatest use to his country. When it was proposed to him, he paused for some minutes, and then, shaking his head, said, "I go Injeree,—father, mother, childs, wife, house, all cry! not go; no, no, all cry!"

In our absence a number of watch-houses had been erected on the heights round the anchorage; they are mere sheds of cane thatched over, in which three or four of the natives remain, day and night, in order to be ready to accompany any person who may happen to land, wherever it be. They have also erected a long shed, with a floor of split bamboo; in this place, which is on the top of the hill above the usual landing place, the chiefs generally assemble in the morning; they invite every one who passes to drink tea and smoke pipes, which is very convenient when the boats happen not to be ready to take us on board. Each of the chiefs is attended by a boy, generally his son, whose business it is to carry a little square box, in which there are several small drawers, divided into compartments, filled with rice, sliced eggs, small squares of smoked pork, cakes, and fish; and in one corner a small metal pot of sackee, besides cups and chopsticks. By having this always with them, they can dine when and where they choose. They frequently invite us to dine with them, and if we agree to the proposal, they generally ask any other of the chiefs whom they meet to be of the party and join dinners. The place selected for these pic-nics is commonly under the trees, in a cool spot, where a mat is spread on the grass; and every thing being laid out in great order, the party lies down in a circle, and seldom breaks up till the sackee pot is empty.

An artist of the island brought a drawing of the Alceste on board to-day for Captain Maxwell: it is about two feet by one and a half, and is altogether a most extraordinary production, in which perspective and proportion are curiously disregarded. The captain and officers are introduced in full uniform, and a number of the sailors on the rigging and masts. With all its extravagance, however, it has considerable merit; there is nothing slovenly about it, and there is enough of truth in it to shew that it was sketched on the spot.

A dispute has arisen between John the interpreter and the chiefs, who it seems had positively promised to get a horse for Captain Maxwell to ride; as they have not kept their word,

John declares that he will have nothing to say to people who do not speak truth. They have again promised, however, that a horse will be got ready, and in the mean time, a fresh stock of beef and vegetables has been sent to both ships, which has pacified John a little. We have had much occasion to lament not having been accompanied by one of the gentlemen of the factory acquainted with the Chinese language, for although to have John is much better than to be without any interpreter, it is probable that he is not very delicate in his requests, and makes use of expressions and arguments unsuited to our character, and contrary to our wishes and instructions.

19th of October.—In the morning, before breakfast, Captain Maxwell was informed by one of the chiefs, that a horse was ready for him on the beach; he landed accordingly, and found a little pony saddled, and two of the chiefs mounted. They objected to his riding in the country, where the roads were uneven, so that for the present his ride was confined to the beach. The saddle is made of wood, and so uneven as to be very unpleasant: it is proposed to have one made of a blanket and mats in future. To the stirrup there is tied a box, large enough to receive the whole foot.

A dinner was given to-day by Captain Maxwell to the chiefs Ookooma, Shayoon, Issacha Sandoo, Jeema, and Issacha Hackeeboocoo; Jeeroo was also invited to it, but did not attend; being the junior, he had probably been left in charge of the beach and store-rooms. Mádera also made one of the party, though not originally included in the invitation. As he had never laid any claim to an equality in rank with the chiefs, it had not been thought right to invite him along with them: but Mádera, who probably knew that he would be very welcome, put himself in Captain Maxwell's way just before dinner, and was prevailed upon, after a little persuasion, to remain.

Dinner was served at five o'clock in as sumptuous a style as possible. Ookooma was placed on Captain Maxwell's right, and Shayoon on his left; I sat beside the former, and Mr. Clifford next the other; then the two chiefs next in rank, and beside them two of the officers of the ship: the first lieutenant, Mr. Hickman, sat at the foot of the table, with Hackeeboocoo on his right, and Mádera on his left. They were all in great spirits, and ate and drank freely, and though they complained of the size of the glasses, and of the strength of the wine, tasted every thing from punch to champagne: the briskness of the last indeed surprised them not a little, and effectually muddled two of them for some time. Cheese was the only thing they all objected to, probably on account of its being made of milk, which they never taste. The interpreter not being present, the conversation was carried on through Mr. Clifford and Mádera, and partly by signs. Whether intelligibly or not, every body was talking. Mádera has dined often on board the ship, and is quite perfect in our customs. On this occasion he took great charge of the chiefs at his end of the table, speaking sometimes in one language and sometimes in the other. Observing Jeema eating ham without mustard, he called to Captain Maxwell's servant, and pointing to Jeema, said, "Tom, take mustard to him." When the desert was put on table, and the wine decanters ranged in a line, they exclaimed in astonishment, "Moo eeyroo noo sackee," six kinds or colours of wine; but the sweetmeats and prepared confectionary pleased them most.

After sitting about an hour and a half after dinner, and drinking with tolerable spirit, they rose to depart; but this they were not allowed to do, and they were informed that it was the English custom to sit a much longer time. They represented that the sun had set, and they would never be able to find their way on shore, but would all be drowned in attempting it. This alarming difficulty was easily overruled by a promise of the barge, and they sat down again. While the discussion was going on between Captain Maxwell and his guests, Mádera kept his seat, and looked about him in his keen observant way, to discover, if he could, what was likely to be the issue of this adventure. Having observed that in general we were anxious to keep our company at table as long as we could, he naturally enough thought that we would not let this opportunity pass of entertaining the chiefs according to our fashion. He appeared to have settled this question with himself just as the chiefs resumed their seats, for rising half off his chair, and with a mixture of archness and simplicity, as if he had made an amusing discovery, cried out in English, "When all drunk then go ashore!" Though Mádera, as will be seen, was not quite right in his guess, there was enough of truth in his remark to raise a hearty laugh among those who understood him; and as he joined in this laugh at his own joke, it was some time before he could explain what he had said to the chiefs, who, being in a merry humour themselves, took it in perfect good part, though their mirth was evidently dashed by a little apprehension of the fate which Mádera had anticipated for them.

The health of his Royal Highness the Prince Regent was then given, all the company standing in the most respectful manner. This was followed by the health of the King of Loo-choo, which was drank with similar observances. On sitting down after the latter toast, the chiefs conferred a few minutes across the table, and then all rose to propose Captain Maxwell's health; their wishes being explained by Mádera. When they sat down, Captain Maxwell proposed the health of Ookooma and the other chiefs, but as we in return stood up to drink to them, their modesty disclaimed this part of the compliment, and they rose likewise; nor was it till a good deal of persuasion had been used, that they consented to be seated while we were standing.

These four bumpers made the party very merry, and it now was intimated to them, that as all the usual formalities had been observed, they might drink just as much as they liked, or pass the bottle altogether; a permission of which few of them took advantage. They lighted their pipes, laughed, joked, and seemed so happy, that it was agreed on all hands, that conviviality is no where better understood than at Loo-choo. After a time, at our request, they played some games, of which we had heard them speak. The object of these games was drinking; a cup of wine being the invariable forfeit. That every thing might be in character during the games, some of their own little cups were put on table. One person holds the stalk of his tobacco-pipe between the palms of his hands, so that the pipe rolls round as he moves his hands, which he is to hold over his head, so as not to see them. After turning it round for a short time, he suddenly stops, and the person to whom the bowl is directed has to drink a cup of wine. Another is a Chinese game: one person holds his hand closed over his head, he then brings it quickly down before him with one or more fingers extended; the person he is playing with calls out the number of them, and if he guesses right, he has to drink the cup of wine. These and other games caused a good deal of noisy mirth, and at length it was proposed by them to go out, in order to look at the sailors who were dancing on deck. Before leaving the cabin, they shewed us a Loo-choo dance round the table: Mádera placed himself at the head before Ookooma, while the others ranged themselves in a line behind him; he began by a song, the air of which was very pretty, and nearly at the same time commenced the dance, which consisted principally in throwing the body into a variety of postures, and twisting the hands about. Sometimes the hands were placed flat together, at others separate, but generally the former; the movements both of the body and hands were regular and of a waving description. The head was made to incline slowly from side to side, so as almost to touch the shoulders; the feet were moved with a slight shuffling motion, with an occasional long sweeping step to one side and then back again; but the perfection of the dance appeared to be in the proper use of the hands and body. The words of the dance song were "Sasa sangcoomah, sangcoomee ah! sangcoomee ah! kadee yooshee daw;" when they came to the last word they all joined in the chorus and clapped their hands. Although Mádera was the leader both in the dance and song, he was occasionally joined in the latter by several of the others, the whole party repeating the last word several times over. In this way they went several times round the table. Mádera had a graceful carriage, and his dancing, though fantastic, was really elegant; his singing too was in good taste. The others danced clumsily, though in perfect good time, and joined with some spirit in the chorus.

The ship was illuminated, and the sailors were dancing on the upper deck. The chiefs were much pleased with this scene, which was lively enough. After watching the dance of the sailors for a few minutes, Mádera, who, to use a common phrase, "was up to every thing," ran among the sailors, and seizing one of them by the shoulders, put him out of the dance, took his place, and kept up the reel with the same spirit, and exactly in the same style and step as the sailors. The other dances were left off, and the whole ship's company assembling round Mádera, cheered and clapped him till the dance was done. The chiefs joined in the applause, seeming no less surprised than ourselves at Mádera's skill, for his imitation of the sailors' odd steps and gestures was as exact as if he had lived amongst seamen all his life. The officers then danced a country dance, after which the chiefs, unasked, and with a sort of intuitive politeness, which rendered every thing they did appropriate, instantly stepped forward and danced several times round the quarter-deck, to the infinite gratification of the sailors.

On returning to the cabin to tea, they were all in high spirits, and while amusing themselves with a sort of wrestling game, Ookooma, who had seen us placing ourselves in the boxer's sparring attitudes, threw himself suddenly into the boxer's position of defence, assuming at the same time a fierceness of look which we had never before seen in any of them. The gentleman to whom he addressed himself, thinking that Ookooma wished to spar, prepared to indulge him; but Mádera's quick eye saw what was going on, and by a word or two made him instantly resume his wonted sedateness. We tried in vain to make Mádera explain what were the magical words which he had used to Ookooma. He appeared anxious to turn our thoughts from the subject, by saying, "Loo-choo man no fight; Loo-choo man write—no fight, no good, no, no. Ingerish very good, yes, yes, yes; Loo-choo man no fight." Possibly he considered that Ookooma was taking too great a liberty; or, perhaps, he thought even the semblance of fighting unsuitable with the strict amity subsisting between us.

Before they went away, Captain Maxwell, who had remarked the satisfaction with which the chiefs received any attention shewn to their children, ordered a large cake to be brought him, which he divided into portions for the family of each. The chiefs were in a proper mood to feel this kindness, and they expressed themselves, as may be supposed, very warmly upon the occasion. When they put off for the shore they began singing, and never left off till they landed.

20th of October.—The forenoon was passed at the Observatory, and afterwards we walked in the country without being observed, for the chiefs had not yet recovered from the effects of last night's gaiety: but we had not gone a mile before Jeeroo overtook us. We were very anxious to gain the brow of a neighbouring hill, from which we imagined there would be a good view of the palace; but although Jeeroo was the most obliging creature in the world on every other occasion, he was resolute now in not letting us go far beyond our usual limits; we tried to overrule his objections by telling him that we should do no mischief, and would not go farther than the adjoining height. He would listen, however, to nothing; and as we still walked slowly on, he at last sent off a messenger for assistance, but before this reinforcement arrived we had turned back, to Jeeroo's great relief. Although the object proposed had not been accomplished, we got a better sight of the palace than we had yet obtained. It is so much enclosed by trees that parts only can be seen, but it is undoubtedly a very large building. On returning we met Hackeeboócoo, the fat chief, coming puffing and blowing up the hill; he had set out to overtake us on being told by Jeeroo's messenger what we were proposing to do. He had drank a good deal of wine yesterday on board, and said he had been "weetee" (drunk), and that his head ached very much. After he joined us we passed near a village, where we met two women at the turning of a road: they did not see us till within a few yards, and their alarm was great; they threw down the baskets, which they were carrying on their heads, and fled into the wood. Our two companions were very uneasy at this rencontre, and would not listen to our reasoning upon the absurdity of their apprehensions, looking quite miserable till the subject, which seems to be an interdicted one, was changed. We went afterwards to the high ground behind the hospital, in order to fill up by eye the edges of the reefs in our charts, for which regular triangles could not be taken in the survey. While I was thus engaged, Mr. Clifford endeavoured to learn from Jeeroo whether or not the King lived in the large house spoken of before; Jeeroo as usual denied any knowledge of the King, and could not be prevailed upon to say what the house was, or who resided there; a peasant, however, who happened to be along with us was more communicative, and was giving all the information desired, when Jeeroo, observing what he was about, reprimanded him sharply. On coming down from the height we found all the chiefs seated in a long room erected on the outside of the garden gate: they were very merry on the subject of last night's adventure.

21st of October.—While Mrs. Loy was employed at the well to-day washing clothes, at a moment when every body else was out of the way, she was visited by a Loo-choo lady, accompanied by a numerous guard of men. She describes her as being about eighteen years of age, well dressed, fair in complexion, with small dark eyes, and not without beauty; her hair was of a glossy jet black, made up into a knot on one side of the head. She wore a girdle tied at the side, and had on sandals like the men. Mrs. Loy wished to touch her, but she shrunk back in alarm. Whether these details be quite correct or not, the circumstance of a lady of rank having visited Mrs. Loy is so far interesting as it denotes a considerable degree of curiosity on the lady's part, together with the power of gratifying it, which, in a country where the women are strictly secluded, perhaps would not be allowed.

22d of October.—Ookooma and Jeeroo came to the Observatory to-day, together with a number of the most respectable of the natives; they were desirous of seeing the reflected images of the sun in the artificial horizon through the telescope of the sextant. As this was placed on a stand there was no difficulty in satisfying their curiosity, for they had only to place their eye to the tube, the angle having been previously arranged. Many of them were amused by the changes of colour in the reflected images by means of the different shades; others were more struck with the apparent motion of the two suns, which is very perceptible when a high magnifying power is used; a few endeavoured to understand the meaning of what they saw, but with the exception of Jeeroo, I think they had no conception of its cause. Jeeroo appeared to have some notion of astronomy; his idea of eclipses was more accurate than could have been expected. From him Mr. Clifford got the names of the days and months, and the various points of information respecting Time, which will be found in the Vocabulary. Whenever we were actually taking observations, the natives invariably remained at a considerable distance. They had been told that the least motion disturbed the surface of the quicksilver, and prevented our taking observations. They had much patience, and sometimes sat quite still and silent for several hours, till invited to come forward to look at the instruments. When Ookooma and Jeeroo came to us, we observed that they were in great distress, and upon our asking the cause, the former explained that Captain Maxwell during his ride this morning had fallen down, or rather that his horse, which was too weak for his weight, had fallen with him, and that his finger was broken: "Tayin ma tawrittee, Tayin no eebee ootee" (the Tayin's horse fell, Tayin's finger broke). A Loo-choo doctor, he said, had gone on board, who would soon cure it.

On going to the Alceste we found that the Loo-choo surgeon had placed Captain Maxwell's broken finger in a thick paste made of eggs, flour, and some other substance which he brought along with him. He then wrapped the whole in the skin of a newly-killed fowl. This skin dried in a short time and held the paste firm, by which the broken finger was kept steady. The doctor went through a number of ceremonies, such as feeling the pulse, looking at the tongue, and so on. He had a box along with him, containing upwards of a hundred medicines.

Captain Maxwell mentioned, that while he was sitting in a shed after the accident, he was surprised to see a person enter the door crawling on all fours, and half dead with terror. This it appeared was the surgeon, who had been sent for by the chiefs. He was horror-struck at the accident, but soon recovered himself on observing Captain Maxwell's perfect tranquillity.

Captain Maxwell's gentleness and forbearance, and his uniform attention to the wishes of the natives, and the great personal kindness which he had shewn to so many of them, had very early won their confidence and esteem. As our intercourse became more intimate, these feelings naturally became stronger, and the concern which the natives felt upon this occasion was very general, and was expressed, not only by Mádera and the chiefs, but by the lower orders, in a manner highly flattering to Captain Maxwell.

23d of October.—A deputation of the chiefs went on board the Alceste early this morning to say, that the Prince of the island, who was the next person in rank to the King, and heir to the throne, meant to come on board the frigate this afternoon, as well for the purpose of paying a visit of ceremony, as of enquiring into the state of Captain Maxwell's health after the accident.

At noon the four senior chiefs, dressed in their state robes and hatchee-matchees, came to announce the Prince's approach, and in about half an hour afterwards he was brought in a closed sedan-chair to the boat, through a concourse of people, to whom he seemed as much a show as to us. The state boat was a large flat-bottomed barge, covered with an awning of dark blue, with white stars on it, the whole having much the appearance of a hearse. It was preceded by two boats bearing flags with an inscription upon them, having in the bow an officer of justice carrying a lackered bamboo, and in the stern a man beating a gong. A vast number of boats were in attendance, some bearing presents, and others following out of mere curiosity. One of the Chiefs came on board with the Prince's card, which was of red paper forty-eight inches long, and eleven wide[12], and shortly afterwards the Prince's barge put off from the shore; upon which the rigging of both ships was manned, and a salute of seven guns fired; when he came on board he was received with a guard, and under a like salute. Captain Maxwell, who had been confined to the cabin ever since his accident, desired me to receive the Prince. No arrangement having been made with us respecting the ceremony of reception, I merely took off my hat and bowed: but all the chiefs fell on their knees the instant he came on the quarter-deck. I took his hand from one of the chiefs who had assisted him up the accommodation ladder, and led him to the cabin.

When seated beside Captain Maxwell, the Prince made several anxious enquiries about his finger, expressing much regret that so disagreeable an accident should have occurred at Loo-choo. He then called to his pipe-bearer, and having prepared a pipe, presented it to Captain Maxwell, who returned him this compliment, by giving him one of his own. The usual questions as to our ages and families, and various complimentary speeches, having passed, he said he had heard much of the wonders of the ship, and should like to see them himself: he rose upon this and went to the globes, which he examined with great care. He begged to be shewn Ingeree, Loo-choo, Quantoong (China); Niphon (Japan); Manilla, and Pekin. The chiefs would not sit down in his presence, and never spoke to him without kneeling. On his expressing a wish to look at the different parts of the ship, he was conducted all round the decks. He observed every thing with attention, but without betraying any great degree of curiosity: he had heard of the boatswain's wife, and asked to see her; the lady, in her best dress, was presented to him; he stood for about half a minute looking at her with a sort of pleased surprise, and then, as if suddenly recollecting that this was somewhat rude, he drew his fan from his breast, and with an air of the utmost politeness, held it towards her, and upon Mrs. Loy curtsying in acknowledgment, he sent it to her by Mádera. He asked to see the fire-engine worked, and appeared much gratified by seeing the water thrown to so great a height. He had heard of the African negro, and begged that he might be sent for. When the black man was brought before him he looked exceedingly surprised, and probably was in doubt whether the colour was natural, as one of his people was sent to rub his face, as if to discover whether it was painted or not. The natives, who had flocked on board in crowds, fell on their knees whenever the Prince passed.

[Illustration: THE PRINCE of LOO-CHOO.]

On returning to the cabin, the Prince was invited to a collation prepared for him in the foremost cabin: for a long time he refused to sit down, nor could we conjecture what his objection was; at length, however, he complied, while the chiefs, who are neither allowed to sit down nor eat in his presence, retired to the after-cabin. He tasted every thing which was offered him, but seemed afraid of the wines, having probably heard of the proceedings on the evening of the 19th. In about half an hour he rose and went to the after-cabin; the chiefs and the people of his suite, to the number of fifteen, then sat down at the table he had left, and made ample amends for the temperance and moderation of his royal highness.

As soon as they rejoined the party in the after-cabin, business was entered upon by Captain Maxwell's returning thanks, in the name of the English government, for the liberal way in which we had been supplied with every kind of refreshment, and for the other assistance which had been given to us. The Prince replied, that the King of Loo-choo was anxious to do every thing in his power for the King of England's ships. Upon this Captain Maxwell observed, that he was very desirous of seeing his majesty, for the purpose of expressing in person his gratitude for the kindness we had received in this country. The Prince answered, that it was contrary to the laws and customs of Loo-choo, for any foreigner to see the king, unless sent by his own sovereign, and charged with complimentary presents. Coming from such high authority, this assurance was conclusive, and as nothing further could now be said on the subject, the hope of opening a communication with this court, which had been so anxiously desired, seemed now destroyed. The Prince, however, unexpectedly resumed the subject, by saying that a letter would be written to the King of England, if Captain Maxwell would undertake to deliver it; his answer was, that nothing could give him more satisfaction than being made the bearer of such a communication: that he had earnestly desired the honour of paying his respects to his majesty, but from the moment that he had heard that it was contrary to the customs of the country, he had ceased to think of it. As soon as it was interpreted that Captain Maxwell was willing to carry the letter alluded to, and that he no longer urged his desire to see the King, the Prince rose and pressed Captain Maxwell's hand and mine between his, while all the chiefs fell on their knees in a circle round us, shewing by the expression of their countenances, how great the anxiety had been from which they were relieved by Captain Maxwell's ready acquiescence with their wishes: the Prince in particular, who had hitherto looked full of anxiety, became all cheerfulness, and his manner assumed a totally different character.

The inference from this curious scene is, that the real object of the Prince's visit was to dissuade Captain Maxwell from urging his request to be allowed an interview with the King; and we conjectured that the circumstance of his accident was taken advantage of to pay a visit to the Alceste, where they naturally thought that the remonstrances of a man of such high rank as the Heir Apparent to the throne, would carry more weight than any which had yet been tried.

When the Prince again alluded to the letter, it appeared that it was to be written by the minister, and not by the King. This altered the case materially, and Captain Maxwell most respectfully informed the Prince, that such a letter as he described could not be received, as it would be an indignity to our sovereign to offer his majesty a letter written by another king's minister. The Prince at once seemed sensible of the propriety of what Captain Maxwell had said, and calling the chiefs round him, entered into a long discussion with them: at the close of which, he declared himself incompetent to decide upon so important an occasion, but said that he would consult with the King, whose pleasure would be communicated in a few days. Captain Maxwell expressed his willingness to abide by his majesty's decision as far as was consistent with the respect due to his own sovereign. The Prince seemed entirely satisfied with this answer, and said something to the chiefs, upon which they again fell on their knees before Captain Maxwell, notwithstanding all his efforts to prevent them. Nothing more of any consequence passed.

In the early part of the interview the present was brought in, or at least such parts of it as were capable of being thus displayed. The whole consisted of two bullocks, three hogs, three goats, and a quantity of vegetables and fruit; besides fifteen webs of the cloth of the island, thirty fans, and twelve pipes. The Prince said he had sent a present to me, which I found to consist of half the above mentioned things. He shortly afterwards rose to take leave. The rigging was manned on his going away, and similar honours were paid him as were shewn when he came on board.

The Prince of Loo-choo, whose name is Shang Pung Fwee, and title Pochin Tay Foo, belongs to the highest of the nine orders of chiefs on the islands, the distinction of which rank is a hatchee-matchee of a pink ground, with perpendicular rows of black, yellow, blue, white, and green spots. He was clothed in a robe of light blue silk, lined with silk a shade lighter, over which he wore a girdle richly embossed with flowers of gold and different coloured silks: in other respects his dress was like that of the chiefs. He is about fifty years old, his beard is full and white, and his figure well proportioned. In manners he is genteel and sedate, but occasionally a little awkward, which his retired habits sufficiently account for. Towards the close of his visit, when his reserve had in some degree worn off, we observed him smile for an instant, now and then, with a shrewd expression in his eyes, as if he was observing what was passing more narrowly than we at first suspected. It was thought, too, that in making inquiries about different things on board, he shewed more discrimination than most of those who had preceded him; but on the whole, there was nothing very interesting in him besides his rank. While he was looking over the books and other things in the cabin, a picture of his majesty King George the Third was shewn to him. As the interpreter was not present, we could not immediately explain who it was intended to represent, till it occurred to us to join our hands and bow to it in the Loo-choo manner: the Prince instantly saw what was meant, and turning towards the picture, made a low and respectful obeisance.

His suite consisted of several chiefs whom we had not seen before, and six or seven personal attendants, two of whom stood behind to fan him and light his pipe. It is curious that these men, who from their dress and manner were certainly servants, derived a sort of rank from being about the Prince's person; for when the chiefs sat down to table after he had left it, they all stood by as if expecting to be invited to sit down also; but Mr. Clifford, to whom Captain Maxwell had given the party in charge, having observed how particular they were with respect to the distinctions of rank, did not think of asking them to be seated, till Jeema requested him to do so; still suspecting some mistake, he applied to Mádera, who said it was perfectly correct, and they were accordingly asked to sit down with the rest.

We had never been able to obtain from the natives any clear account of former visitors, and as the Prince was thought a likely person to be in possession of the desired information, questions were asked him upon this subject. He said that a vessel had been here about twenty years ago, and that she went away immediately without holding any communication with the court. This must have been the schooner in which Captain Broughton visited Napakiang in July, 1797, after he had been wrecked in his majesty's ship Providence, on the island of Typinsan[13]. He said that he knew of no other stranger who had visited Loo-choo. On being interrogated as to the knowledge of other countries, he declared that they knew nothing of the English or French, or any nation indeed but the Chinese, Corean, and Japanese. Something was said about Manilla, and from its not being very remote, it is possible that some communication may have existed between that place and Loo-choo. Their accounts, however, were vague and unsatisfactory, and it is not impossible that we ourselves may have first suggested the name, and afterwards ascribed the use of it to them[14].

Nothing, however, that occurred to-day, attracted more notice than Mádera's assumption of his long concealed rank. He came for the first time dressed in the robes and hatchee-matchee of a chief, and not only took precedence of all our old friends, but during the discussion in the cabin with the Prince, maintained a decided superiority over them all. While all the rest were embarrassed in the Prince's presence, and crouching on their knees every time they spoke, Mádera, though always respectful, was quite at his ease; and we could not help fancying that he addressed the Prince as if accustomed to his society. It was no less remarkable, that the Prince referred much oftener to him than to any of the rest, and listened to what he said with greater attention. Whether Mádera owed such distinction to his actual rank, which may have placed him about the court, or to the ascendancy of his talents, or to the accidental circumstance of his having had better opportunities of knowing us than any other of the natives, we could never discover. He admitted, when interrogated, that he had often seen the Prince before, while the other chiefs confessed their ignorance even of his person, before to-day.

As soon as the Prince was placed in his chair and carried away, Mádera came on board, and entered with great good humour into all the jokes which were made upon his new character. He declined telling why he had kept his rank so long out of sight, but it was sufficiently obvious that his main object was to establish an intimacy with all the different classes on board the ships, and in this he completely succeeded; for he had gradually advanced in his acquaintance, first with the sailors, then the midshipmen, next with the officers, and last of all with the captains. By this means he gained the confidence and good will of each class as he went along; and by rising in consequence every day, instead of putting forward all his claims at once, acquired not only substantial importance with us, but gained a much more intimate knowledge of our character and customs than he could have hoped to do in any other way.

24th of October.—Mr. Clifford went along with me to-day for the purpose of sketching the bridge, which, though not above three hundred yards from the landing place, the chiefs have always objected to our examining. We took Jeeroo with us without telling him our object, which he no sooner discovered than he became quite alarmed, and sent off for Mádera, who came to us immediately, and upon learning that nothing further was proposed than a mere examination of the bridge, he said that we might go on; having first made us promise solemnly not to go any further. While Mádera was binding us down in this way, I expressed some little impatience at his doubting our simple declaration of nothing more being intended than what we avowed; but his duty I suppose was imperative, and he would not leave us till the matter was arranged in his own way. As soon as he was satisfied on this point he said something to Jeeroo and left us; but turning back again, he came up to Mr. Clifford, and whispered, "captain no sulky?" meaning, we supposed, to express his apprehension that I had been angry at the stipulations so positively required by him. Mr. Clifford, having assured him that I was not sulky with him, detained him to ask him what it was he feared? what he had seen in us to excite such dread of our going near the town? He replied, "Loochoo woman see Ingeree man, Loochoo woman cry!" He then returned; and Jeeroo, who remained in a boat close to the bridge while I was employed measuring it and drawing it stone by stone, was greatly interested by Mr. Clifford's account of the great age of our venerable Sovereign, and the number of his family, which excited his astonishment and admiration. He conversed freely while the subject was the King of England, but the moment the slightest turn in the discourse was made towards the King of Loo-choo he drew up, and became impenetrable. "He did not know," he said, "how old he was, nor how many children he had;" in short he seemed scarcely to admit that he had ever heard any thing about him.

From Mádera, however, who had no concealments, we learnt afterwards that the King has only one wife, but has twelve concubines; he is an old man, and has seven children. It is curious that none of the chiefs will inform Captain Maxwell whether or not the Prince who visited the ships yesterday has any children; it is hardly possible that they can be ignorant of the fact; but either they are kept strangely in the dark as to what passes in the palace, or they carry their reserve on royal topics to a singular length.

From the bridge we went to the top of the hill above the well, where Jeeroo sung several songs. On the way up we stopped at one of the large horse-shoe tombs mentioned before, which resembles in all respects the tombs of China. On this similarity being pointed out to Jeeroo, he became anxious to explain that it was a Loo-choo tomb, and not exclusively Chinese; meaning probably that Loo-choo persons were contained in it. He informed us that these tombs did not contain a single person only, or a single generation, but were used as cemeteries from age to age. The bodies, according to his account, are put into coffins, and allowed to lie untouched for seven years, by which time the flesh is entirely decayed; the bones are then collected, and being put into cases are preserved by the families of the deceased with great care.

25th of October.—This being the anniversary of His Majesty's accession to the throne, the ships were dressed in colours, and a royal salute fired. Upon the natives this produced a great effect; they had never seen any other flags than the single ensigns hoisted on Sundays, and this display of several hundred flags was well calculated to surprise and delight them. They were informed some days before that there would be some ceremonies in honour of our King, and great numbers of people had assembled on the shore in consequence. This morning had also been fixed upon for returning the Prince's visit; accordingly we left the Alceste at one o'clock, forming a procession of four boats, with flags in each. Captain Maxwell took twelve of his officers and young gentlemen, and six accompanied me from the Lyra, all being dressed in full uniform. We entered the harbour, and landed at the same part of the causeway as before, where the chiefs were in attendance, as on the occasion of our visit on the 23d ult.

The Prince advanced a few yards on the outside of the gate, and having taken Captain Maxwell's hand, conducted him to the temple, where an ingenious device was adopted to preserve the etiquette, requiring that none of inferior rank shall sit down in the Prince's company. The temple was divided into three rooms by ranges of columns, which were deemed a sufficient separation; and, at the same time, no person in the other rooms could feel himself slighted by the exclusion, since the division by the pillars was merely nominal. The feast was sumptuous, consisting of twelve regular courses, besides tea and sackee. There were many new dishes, principally of meat, dressed in various ways in large bowls. We saw what seemed to be wheaten bread for the first time to-day. It being necessary to make some return for the presents brought on board by the Prince two days ago, Captain Maxwell now gave him several pieces of scarlet and blue superfine cloth, and samples of every species of cloths, from the finest damask to the coarsest sail canvas; also a set of cut crystal decanters and glasses, and three dozen of wine of ten different sorts, with several books, and a number of smaller articles. It was also stated to the Prince, that a cow and calf had been left on shore in order to be offered to the King as a small mark of our sense of the kindness which we had experienced. The Prince expressed much satisfaction at this gift, as the calf had become a great favourite with the natives. My present consisted of half the quantity of wine given by Captain Maxwell, a mirror taken from a dressing-stand, samples of English stationary, Cary's map of England, an atlas, and a small brass sextant; which latter present had been suggested by the wonder which it had invariably excited at the observatory. Mr. John Maxwell, to whom the Prince had sent a present of cloth and pipes after he landed yesterday, gave him a spy-glass and a map of London; the map was coloured, and round the edges were the palaces, Greenwich Hospital, and other public buildings, all of which he examined with great attention. After he had looked over most of the things, and was satisfied with the explanations, he rose and said that a great deal too much had been given, to which it was replied, that a great deal too little had been given, and that they were not offered as being, in any respect, an equivalent for the supplies sent on board, but merely to shew our sense of the kindness and attention with which we had been received[15]. During the time that we sat at table to-day, the interpreter was hardly ever called in, as Mádera and Mr. Clifford contrived between them to explain every thing, if not as clearly as could have been wished, yet in a more satisfactory manner than could have been done through the medium of John the Chinaman, of whose fidelity we were nowise certain, and whose taste and delicacy in conveying our sentiments we had great reason to doubt.

The Prince, after a time, rose and proposed the King of England's health, which was accordingly drank in a cup of sackee. In return we gave the King of Loo-choo. As the surgeon had desired Captain Maxwell to drink no wine, there was very little drank at the Prince's table; but at the others every art was used to circulate the sackee pot. Indeed, little persuasion was required, for the sackee, though not strong, was very good. Ookooma presided at the table occupied by the officers, and Jeero at that where the midshipmen sat.

Ookooma having remarked on board, that whenever the King's health was drank, whether his Majesty of England, or of Loo-choo, the cups were always freely emptied, took advantage of this loyalty of sentiment, and gave "The King of Injeree's health" three or four times over, to which, of course, the officers were obliged to reply, by giving "The King of Loo-choo" as often. He carried this rather farther than is customary with us on similar occasions, for observing that the company were rather backward in eating a bowl of sweet rice-meal porridge, he stood up with his bowl in his hand, and calling out "King of Injeree health!" swallowed the whole of it, and invited the rest to follow his example.

The Prince seemed to enjoy the mirth of the other tables very much; he was himself more cheerful and disengaged than when we first saw him, though he appears to be naturally a silent man. Ookooma, by overacting his part, got, we thought, a little tipsy, and came several times into the state chamber, talking louder than was proper, but of this the Prince took no notice. When Ookooma came near my chair, I whispered to him, "Ya weetee," (you are drunk;) he turned round, and affecting to be angry, called out, "Weetee nang," (I am not drunk) in a voice and manner which were in direct contradiction to his assertion: his subsequent behaviour, however, was so correct and sedate when the feast broke up, and all were again upon duty, that he was probably merely pretending to be tipsy, in order to suit what was considered to be the humour of the company.

On rising to depart, the Prince led Captain Maxwell by the hand, not only through the gate, but about twenty yards along the causeway; here he stopped and took leave. Captain Maxwell availed himself of this opportunity to repeat, for the last time, his thanks in the name of his government, for the numerous attentions and marks of kindness which we had received. He requested that what he had said might be communicated to the King, and assured the Prince, in the most earnest and respectful manner, that all the circumstances of our reception and entertainment should be stated to our own government. The Prince bowed to this in a manner which seemed to express his satisfaction at what was promised. Captain Maxwell next observed, that besides the high public benefits of which he had just been speaking, he felt individually greatly honoured and obliged by the particular attention which had been shewn to himself, and to the captain of the little ship, and hoped that the Prince would accept from himself a small mark of his respect and gratitude. As soon as this was interpreted to the Prince, Captain Maxwell took from his neck a small thermometer, set in silver, and presented it to the Prince, who leaned his head forward, and requested that it might be hung round his neck.

This may be supposed a curious place to hang a thermometer, but we had learned during our intercourse with the chiefs, that some management of this kind was necessary whenever it was intended to offer them presents; for their extreme delicacy made them unwilling to accept any thing of value, lest it might appear in the light of remuneration for their hospitality. Whenever any thing merely ornamental, or of little value, was offered, and particularly if worn about the person, no objection was made to receiving it. It thus became the practice, as being the most convenient method, to tie the proposed gift by a ribbon round the neck; and after a time, every one had rings, seals, watch-keys, or bank tokens with holes drilled in them, prepared for these occasions. The thermometer which was given to the Prince had particularly attracted his notice when he was on board.

After Captain Maxwell had given his present, the Prince turned to me, and I put over his neck a cornelian ornament, suspended by a ribbon, in the same manner as the thermometer.

He was greatly delighted with these compliments, and immediately resuming Captain Maxwell's hand, led him along the whole length of the causeway to the boat, and then stepped upon the top of the parapet to see us row away.

As soon as we had put off, every one in the boats stood up and gave three cheers; to which the Prince bowed several times, with his hands closed and raised to his breast. He remained on the parapet, and continued waving his fan to us as we rowed down the harbour, as long as we could see him. As the boats rowed in procession out of the harbour, all the chiefs ran along to the end of the causeway, where they continued, along with a vast crowd of natives, waving their handkerchiefs and fans till we were a great way from the shore. On each side of this group of chiefs a gong was beat incessantly. On every side, the rocks, the trees, houses, and boats, in short, every spot was crowded with people, waving their hands, and cheering us as we went along. This brilliant scene had less of novelty in it, to be sure, than what we had witnessed at the same place on the twenty-third of last month, but it was still more pleasing, for we had now become acquainted with many of the individuals forming this assemblage, and could feel assured that their expressions of kindness and respect were sincere. On the first occasion, too, the natives being ignorant of our intentions, were very generally alarmed at our appearance; and accordingly, though there was much curiosity shewn, a profound silence and stillness prevailed over the whole crowd, very different from the friendly shouts and signs with which they greeted us as we passed among them to-day.

Precautions had been taken to prevent the ladies from indulging their curiosity as they had done on the first visit, not a female being seen any where.

26th of October.—Last night both the Alceste and Lyra were illuminated. At nine o'clock a *feu de joie* was fired, and a number of fire-works let off from the yard-arms. A great concourse of the natives, who had been apprised of our intentions, assembled on the shore, and were very highly delighted with this brilliant exhibition.

[Illustration: SCENE after the PRINCE of LOO CHOO'S FEAST.]

The sick, as well as the remaining stores belonging to the Alceste, were removed on board this morning, and every preparation made for sea. While employed in completing the series of observations at the observatory, Mádera joined us, having in his hand the sextant which I had given to the Prince yesterday. It seemed that he had been ordered to make himself acquainted with the use of it; and a more hopeless enterprise could not have been proposed to any man. But Mádera was not a man to be thrown into despair by difficulty; on the contrary, he persevered in observing with this sextant, and the more the difficulty was made apparent, the more keenly he laboured to overcome it. The progress which he made in a few hours in the mere practical operation of taking angles and altitudes was not surprising, because there is in fact not much difficulty in it; but he was nowise satisfied with this proficiency, and seemed anxious to apply his knowledge to some useful purpose.

With a sextant on a stand, I made him take the distance between the sun and moon, four or five times; on every occasion he was wonderfully near the truth. We endeavoured to confine him to one object, merely to ascertain the time of apparent noon; and I think we succeeded in explaining to him how this was to be done. He expressed repeatedly his regret at our approaching departure, in which sentiment he was joined by Jeeroo and the rest of the chiefs, who were quite out of spirits. Jeeroo, poor fellow, had prepared a handsome dinner for us under a tree near the observatory. He made us drink what he called "wackaríttee," or the parting cup, several times over. We had a number of visitors at the observatory, who saw the instruments packed up and sent off with looks of real regret. They all said they were sorry we were going away. One man gave Mr. Clifford, as a farewell gift, a curious drawing of the Alceste dressed in flags, and executed, he said, by his son. The children, too, were all much affected by our preparations, and the wonted hilarity of the lower orders was quite gone.

Having taken our final leave of the shore, we went to the Alceste, where we found the chiefs in conference with Captain Maxwell, who made each of the chiefs a present of a cut wine glass, which he knew they had long desired to possess. To Ookooma he gave a finely cut tumbler, in a red morocco case. This was much beyond his expectations, and perhaps his wishes, for he appeared to observe the wine glasses of the others with somewhat of a disappointed look. Captain Maxwell perceiving in a moment that Ookooma had set his heart upon a wine glass, opened the case, and placed one inside the tumbler, to Ookooma's great satisfaction; and soon afterwards the whole party went on shore, saying, before they left the ship, that in the morning the Bodzes would come on board in order to perform some sacrifice. As they never came, it is probable that the interpreter misunderstood them, particularly as Isaacha Sandoo said to Mr. Clifford, "Acha hoonee nittee Doochoo mang hoonee oocooyoong." "To-morrow the ships will go, and all the Loo-choo people will pray for them, or wish them well;" which was probably what was meant when the interpreter reported that the Bodzes were to come on board.

While we were at dinner, Mádera came into the Alceste's cabin for the purpose of asking some questions about the sextant. He had not been aware of our being at dinner, and looked shocked at having intruded; and when invited to sit down, politely, but firmly declined. From the cabin he went to the gun room, to see his friend Mr. Hoppner, the junior lieutenant of the Alceste, with whom he had formed a great friendship. Mr. Hoppner gave him a picture of the Alceste and some other presents; upon which Mádera, who was much affected, said, "To-morrow ship go sea; I go my father house, two day distance: when I see my father, I show him your present, and I tell him, me, Henry Hoppner all same (as) brother," and burst into tears!

Sunday, 27th of October.—At daybreak we unmoored, and the natives, on seeing us take up one of our anchors, thought we were going to get under weigh immediately, and give them the slip, which was not at all intended. This alarm, however, brought the chiefs off in a great hurry; not in a body in their usual formal way, but one by one, in separate canoes. Old Jeema called on board the Lyra on his way to the frigate; he was a good deal agitated, and the tears came into his eyes when I put a ring on his finger. He gave me in return his knife.

The other chiefs called alongside on their way to the frigate, but went on when I told them that I was just going to the Alceste myself. In the mean time Mádera came on board, with the sextant in his hand; he was in such distress that he scarcely knew what he was about. In this distracted state he sat down to breakfast with us, during which he continued lighting his pipe and smoking as fast as he could; drinking and eating whatever was placed before him. After he had a little recovered himself, he asked what books it would be necessary to read to enable him to make use of the sextant; I gave him a nautical almanack, and told him that he must understand that in the first instance: he opened it, and looking at the figures, held up his hands in despair, and was at last forced to confess that it was a hopeless business. He therefore put the sextant up and bade us farewell. Before he left the Lyra he gave Mr. Clifford his pipe, tobacco pouch, and a crystal ornament; saying, as he held out the last, "You go Ingeree, you give this to your childs."

Mr. Clifford gave him a few presents in return, and expressed his anxiety to be considered his friend. Mádera, with the tears streaming down his cheeks, placed his hand several times upon his heart, and cried, "Eedooshee, edooshee!" My friend, my friend!

To me he gave a fan and a picture of an old man looking up at the sun, drawn, he said, by himself: he probably meant in his picture some allusion to my usual occupation at the observatory. After he had put off in his boat, he called out, "Ingeree noo choo sibittee yootoosha," I shall ever remember the English people. When he went to the Alceste, one of the chiefs remarked that he had neither his hatchee-matchee on nor his robes, and told him that it was not respectful to wait upon Captain Maxwell for the last time, in his ordinary dress; particularly as all the others were in full array. Mádera, who, poor fellow, had been too much concerned about other matters to think of dress, was shocked at this apparent want of politeness, and went immediately to apologize to Captain Maxwell, who took him by the hand, and gave him a present, telling him, at the same time, that he was always too happy to see him, to notice what dress he had on.

On going into the cabin, I found the chiefs seated in a row, all very disconsolate, and apparently trying to conceal emotions different, in all probability, from any which they had ever before experienced. Captain Maxwell had made them his parting present, and I therefore gave to each chief some trifle, receiving from them in return, their knives, pipes, pouches, and fans. In the mean time the anchor was hove up, and every thing being ready for making sail, the chiefs rose to take leave. Ookooma wished to say something, but was too much affected to speak, and before they reached their boats they were all in tears.

Mádera cried bitterly as he shook hands with his numerous friends, who were loading him with presents.

The chiefs, as well as the people in the numerous canoes which had assembled round the ships, stood up, and continued waving their fans and handkerchiefs till we were beyond the reefs, and could see them no longer.
　　* * * * *

Almost every thing respecting the manners and customs of Loo-choo, with which we have had an opportunity of becoming acquainted, has been laid before the reader in the foregoing narrative. It is proposed to insert here a few particulars which in the hurry of the moment were noted down without date. They might easily have been embodied with the narrative, but it has been considered of less consequence to sacrifice arrangement, than to interfere in any way with the integrity of the Journal, in which nothing has been inserted out of the exact order in which it is known to have happened.

The religion of Loo-choo appears to be that of Fo, said to be introduced by the bodzes one thousand years ago[16]. We found great difficulty in discovering any thing precise on this subject from the natives; but from all that we could gather, religion does not appear to be made a matter of general instruction as in Europe, being left, as in China, to the priests. This we infer from the careless way in which the subject was at all times treated by the natives, and the ignorance which they professed of the forms and ceremonies used in the temples. The bodzes are not respected or esteemed in society; they are prevented from marrying, and are not allowed to eat meat: few people associate with them, and even the children turn them into ridicule. On the occasion of the Loo-choo funeral service over the grave of the seaman, the bodzes stood behind, and were not called upon to officiate, the service being entirely performed by Jeeroo.

In the large temple we saw three gilt idols and various pictures; but with the exception of the funeral service just alluded to, we never met with any thing in the least degree resembling a religious ceremony. The bodzes kept the temple clean swept, and took care of the walks and hedges, and this appeared to be their only employment. It is fair to suppose, however, that the occupation of the temple by us may have caused a temporary cessation of their religious observances.

They have large tombs or cemeteries for their dead, being mostly of the Chinese form, viz. that of a horse-shoe. They are formed of stones and mortar, and are covered with a coat of cheenam, (shell lime), which is always kept nicely whitewashed and clean swept: some are more highly finished than others; their size varies from twenty to thirty feet in length, by twelve to fourteen broad. The coffin, when closed, is placed in the vault under the tomb, and is not touched for six or seven years, by which time the flesh is found to have separated and wasted away; the bones are then collected, and put into jars ranged in rows on the inside of the vault. Burning is never used at any stage of the proceedings, nor under any circumstances. In the course of time, when these vaults become crowded, the vases are removed to houses appropriated to their reception above ground: such must have been the building described by Mr. Clifford in the village near Port Melville. The lower orders, who cannot afford these expensive tombs, take advantage of hollow places in the rocks, which by a little assistance are made secure vaults. In the cliffs behind the village of Oonting, the galleries cut for the reception of the vases must have been the work of men possessed of power and authority. Not being fully aware what the Chinese customs are with respect to the dead, in ordinary cases, it is impossible for us to say how nearly they resemble those of Loo-choo, but there are certainly some points of resemblance.

From Mr. Clifford's notes on the Loo-choo inscriptions, I have extracted the following particulars.

"A number of carved stones, called by the natives Kawroo, were found at many places, particularly in the groves on the hill. The Kawroo is two feet long, by one wide, and one high; it is excavated a little on the upper part, on which an offering of rice is placed. On the sides of this stone are carved a variety of characters, denoting the rank of the person who makes the offering, as well as the object of his petition, together with the date.

"Two of these inscriptions, copied at the time, have since been translated by a gentleman acquainted with the Chinese characters. The first gives an account of a man about to sail for China, in the reign of Kien Lung, the late monarch of that country; this person implores the divine aid in protecting him during his voyage. The other is dated in the twenty-first year of the reign of Kia-King, the present emperor of China, answering to the year 1816, in which we visited Loo-choo. This is an invocation to the deity for success in a literary pursuit.

"Two narrow strips of paper, with characters inscribed on them, which by consent of the natives were taken from a pillar in the temple, and which have since been translated, prove to be invocations, one to the supreme deity, and the other to the evil spirit. The first is on a slip of paper, two feet long, by two inches wide, and contains a supplication for pardon. The latter invocation begins by seven rows of the character symbolical of the Devil. In the upper line there are seven, and in the last one, so that a triangular page is formed of twenty-eight characters, each signifying the Devil; and the prayer itself is written in a narrow perpendicular line underneath; the whole inscription resembling in form a kite with a long tail attached to it."

Polygamy is not allowed in Loo-choo as in China, and the king, it appears, is the only person permitted by law to have concubines; they invariably spoke with horror of the Chinese practice, which allows a plurality of wives, and were much gratified on learning that the English customs in this respect were similar to those of Loo-choo. The women are not treated so well as we were led to expect from the mildness of character in the men, and their liberality of thinking in general. The upper classes of women are confined a good deal to their houses, and the lower orders perform much of the hard work of husbandry. We saw them at a distance, in great numbers, carrying loads on their heads. Mádera says that the women are not treated with much indulgence, being even restricted from using fans; and that when they are met out of doors by the men, they take no notice of one another, whatever may be the degree of relationship or intimacy subsisting between them. The perseverance with which they kept the women from our sight is curious, and leads us to conjecture that the general practice of the island is to seclude the women at all times. In this respect they differ from the Japanese, who are said to allow wives to every stranger. This degree of seclusion does not prevail in China, as we had opportunities of observing at several places never before visited by Europeans. The Chinese account quoted in the Lettres

Edifiantes et Curieuses, vol. 23, states that the young men and women marry on this island by choice, and not, as in China, by a contract made without any personal knowledge of each other. We took every opportunity of interrogating them on this subject, but as the question was always evaded, we fear that their practice in this respect is not so praiseworthy as that account would make it appear.

Of their literature we could get but few satisfactory accounts; they say that they have few books in their own language, the greater number on the island being Chinese. The young men of rank are sometimes sent to China to be educated. Jeeroo had been there when a boy. None but the upper classes understand the spoken Chinese, and the peasantry are in general ignorant both of the spoken and written Chinese language.

They appear to have no money, and from all we could see or hear, they are even ignorant of its use. Those, however, who have visited China cannot be so ill informed, and yet none of them set any value upon Spanish dollars, or upon any gold coins that we had. Though we were incessantly trying to make out from Mádera and the others, what their medium of exchange was, we could never learn any thing distinct upon the subject, nor could they be made to comprehend our questions about money; a difficulty, it may be observed, which we should expect to meet with among people whose only mode of purchase was by barter. The only circumstance which came to our knowledge bearing at all upon this question, was during the time when the garden was under preparation for the reception of the Alceste's stores; it was then remarked that each of the labourers employed had a little piece of paper stuck in his hair, with a single character written on it; this naturally excited our curiosity, but the inquiries we were enabled to make at that early stage of our knowledge of the language, led to nothing conclusive. Afterwards, when our means in this respect were more ample, we could not recall the circumstance to the recollection of the chiefs. As these papers were called by the people wearing them, "hoonátee," and as "hoónee" means ship, Mr. Clifford has conjectured that they may have been written passes to enable them to enter the gate on the ship's business.

We saw no arms of any kind, and the natives always declared that they had none. Their behaviour on seeing a musket fired certainly implied an ignorance of fire-arms. In a cottage at the north end of the island, we saw a spear which had the appearance of a warlike weapon, but we had every reason to believe that this was used for the sole purpose of catching fish, having seen others not very dissimilar actually employed in this way. They looked at our swords and cutlasses, and at the Malay creeses and spears, with equal surprise, being apparently as little acquainted with the one as with the other. The chiefs carried little case knives in the folds of their robes, or in the girdle, and the lower orders had a larger knife, but these were always of some immediate practical utility, and were not worn for defence nor as ornaments. They denied having any knowledge of war either by experience or by tradition.

We never saw any punishment inflicted at Loo-choo: a tap with the fan, or an angry look, was the severest chastisement ever resorted to, as far as we could discover. In giving orders, the chiefs were mild though firm, and the people always obeyed with cheerfulness. There seemed to be great respect and confidence on the one hand, and much consideration and kind feeling on the other. In this particular, more than in any other that fell under our notice, Loo-choo differs from China, for in the latter country we saw none of this generous and friendly understanding between the upper and lower classes.

One day when we were drinking tea and smoking pipes with the chiefs, on the top of the hill, a boy began to exhibit feats of tumbling before us; in a short time all eyes were turned towards him, and his modesty caused him to desist. We offered him buttons and various things, but he would not resume his tumbling: we then asked Jeema to interfere; he did so, and told the youngster to go on; but he kept his seat, and Jeema became angry, or rather pretended to be so, yet the tumbler sat obstinately still. "Well," said Jeema to us, "what is to be done? It was for his own amusement that he began, and probably for his amusement he will do so again." The boy, when left alone, in a short time resumed his tumbling. I mention this to shew Jeema's good sense in not forcing the boy to do that as a task, which he had begun as an amusement, and which he had discernment enough to know would be unpleasant for us to witness in any other way. By this treatment of their children, mutual cordiality and freedom of intercourse are encouraged. It was probably owing to this mode of education that the children became at once familiar with us. One day while I was employed sketching the village and trees near the bridge, a boy stopped near me, and without saying any thing, endeavoured to attract my notice by performing various gambols before me. I took no notice of him for some time, but at last looked up and smiled; upon which the boy cried out in perfectly good English, "How do you do? Very well, I thank you;" and ran off, quite delighted at having displayed his proficiency in English.

The chiefs were generally accompanied by one or two of their sons, who took their places near them, and were always put forward when there was any thing curious to be seen. In this way they were encouraged to make themselves acquainted with every thing, and yet nothing could be more respectful or affectionate than they always were. Great pains were taken to form the manners of the children, and we never observed an instance of rudeness in any one of them, though they were as full of life and spirits as the wildest English school-boys. John the Chinaman afforded them much amusement: he was a great coxcomb, and therefore fair game for the boys; they used to surround him and pretend to pull his long tail; but they never actually pulled it, but merely teazed him a little, and then ran away. These little traits seem worthy of notice, as they belong to a style of education quite different from what we had seen in China and some other eastern countries, where the children are made to look like men in miniature.

During our intercourse with these people, there did not occur one instance of theft. They were all permitted to come on board indiscriminately; to go into the cabins, store-rooms, and wherever they liked, unattended. At the temple the Alceste's stores of every kind were lying about, as well as the carpenter's and armourer's tools; and in the observatory, the instruments, books, and pencils were merely placed under cover; yet there was not a single article taken away, though many hundreds of people were daily admitted, and allowed to examine whatever they pleased. This degree of honesty is a feature which distinguishes the people of Loo-choo from the Chinese, as well as from the inhabitants of the islands in the South Sea and of the Malay Archipelago; among whom even fear, as was ascertained by Captain Cook and other voyagers, is altogether insufficient to prevent theft. At Loo-choo the people are considerably civilised; but they have few wants, and they appear to be perfectly contented. Honesty is perhaps the natural consequence of such a state of society.

We saw no musical instruments of any kind; they were, however, aware of their use. The natives almost all sing, and we heard several very sweet airs, principally plaintive: they had many jovial drinking songs, one of which we wrote down from their singing; it was inscribed on a drinking cup, and is as follows:

"Ty´wack koo, tawshoo, shee kackoofing,
"Chaw ung, itchee shaw, shooha neebooroo;
"Ting shee, you byee, chee taroo shoo ninnee
"Nooboo cadsee meesee carra shaw jeeroo
"Shing coodee sackee oochee noo shing."

The Chinese characters on the drinking-cup were thus translated in China, "Tywack hoo[17], inspired by a jar of wine, writes an hundred pages of odes or verses without end. At the market town of Chaw-ung[18] he entered a wine shop to sleep. The Emperor summoned him to appear; in his haste to obey the summons, he forgot to put on his neckcloth, and rushing into the royal presence, exclaimed, 'I am the wine-loving immortal.'"

The Loo-choo dress has been so frequently mentioned, that a brief notice, in recapitulation, will suffice in this place. Their loose robe was generally made of cotton, and of a great variety of colours. The robe of a grown up person was never flowered or printed over with figures, being generally of a uniform colour, though instances occurred of striped cloths being worn by the chiefs. This robe opened in front, but the edges overlapped, and were concealed by the folds, so as to render it difficult to say whether or not the robe was continued all round: the sleeves were about three feet wide: round the middle was bound a belt or girdle about four or five inches wide, always of a different colour from the dress, and in general richly ornamented with wrought silk and gold flowers. The folds of the robe overhang the belt, but not so much as to hide it: the whole of the dress folds easily, and has a graceful and picturesque appearance. The garments worn by the children were often gaudily printed with flowers. In rainy or cold weather, a sort of great coat was worn by the chiefs only, of thick blue cloth, buttoning in front over the robe, and tighter both in body and sleeves than the other. This cloth resembled the coarse cloth used in China; and it looked like woollen manufacture, and may possibly have been originally brought from England. The sandals worn by all ranks were exactly the same; they were formed of straw wrought into a firm mat to fit the sole of the foot, smooth towards the foot, and ragged underneath: a stiff smooth band of straw, about as thick as one's little finger, passes from that part of the sandal immediately under the ancle and over the lower part of the instep, so as to join the sandal at the opposite side; this is connected with the foremost part of the sandal by a short small straw cord which comes between the great toe and the next one. The upper classes wore stockings of white cotton, not unlike our half stockings, except that they button at the outside, and have a place like the finger of a glove for the great toe.

[Illustration: GENTLEMAN of LOO CHOO in his CLOAK.]

Their hair is of a jet black, and is kept glossy by juice expressed from a leaf. There is no variety in the fashion of dressing it; it is pulled tight up all round, and is formed at top into a compact knot, so as to conceal the crown of the head, which is shaved; through the knot are thrust two metal pins, one of which has a square point and flowered head consisting of six leaves or divisions: the other pin has one end sharp, and the other shaped like a scoop: the length of these pins is from four to six inches. We did not see the Prince's, as he remained covered during all the time of his visit; but the Chief of high rank, who visited the Alceste on the 23d of September, had the flowered end of one pin studded with precious stones. The higher orders wear, on state occasions, what they called a "hatchee-matchee," which is a kind of turban, apparently made by winding a broad band round a cylinder, in such a way, that a small segment of each fold is shewn at every turn, in front above, and behind below; this is effected by giving a slight diagonal direction to each fold. The lower orders occasionally tie a coloured cloth or handkerchief round the head; this they call "sadjee:" next the body they wear a thin cotton dress. The men wear no ornaments through their flesh, nor are they tattooed: we saw, indeed, some fishermen who had fish spears marked on their arms, but this does not prevail generally. An etching of these marks is given by Mr. Clifford in the second part of the Vocabulary.

The cattle on this island, which are of a small black breed, are used exclusively for agricultural purposes. Hogs, goats, and poultry, with rice and a great variety of vegetables, form the food of the inhabitants: milk is never used. We saw no geese, so that those left by Captain Broughton most probably did not thrive. They have no sheep nor asses. Their horses are of a small slight make, and the natives are very fond of riding. We saw no carts or wheeled carriages of any kind, horses being used to carry loads; for this purpose the roads are numerous, and kept in excellent order, being from six to ten feet wide.

Their mode of dressing the ground is neat, and resembles the Chinese, particularly in manuring and irrigating it. This is most attended to where the sugar-cane is cultivated: they have, besides, tobacco, wheat, rice, Indian corn, millet, sweet potatoes, brinjals, and many other vegetables. The fields, which are nicely squared, have convenient walks on the raised banks running round each. Along the sides of the hills, and round the villages, the bamboo and rattan grow to a considerable size. The pine is the most conspicuous tree on the island, growing to a great height and size, which we infer from seeing canoes built with planks several feet wide; the trees, however, near the temple at Napakiang were not above ninety feet high, and from three to four in girt. The banyan-tree of India was seen at several places; the finest one overhung the small temple at Napakiang, which circumstance led to the enquiry whether, as in India, this tree is held sacred, but we could gain no information on this subject.

In a little plot of ground in the temple garden, Mr. Phillips, purser of the Alceste, sowed mustard-seed, peas, and a variety of other seeds, the natives taking his directions for their culture. Our total ignorance of botany prevented our making any observations on this subject while at Loo-choo; but to supply this deficiency, we collected specimens of every plant at the place. These were preserved between sheets of brown paper, and given afterwards to Mr. Abel, the naturalist of the embassy, in order to be arranged; but they were subsequently lost, along with the whole of that gentleman's collection.

Of their manufactures it is difficult to speak with certainty. By their own account the silks which they wear are Chinese, but the cotton cloths are made on this and the neighbouring islands; the printed patterns of these are not without elegance. We saw no weaving looms, but as we were only in a few houses, this is not surprising: the webs are thirty-six feet long, and fourteen inches broad. Tobacco-pipes and fans are made at Loo-choo; as well as the sepulchral vases, of which there is a manufactory at Napakiang, from whence they are exported to Ooting, and other parts of the island. Some of the pouches of the chiefs were made of cloth, which they say comes from China; it is exactly like our broad cloth. We tried in vain to learn what goods they send to China in exchange for silks: perhaps sulphur forms a part, which these islands are said to produce, as well as tin. From the number of vessels constantly sailing out and in, it appears that they must have some trade, but our enquiries on this and many other topics, though sedulously pursued, led to nothing satisfactory, owing probably rather to our ignorance of the language, than to any wish on their part to withhold information; because, on topics which had no reference to the royal family or the women, they in general spoke freely.

We had frequent opportunities of seeing their method of making salt, and an account of it may, perhaps, be interesting. Near the sea, large level fields are rolled or beat so as to have a hard surface. Over this is strewn a sort of sandy black earth, forming a coat about a quarter of an inch thick. Rakes and other implements are used to make it of a uniform thickness, but it is not pressed down. During the heat of the day, men are employed to bring water in tubs from the sea, which is sprinkled over these fields by means of a short scoop. The heat of the sun, in a short time, evaporates the water, and the salt is left in the sand, which is scraped up and put into raised receivers of masonry about six feet by four, and five deep. When the receiver is full of the sand, sea water is poured on the top, and this, in its way down, carries with it the salt left by evaporation. When it runs out below at a small hole, it is a very strong brine; this is reduced to salt by being boiled in vessels about three feet wide and one deep. The cakes resulting from this operation are an inch and a half in thickness.

Of the population of this island we know nothing satisfactory: the natives invariably pleaded ignorance themselves; and as we had no precise data, our estimates were made at random, and as they never agreed with each other, they are not worthy of notice. From the south point of this island, to five or six miles north of Napakiang, an extent of sixteen or eighteen miles, the country is highly cultivated, and is almost entirely covered with villages. All round Port Melville too there are populous villages, but the north, north-east and eastern places are thinly peopled, and not cultivated to any extent. We saw nothing like poverty or distress of any kind: every person that we met seemed contented and happy. We saw no deformed people, nor any who bore indications of disease, except a few who were marked with the small-pox.

The style of living of those with whom we associated is generous and free; their custom of carrying about their dinner in boxes, and making little pic-nic parties, is peculiarly striking, and they appeared fully sensible of the advantage of bringing people together in this way, and expressed much satisfaction at the ready way in which we fell into a custom from which all formality was dismissed. They shewed, moreover, a good deal of discernment, and could adapt themselves to the character of the particular persons they happened to be in company with, in a manner very remarkable; but this was evidently the result not of cunning, but of correct feelings, and of a polite habit of thinking.

Of their manners, little need be added here to what every page of the narrative will show. It ought to be particularly noticed, however, that they are an exceedingly timorous people, and naturally suspicious of foreigners. A stranger visiting Loo-choo ought therefore to keep these features of their character constantly in mind. By imitating Captain Maxwell's wise plan of treating the natives with gentleness and kindness, and shewing every consideration for their peculiarities, he will stand the best chance of gaining their good-will and confidence. But if he should betray any impatience, or be at all harsh in treating with them, he may rest assured that he will lose much time, and in all probability fail at last in his attempts to establish an unreserved and friendly intercourse.

As Loo-choo, however, lies quite out of the track of trading ships, and does not appear to produce any thing of value itself, and as the inhabitants seem indifferent about foreign commodities, and if they wished to possess them are without money to make purchases, it is not probable that this island will be soon revisited.

[Illustration: BRIDGE AT NAPAKIANG.]

FOOTNOTES:

[Footnote 11: We first discovered the meaning of this word by hearing one of the natives apply it to the castle on the chess board: he used the same term when drawings of towers and castles were shewn to him.]

[Footnote 12: The literal translation of the card is "Loo-choo nation, extender of laws, Great Person (called Ko), Heang, bows his head and worships," (the common visiting expression among the Chinese.) It ought to be remarked, that the Prince's name is placed on one corner of the card, which is the most respectful mode that can be used, according to Chinese usage.]

[Footnote 13: See Broughton's Voyage, Book II. Chap. 2. for a very interesting account of the natives of Typinsan, who appear to resemble the people of the Great Loo-choo Island. In Book II. Chap. 3. Captain Broughton gives an account of his visit to Napachan. He was received by the inhabitants with great kindness; they supplied his wants, but objected to his landing, and sent back to the schooner some of the officers who had been sent on shore to examine the town. We found Captain Broughton's account of the people quite accurate.]

[Footnote 14: At Manilla we found that the Great Loo-choo Island was known only by name. There appeared to be no intercourse between the two places.]

[Footnote 15: LIST OF SUPPLIES RECEIVED AT LOO-CHOO BY H.M. SHIPS.

	Alceste.	Lyra.
Bullocks	19	8
Pigs	23	10
Goats	15	7
Fowls	*216	102	*Not including
Fish	29	12	extra supplies
Eggs	920	455	to the officers.
Bags of sweet potatoes	*59	27	*Not including
Squashes	34	14	ditto.
Jars of Samchoo, each containing about		
fifteen gallons	6	3
Baskets of oranges	9	4

Bundles of gingerbread | 8 | 3 |
——————Onions | 16 | 8 |
——————Radishes | 30 | 12 |
——————Celery | 12 | 5 |
——————Garlick | 8 | 4 |
——————Candles | 7 | 3 |
——————Wood | 16 | 8 |
Pumpkins | 60 | 30 |
Baskets of vermicelli | 7 | 3 |
Boxes of sugar | 2 | 1 |
Rolls of printed linen | 14 | 7 |
Bundles of paper | 6 | 3 |
]

[Footnote 16: See Lettres Edifiantes et Curieuses, vol. 23.]

[Footnote 17: A man celebrated in the Tung dynasty for his convivial disposition: he is known in China by the name of Jai-pe.]

[Footnote 18: The town of Chang-ngan in China, near the Great Wall.]

APPENDIX:

CONTAINING

CHARTS

OF THE GULF OF PE-CHE-LEE, THE WEST COAST OF COREA, THE GREAT LOO-CHOO ISLAND, NAPAKIANG ROADS, AND PORT MELVILLE: WITH BRIEF EXPLANATORY NOTICES.

TABLE OF OBSERVATIONS

MADE WITH DR. WOLLASTON'S DIP SECTOR: WITH AN ENGRAVING, AND A DESCRIPTION OF THIS INSTRUMENT, AND DIRECTIONS FOR ITS USE.

METEOROLOGICAL JOURNAL,

FROM JULY TO NOVEMBER 1816, WHILE THE SHIPS WERE IN THE YELLOW AND JAPAN SEAS.

ABSTRACT OF THE LYRA'S VOYAGE,

FROM LEAVING ENGLAND TILL HER RETURN; SHEWING THE DISTANCE BETWEEN THE DIFFERENT PLACES AT WHICH SHE TOUCHED, AND THE TIME TAKEN IN PERFORMING EACH PASSAGE.

GEOLOGICAL MEMORANDUM;

BEING A DESCRIPTION OF THE SPECIMENS OF ROCKS COLLECTED ON THE SHORES OF THE YELLOW SEA, COREA, LOO-CHOO, MACAO, AND THE LADRONE ISLANDS.

CHARTS

OF THE

GULF OF PE-CHE-LEE, THE WEST COAST OF COREA, THE GREAT LOO-CHOO ISLAND, NAPAKIANG ROADS, AND PORT MELVILLE.

WITH BRIEF EXPLANATORY NOTICES.

[Illustration: Track of His Majesty's Sloop LYRA *and Honble. Comps. Ship INVESTIGATOR along the Shores of the* GULPH OF PETCHELEE By Captain Basil Hall R.N. 1816.

East of Greenwich]

NOTICE EXPLANATORY OF A CHART

OF

THE SOUTH SIDE OF THE GULF OF PE-CHE-LEE, YELLOW SEA.

[Sidenote: First meridian used in constructing the chart.]

In constructing this chart, I have assumed the longitude of the fort at the mouth of the Pei-ho to be 117° 49' east of Greenwich, or 11' west of the place where the squadron lay at anchor. From this the difference of longitude was measured by two chronometers. The latitudes were ascertained by frequent observations of the stars, as well as of the sun.

[Sidenote: Aspect of the south and south-west coasts.]

[Sidenote: Soundings.]

The coast on the south and south-west sides of this Gulf is very low, resembling, in this respect, the shore at the entrance of the Pei-ho, or Pekin river, where it is uniformly low and sandy; occasionally a few houses are to be seen, and also square mounds or buildings like forts, but generally, a low white beach is all that can be discovered. The coast is not visible till within about three leagues distance, and the eye elevated eighty feet from the sea, which is the height of the Lyra's foretop-gallant yard. The depth of water when the land first came in sight, was generally five fathoms; at some places only four fathoms, and at the very bottom of the Gulf, it could not be discerned till in three and a half fathoms. It may be said generally, that at ten miles distance the soundings are from four and a half to six fathoms; at twelve miles, from six to eight fathoms. There is a wonderful uniformity in the depth from the Pei-ho round to the south-east corner of the Gulf; the bottom is mud, sometimes a little gritty, particularly towards the southern parts.

[Sidenote: Colour of the water.]

The colour of the water was mostly of the same dirty yellow or green which was observed off the Pei-ho, but we did not observe any red coloured water, as was frequently noticed at that place; indeed, at the bottom of the Gulf, there were several changes in the colour of the water, accompanied by long lines of foam, indicating, it would seem, the vicinity of a great river.

[Sidenote: Tides on the western side of the Gulf.]

On the west side of the Gulf the ebb tide runs to the south-east by south, and the flood north-west by west; the periods are very regular, being generally about six hours: they vary, however, in rapidity. As we anchored on the flood we were enabled to measure its velocity; as we got deep in the Gulf it decreased: at the Pei-ho it frequently ran two and two and a half knots, but far south it was sometimes hardly perceptible; it is worthy of notice, too, that the perpendicular rise and fall decreased from ten feet off the Pei-ho, to one, or at most two feet, in the bottom of the Gulf.

[Sidenote: Bottom of the Gulf.]

The most southern point of our track was 37° 15' north; at this time we could perceive the low coast stretching to the east and west; the distance it is difficult to assign very accurately, but it was probably seven or eight miles, for with a glass we could perceive a number of people on the shore. I took great pains to ascertain the latitude stated above, by the meridian altitudes of several stars; the longitude is 1° 39' east of the Pei-ho, or 119° 28' east of Greenwich.

[Sidenote: South-eastern side different from the opposite.]

The coast from the south-west corner of the Gulf to the peninsula of Teu-choo-foo, is of a totally different character from that opposite to it, for it is high, and well marked: a range of mountains stretches from south-west to north-east, at the distance of three or four leagues inland; their outline is peaked, and they are intersected by deep ravines without any verdure; the summits are also barren.

[Sidenote: Mount Ellis.]

One of these mountains is very remarkable, having two peaks or paps by which it can be distinguished at the distance of fifty miles, and bears the same aspect when viewed from all parts of the Gulf. It lies in 37° 6' north, and 2° 11' east of the Pei-ho, or 120° east of Greenwich. It has been called Mount Ellis, in honour of Mr. Ellis, the third commissioner of the Embassy.

[Sidenote: Aspect of the coast.]

[Sidenote: Jane's Isle.]

[Sidenote: Douglas Island.]

Between this range of hills and the shore, there is a lower belt of elevated ground in a state of high cultivation, covered with many towns and villages, and interspersed with scattered trees and several extensive woods; the ground, too, presents a varied surface, so that the whole offers a pleasing contrast with the rugged land behind. There are two small islands on this line of coast; the southern one lies in 37° 21' north, and 2° 5' east of the Pei-ho; the other is in 37° 28' north, and 2° 19' east of the Pei-ho.

[Sidenote: Dangerous shoal.]

There is a dangerous shoal about five leagues off the shore, abreast of these islands, upon which the Lyra nearly struck at midnight on the 17th instant. When at anchor just outside the shoal, the south island bore south 20° east, and the other, east 21° south; on the shoal there was two and a half fathoms, hard bottom. It seems to extend in a north and south direction, and is very narrow. It lies in 37° 32' north, which I ascertained by altitudes of the pole star, under favourable circumstances. It is 1° 58' 30" east of the Pei-ho.

[Sidenote: Soundings and tides.]

The soundings on this side of the Gulf are somewhat deeper than on the other, but not so deep as might have been expected from the bold nature of the land. The ebb tide runs to the north-eastward, and the flood into the Gulf.

[Sidenote: Winds.]

[Sidenote: Melville Point.]

[Sidenote: Teu-choo-foo city.]

The wind was south-east and quite light, from the 11th August to the 17th, when it shifted to north north-east till about eight P.M. when close in shore near the southern of the two islands; it then blew off, with all the appearance of a regular land breeze. On the 19th it blew a gale of wind from the north-east, with a short, high sea; during the gale we lay at anchor off a remarkable point, connected with the main land by a low sandy neck; the ground felt soft to the lead, but it was probably rocky under the mud, as both ships lost a bower anchor by the cables being cut. This point lies in 37° 42' north, and 2° 35' east of the Pei-ho. We found the city of Teu-choo-foo to lie in 3° 4' east of the Pei-ho. The latitude observed in Teu-choo-foo roads was 37° 53' north, and the longitude 2° 54' east of the Pei-ho. The western Meadow Island bearing north.

[Sidenote: Cheatow Bay.]

The latitude of a small island at the north-east corner of the Bay of Cheatow or Zee-a-tow, was determined by the sun's meridian altitude on shore, to be 37° 35' 52" north, and longitude east of the Pei-ho 3° 45', or in 121° 34' east of Greenwich.

[Sidenote: Oei-hai-oei.]

The latitude of Oei-hai-oei was observed on shore to be 37° 30' 40" north, and lies 4° 25' east of the Pei-ho.

[Sidenote: Variation of the compass.]

The variation of the compass in the Yellow Sea was found to be 2° 16' westerly.

The rise and fall of the tide at the anchorage of the squadron off the Pei-ho was twelve feet. It was high water at full, and change at III. The flood tide runs to the west-south-west, and the ebb generally about east and east-south-east. Its strength and direction are a good deal influenced by the prevalent winds.

NOTICE TO ACCOMPANY THE CHART OF THE WEST COAST OF COREA.

[Sidenote: Inadequate time allowed for so extensive a survey.]

This chart extends from 34° to 38° north latitude, and from 124° to 127° east longitude. The time of our stay on the coast being only nine days, no great accuracy is to be expected, and this chart pretends to be little more than an eye-draught, checked by chronometers and meridian altitudes of the sun and stars. Under circumstances of such haste, much has unavoidably been left untouched, and what is now given is presented with no great confidence.

[Sidenote: General remarks on the methods followed in the survey.]

What follows is extracted from notes made at the time by Mr. Clifford and myself. The longitudes by chronometer have all been carefully recomputed, and the greatest care was taken in ascertaining the various latitudes. The true bearings are in every instance set down, the variation being allowed for at the moment. The variation of the compass recorded in this notice, was determined by two azimuth compasses, and the method recommended by Captain Flinders, of repeating the observations by turning the compass first one way and then the other, was invariably followed.

[Illustration: Track *of His Majesty's Ship* ALCESTE *and* LYRA *Sloop along the Western Coast of the PENINSULA of* COREA *by Captain Basil Hall R.N.*]

[Sidenote: The ships leave China.]

[Sidenote: Make the coast of Corea.]

[Sidenote: Sir James Hall's group.]

[Sidenote: Anchorage on the south side of an island.]

His Majesty's ships Alceste and Lyra, after quitting the port of Oei-hai-oei, which is in latitude 37° 30' 40" north, and longitude 122° 16' east, on the north coast of Shantung Promontory, stood to the northward and eastward till in latitude 38° north, and then ran to the eastward. On the morning of the 1st of September, 1816, we saw the land, bearing about east. By sights with chronometer on the meridian of these islands, we ascertained that the west end of the northern one lies in 124° 44-1/2' east. The latitude of the south end of the eastern island was ascertained by meridian altitude of the sun to be 37° 44-1/2' north. There is a rocky white islet off the west end of the middle island. We had from twenty to thirty fathoms on rounding the south-west end of the islands, but on the south side of the southern one there is a bight with seven fathoms, black sand in the centre: here we anchored. There is good anchorage all over the bay, which is sheltered from all winds except between west south-west and south-east, being open to the southward. There are two villages here. From the top of the highest peak on this island, which is about seven or eight hundred feet high, we could discern the main land of Corea, high and rugged, stretching north north-west and south south-east, distant from eight to ten leagues. Along the coast abreast of us there were seen many islands. The channel between the middle island of the group and the one we were upon appeared clear and broad; but the northern and middle islands seemed connected by a reef which shews above water at several places.

[Sidenote: Character of the inhabitants.]

The inhabitants were suspicious and unfriendly: we saw some cattle and many fowls, but neither money nor any thing else that we had could induce them to part with either.

[Sidenote: Lose sight of the coast.]

In the evening we weighed and stood to the southward; next morning there was no land in sight. At noon we were in longitude 124° 47' 52" east, and latitude 36° 44-1/2' north, no land in sight. We hauled in shore to the eastward, and anchored in the night in deep water.

[Sidenote: Group of five islands.]

[Sidenote: Bearings.]

3rd of September.—Weighed at 3.30 and stood in shore; at 7.45 A.M. we were due south of the western of a group of islands. Many sights were taken as we passed to settle the place of this group: it lies between 125° 42-1/2' east, and 125° 57-1/2' east, and in latitude 36° 44' north. After passing this group we stood to the south-east towards a vast cluster of islands: at noon, when we were just entering the cluster, the latitude was observed 36° 18' 21" north, and longitude 126° 10' east. The south-west extreme of the islands bore south 40° west. There were eight islands near us between south-east and south-west, and a high bluff dark rock south one-quarter east, four miles: and on the main land a very high hill, east 19° north. When we had got well among the islands it fell calm, and we anchored in eight and a half fathoms. It remained calm during the night.

[Sidenote: Run among the islands.]

4th of September.—Weighed on a breeze springing up, and stood in shore. Observed in 36° 13' north, longitude 126° 30' east; at this time the following bearings were taken.

[Sidenote: Bearings.]

A remarkable peak on the main land, east.

High mountain on the main land, east 38-1/2° north.

White cliff on the east end of the fourth island to the left of the wide entrance into the cluster, north.

Small round island, north 30° west.

Another, north 35° west.

Extremes of a large bluff island from north 38° west, to north 32-1/2° west.

Rock, north 72° west.

Outer island, north 75° west.

Extremes of the outer cluster, from north 77-1/2 west, to west 1° south.

Large island, from west 14° 30' south, to west 18° south.

[Sidenote: Basil's Bay.]

[Sidenote: Unsocial disposition of the inhabitants.]

These islands being within from ten to fifteen miles, were laid down by estimated distances, but it was quite impossible to assign places to the immense number of others which stretched away to the south and south-east, as far as the eye could reach. We stood in shore for the purpose of discovering whether there was any place of shelter in the main land, but in general it proved shallow and unsafe. At length we discovered a bay which promised shelter, but on running into it, the depth was found not to exceed three or four fathoms. This bay is open towards the south, and is formed by a curved tongue of land on the north and west. The longitude of the south end of this point is 126° 42' 22" east, and latitude 36° 7' 38" north. We remained here during the night, and the forenoon of the 5th. The natives came on board, but made great objections to our landing.

[Sidenote: Tides.]

The tide rose and fell fifteen feet and a half; it was low water at 8 P.M., and high water at 2.30 A.M. This was two and a half days before full moon.

The Alceste's boats were sent to sound in the eastern quarter, but they found shoal water every where.

[Sidenote: Proceed to the south-westward.]

5th of September.—At 11 A.M. we got under weigh and stood to the south-west among the islands, carrying seven, eight, nine, ten, to fifteen fathoms, and occasionally deepening to seventeen fathoms. At 4.45 we observed in longitude 126° 24-1/2' east, and latitude 35° 52' north at this time.

[Sidenote: Bearings.]

Two islands bore north half east, seven miles.

A remarkable small black island, west 32°, north four miles.

Another, west 22° north, seven miles.

A range of islands, from east 10° north, to east 16° south.

A long island, from south 25° east, to south 11° east.

The islands off which we anchored on the 2nd instant bearing about north 10° west.

Two islands, from south 16° west, to south 25° west.

[Sidenote: Main land.]

The main land from south south-east to north-east, high and rugged.

We had a sea breeze to-day, and fine weather. Variation 2° 10' westerly. We ran on by moonlight till 11 P.M., and then anchored among the islands. Latitude, observed by Polaris 35° 26' north. Longitude, at anchor by chronometer next morning 126° 23' 22" east. From this spot the main land was seen from east 12° north, to south 20° east.

[Sidenote: Bearings.]

A rock, west 7° south, four miles.

An island, from west 15° north, to west 31° north, 4-1/2'.

Three islands, extending from west 36° south, to west 45° south, 3'.

Two distant ones in the same direction.

Cluster of islands, from west 64° south, to west 84-1/2° south.

Large island, north 12° west, ten or twelve miles.

A cluster of islands, from north 15° east, to north 28° east.

Two distant islands, north 32° east.

Two others, north 42° east.

[Sidenote: Channels between the islands generally deep.]

6th of September.—Weighed and stood to the southward. At noon observed in 35° 17' north, longitude 126° 28-1/2' east, being then in the centre of a semicircle of islands, extending from north-east to south-east and south-west. During the forenoon the flood tide set strong to the north north-east against us. Most of the channels between the islands were deep, but to-day we tried one which had not more than five and a half fathoms. At 4.30. took sights, when a long bluff island bore east north-east a quarter of a mile. Longitude 126° 6' 37" east; latitude 35° 6' north. This island is the most westerly of the range of islands which lie between the latitude 35° and 36° north. High and connected land was faintly discernible to the eastward. The soundings were generally from nine to fifteen fathoms, deepening in most cases on approaching the bluff islands.

[Sidenote: Flood tide runs to the northward.]

[Sidenote: Windsor Castle.]

[Sidenote: Bearings.]

7th of September.—We anchored last night about ten o'clock in seventeen fathoms; the flood tide had made; it ran north nearly three miles an hour, till four A.M. when we got under weigh, and drifted fast to the southward with the ebb. At 9.30. got sights, which gave longitude 125° 52' 45" east, latitude 34° 42' north; at this time a very remarkable hill on an island bore east 8° south; it has the appearance of a turret or large chimney. The other bearings from this spot were—

Western extreme of a large island stretching west north-west, and east south-east; north 27°, east 4 or 5'.

Round rock, north 18° east, 8'.

Cluster of islands from north 50° west, to north 74° west.

Round bluff small island, west 9° south.

Large island, west 42° south, 7 or eight leagues.

Two small distant islands, west 53° south, 10' leagues.

Small island, south 11° east.

[Sidenote: Soundings.]

[Sidenote: Variation of the compass.]

Extreme of distant land, south 37° east: besides, as usual, innumerable distant islands. The flood tide made against us between ten and eleven. The soundings this morning have been from twenty-three to nineteen fathoms. The weather extremely hot and the water smooth. The ebb made about four, and there being no wind, it carried us rapidly towards some rocks joining two islands. We anchored in twenty-one fathoms. The variation of the compass 2-1/2° westerly. The bearings at anchor this evening were as follows:

[Sidenote: Bearings.]

Small island, south 3° 22' east.

Large island, from south to south 20-1/2° east.

A small island, south 22° east.

Another, south 28-1/2° east.

High bluff island, south 31° east.

Island from south 9° east, to south 18° west.

Sharp peaked rock, south 25° 40' west.

Island from south 63° west, to south 65° west.

Distant island, from south 63-1/2° west, to south 66° west, nine or ten leagues.

Distant small island, west 1° 10' north, seven or eight leagues.

[Sidenote: Bearings.]

Distant island, from west 6° 39' north, to west 9° north, formed of one large flat space and five hummocks, eight or nine leagues.

Island, west 28° 50' north.

Large island, from west 31° north, to west 38° 19' north.

Round bluff island, off which we observed at noon to-day, west 39° 52' north.

Distant small island, west 44° 28' north, four or five leagues.

Large island, from west 71° north, to west 81° 30' north.

An island, afterwards called Thistle Island, south 79° east, to east 14° 52' north, besides numberless islands, in thick clusters, extending as far as the eye could reach, in the north-east and east quarters. In the afternoon a boat went inside Thistle Island, and reported that there was a clear anchorage.

[Sidenote: Sail into Murray's Sound.]

[Sidenote: Latitude observed on shore.]

[Sidenote: Longitude.]

[Sidenote: Tides.]

[Sidenote: Variation of the compass.]

8th of September.—At noon we weighed and sailed round the north end of Thistle Island, carrying seventeen fathoms, till the north end bore south; we then shoaled to ten and eleven, and one cast nine fathoms. On rounding the island we steered south, and anchored in eleven fathoms, soft bottom, about four hundred yards from the middle part of the island. The islands at this place are so situated as to form a capacious and secure anchorage, with passages among the islands in all directions. The latitude observed with an artificial horizon on shore, was 34° 22' 39" north; longitude by mean of two chronometers, agreeing nearly, 126° 2' 52" east. The tides run at the springs at the rate of three and four knots, the flood to the north north-east; the rise and fall is fifteen feet. Strong eddies are felt among the islands. The variation of the compass is 2° 30' westerly.

[Sidenote: Appearance of the Amherst Isles, from the top of a peaked island.]

On the 9th of September Captain Maxwell and a party went to the summit of a high peak, on an island to the south-east of the ships, in latitude 34° 20' north, and longitude 126° 6' east. From this spot, elevated about seven or eight hundred feet above the sea, the view of the islands was very striking: we endeavoured to number them, but our accounts varied, owing to the difficulty of estimating the number in the distant groups; it will serve, however, to give some idea of this splendid scene, to say that the lowest enumeration gave one hundred and twenty islands.

Many of these islands are large and high, almost all are cultivated, and their forms present an endless diversity.

High land was seen to rise above the distant islands in the east and north-east; this probably was the main land of Corea, for it seemed more extensive and connected than any group of islands we had seen.

[Sidenote: Difficulty of estimating the number of islands on this coast.]

We had now ran along upwards of two hundred miles of this coast, and at every part which we approached, the islands were no less thickly sown than here; so that our attempts to enumerate them all, or even to assign places on the chart to those which we passed the nearest to, became after a time quite hopeless.

[Sidenote: Winds and weather.]

During our stay upon the coast of Corea, between the 1st and 10th of September, the winds were principally from the northward; the weather was moderate and clear; and occasionally calm during the heat of the day.

[Sidenote: Barometer and thermometer.]

The barometer rose and fell gradually between 29. 78. and 29. 98. The thermometer was never above 82°, and never, even at night, under 72° For further details respecting the winds and weather, see the Meteorological Journal.

[Illustration: Chart of GREAT LOO CHOO Island
Surveyed in H.M. Sloop LYRA by Captain Basil Hall
1816]

NOTICE TO ACCOMPANY THE GENERAL CHART OF THE GREAT LOO-CHOO ISLAND, AND THE CHARTS OF NAPAKIANG, AND PORT MELVILLE.

[Sidenote: Different names of this island.]

This island is called Loo-choo, and sometimes Doo-choo, by the natives. In our maps it is variously written, but mostly Lekayo: the Chinese know it by the name of Low-kow. The spelling used by Mr. Horsburgh in his directions, Lieou-kieou, or Lieu-chew.

[Sidenote: Geographical limits and general aspect.]

The island lies between 26° 4-3/4' and 26° 52-1/2', north, and between 127° 34' and 128° 18' east, being very nearly sixty miles long in a north-east direction, and preserving a tolerably uniform breadth of about ten or twelve miles. The north end is high and bold, with wood on the top of the hills. The north-east coast is also abrupt, but quite barren. The south-east side is low, with very little appearance of cultivation. The south, south-west, and western faces, particularly the two former, are of moderate height, and present a scene of great fertility and high cultivation: it is to this quarter that the mass of population have resorted. The north-west side is generally rugged and bare.

[Sidenote: Deep bay.]

[Sidenote: Barrow's Bay.]

There are two deep indentures, one on each side of the island; that on the west has at least one hundred fathoms depth, and appears to have no coral in it: while the eastern bight is extremely shallow, and is not only skirted by a broad fringe of coral, but has reefs in the centre; and these last are very dangerous, for they give no warning either by breakers or discoloration of the water, or by soundings: and this remark will apply generally to all the reefs round this island, rendering the navigation, particularly at night, very dangerous.

[Sidenote: General caution respecting coral reefs.]

[Sidenote: Sugar Loaf or Eegooshcoond.]

The most remarkable headland is the island called by Captain Broughton the Sugar Loaf, and by the natives Eegooshcoond (tower or castle); it can be seen distinctly at the distance of twenty-five miles when the eye is elevated only fifteen feet. It is a high conical mountain, varying very little in its aspect when viewed from different quarters: as there is no other peak like it on or near this island, it cannot be mistaken. The latitude of the peak is 26° 43' north; and I have reason to believe that this is within one mile of the truth. Its longitude is 127° 44', or 6' east of the observatory at Napakiang, by two chronometers. The base of the cone and one-third of the way up is covered with houses; and the whole island has the appearance of a garden. When nearly on the meridian of the Sugar Loaf its top seems rounded off.

[Sidenote: Two safe anchoring places.]

[Sidenote: Geographical position of Napakiang.]

There are two places where ships can ride in safety, Napakiang Roads on the south-west, and Port Melville on the north-west side of the island. The first of these is the one in which his majesty's ships Alceste and Lyra lay for upwards of a month. By means of a base of 1319 feet on a coral reef, which dried at half ebb, we were enabled to make the survey which accompanies this notice. The latitude of the observatory was determined to be 26° 13' 34" north, the mean of three meridian altitudes of the sun by a sextant of Cary's, and five by a circle of Troughton's, the extreme difference being 20". The longitude is 127° 38' east; this was ascertained by measuring the difference of longitude between the observatory and Lintin Island off Canton river in a run of six days; on which occasion two chronometers on board the Lyra gave within one mile the same difference of longitude, viz. 13° 50', with that shewn by two others on board his majesty's ship Alceste; the longitude of Lintin being 113° 48' east of Greenwich. The longitude, by lunar observations, is 127° 37' 28". The plan of Napakiang roads will be found sufficient without many directions for ships wishing to enter it. The principal danger lies in the outer reefs, which do not show when the weather is very fine and there is little swell; on such occasions a boat ought to go a-head at least a quarter of a mile, and the ship should put about instantly upon approaching the reefs, which are every where bold. A ship coming from the westward ought to steer between the north-eastern of the group of high islands to the south-westward, and a low green island with extensive reefs to the northward, in latitude 26° 15' north. On passing which she should haul up east by south, giving Reef Island a birth of at least a mile.

[Sidenote: Plan of Napakiang.]

[Sidenote: Directions on approaching Napakiang.]

[Sidenote: Reef Island.]

[Illustration]

[Sidenote: Directions for entering Napakiang roads.]

[Illustration: NAPAKIANG ROADS
on the S.W. Side of the GREAT LOO CHOO Island
Laid down from actual survey by Captain Basil Hall R.N. H.M. Sloop LYRA 1816]

[Sidenote: Capstan Rock.]

[Sidenote: Best anchorage off the mouths of two rivulets.]

[Sidenote: The northern entrance.]

On approaching the main land a conspicuous wooded point will be seen, having rocks on its summit like the ruins of an abbey; this forms the south side of the anchorage, and is considerably more to the westward than the north-east side. The harbour of Napakiang will soon be seen at the south side of the bay; steer directly in for this, giving Abbey Point a birth of half a mile, and when directly between the south end of the outer reefs and Abbey Point haul up east by north. There is a very remarkable rock on the south-east side of the anchorage resembling the head of a capstan. It would be safest to anchor when this bears about south-south-east half a mile at most, in order to avoid a dangerous coral tongue, which lies north a little easterly from it, three-quarters of a mile; but as this anchorage is exposed, the ship may proceed farther in as soon as the exact place of the reef has been ascertained by boats; and if she proposes staying any time, she may warp into Barnpool, taking the precaution of placing a boat on each side of the entrance. There are two rivulets at this place, and probably the best anchorage is off their mouths, the bottom consisting of the mud brought down by the stream. There is a well on the eastern side supplied by a spring, and there are landing places at the entrance of both harbours. There is a safe passage between the reef, on which the base was measured, and the outer ones. The Lyra passed through this three times; and if the object is to go to the northward it ought to be followed, provided the wind will admit of steering north and two points on each side of it. The leading mark for going by this passage is Capstan Fort or Rock, on with a remarkable nose formed by the trees on the highest distant land; these are on when they bear about south by east half east. It would certainly not be advisable for a stranger to enter by this passage, but he may run on coming from the northward along the shore at the distance of two or three miles till Reef Island bears west, and then he should look sharply out for the reefs, keeping outside them till near Abbey Point, then act as before directed. On running down towards Napakiang from the northward a remarkable bluff table land will be seen to the southward of Abbey Point. The west face of Abbey Point ought to be kept just on with the east end of the table land; this will take you further out than is absolutely necessary; but it is safe; and when Reef Island is just on with the northern of the group of distant islands you will be exactly off the north entrance.

[Sidenote: Appearance of land in coming from the northward towards Napakiang.]

[Sidenote: Not to be attempted by a stranger.]

[Sidenote: Dangerous coral reef about four leagues south-west by west from Napakiang.]

On coming from the southward the only danger that lies in the way is a coral reef even with the water's edge; it is of a circular form, and at low water several rocks shew on it. On every occasion that we passed the sea broke high upon it; but from what we saw of other similar reefs, it seems very probable that when the water is smooth it will give no warning: it is about eight miles west, 15° north of the extreme south point of the island, and lies in latitude 26° 7' north, and longitude 127° 26' east of Greenwich.

[Sidenote: Port Melville.]

[Sidenote: Directions to approach it, and to anchor previous to entering the harbour.]

Port Melville is on the north-west side of the island. A ship wishing to enter it ought to make the Sugar Loaf Peak, and steer between it and the cluster of islands to the northward, directly for the bottom of the bight, which lies between the Sugar Loaf and the north end of the island; here Herbert's Island will be seen close to the shore, run in towards its western end, anchor when it bears east one-third of a mile, and the Sugar Loaf west one-quarter north, barely shut in with a low dark green point of land; here you will have from seventeen to twenty fathoms.

[Sidenote: Boats should be sent to buoy the channel.]

The entrance of the harbour is narrow, and ought not to be attempted without previous examination by the boats of a ship wishing to enter it. With a very little trouble the passage might be buoyed: a large ship will probably find it expedient to warp in and out.

[Sidenote: Eye-draught of Port Melville.]

The eye-draught, with the directions on it, render much further notice here superfluous. The harbour is secure, and sufficiently capacious for a numerous fleet. It extends in a north and south direction for about two miles, varying in breadth and form in a very remarkable manner; at the lower or north end there are two basons of a circular form, and have from nine to fifteen fathoms, soft bottom; these are about one-third of a mile across. At some places the steep rocks which form the banks approach within an hundred yards of one another; here the water is sixteen, eighteen, and twenty fathoms. There are many fine coves, some with shelving shores, and others steep-to. Every part of the harbour is secured from the sea, and many parts from all winds: it is well calculated for the re-equipment of ships, for it is not only secure as an anchorage, but offers conveniences for landing men and stores, and also for heaving down or careening a ship.

[Sidenote: Villages of Cooee and of Oonting.]

There are several large villages on the shores of an extensive bay, communicating with the sea to the north-eastward, at the upper or south end of the line of harbours, and one called Oonting on the west side of the lower harbour; there is another of some extent, on the south side of Herbert's Island, called Cooee.

63

By permission of Captain Maxwell, I have named this excellent harbour, Port Melville, in honour of Lord Viscount Melville, First Lord of the Admiralty.

[Illustration: *Draught of* PORT MELVILLE *on the N.W. side of GREAT LOO-CHOO* Island *by Captain Basil Hall and the* OFFICERS *of His Majesty's Sloop* LYRA *11th Octr. 1816.*]

From the top of a range of hills which we ascended, rising on the south side of the upper bay of Port Melville, we could see the south-west corner of the great western bay, the whole range of Port Melville, and the coasts adjacent.

[Sidenote: Geographical position of Port Melville.]
The latitude of Herbert's Island, which lies directly off the entrance of Port Melville, is 26° 42-2/3' north, by meridian altitude of the sun observed on shore. Its longitude, which is also the longitude of Port Melville, is 127° 55' east, or 17' east of Napakiang observatory. The Sugar Loaf bears from the centre of the island, west 4-1/2° north, about ten miles.

[Sidenote: Coast skirted by coral reefs.]
As the whole part of this coast is skirted by dangerous coral reefs, the greatest attention should be paid to the lead, and the ship ought to be put about the instant that the water shoals to eight, seven, or six fathoms. On running in for the west end of Herbert's Island, on the morning of the 11th of October, we passed over a coral ledge having nine fathoms on it. The west point of Herbert's Island bore at this time south 8° 40' west, distant four or five miles. Before and after passing this we had from thirty to sixty fathoms; whether it was shoaler than nine fathoms at any place, was not ascertained, but the circumstance is deserving of notice, and ought to teach the necessity of constant vigilance, when near coral reefs.

[Sidenote: Montgomery islands.]
The cluster of islands to the northward of Port Melville lies between 26° 54' and 27° 4-1/2' north, the north end of the northern one being in longitude 127° 57' east, or 19' east of the observatory. It does not appear that there is any good anchorage about them; and there are dangerous reefs off the south and south-western ones.

[Sidenote: Hope Point.]
The north end of the Great Loo-choo lies in 26° 52-1/2' north, and this is probably within one, or at most two miles of the truth. We observed in 27° 00' 15" north, at which time the northern extreme bore east 59° south, nine miles by estimation, an inference which was checked by the distance run on a direct course afterwards. The longitude is 128° 9' east, or 31' east of the observatory.

[Sidenote: Sidmouth Point.]
The coast from the north point runs south-east by east, with some minor deviations, nearly four leagues: great pains were taken to ascertain this precisely, as the former charts not only place it many miles further north, but make the coast at this end lie east and west. The north-east point lies in 26° 47' north, and longitude 128° 18' east, or 40' east of the observatory. The latitude was determined by the meridian altitude of Sirius and an altitude of Polaris, so near daylight that the horizon was well defined; but as this point, off which there is a small island, was some miles north of the ship at the time of observation, the above latitude may err possibly two miles. It was intended to have examined two islands which lie to the north-eastward of the north point, but a strong current in the night carried us so far to leeward, that we could not effect this object; the situation, therefore, of these two islands, may perhaps not be accurately laid down in the chart.

[Sidenote: Barrow's Bay.]
The deep indenture about the middle of the east side of the island is unsafe to enter during the north-east monsoon: as the wind, however, had westing in it, we sailed up to within three or four miles of the top, carrying from thirty to twenty fathoms water; but when about to haul in for the north side, where there appeared to be a bay, we shoaled suddenly from twenty-four to eight fathoms: the helm was instantly put down, and when head to wind, we had only five fathoms. While in stays the water was observed to wash on a rock not a hundred yards to leeward of us, on which we must infallibly have struck, had we bore up instead of tacking.

[Sidenote: South-east coast dangerous.]
From the north-east to the south-east point, the coast runs south 40° west; the shore to the north-east of this deep bight is bold, and seems clear; that on the south-west side of it presents a formidable barrier of islands and coral reefs, which break to a great distance: in fine weather this part of the coast ought to be approached very cautiously.

[Sidenote: South Point.]
[Sidenote: Reef.]

The southern extreme of this island lies in latitude 26° 4' 46" north, determined with great care by the meridian altitude of the sun on shore; and in longitude 127° 35' east, or 3' west of the observatory. There is good anchorage from twenty to thirty fathoms, south a little easterly, of this point. Between this point and the group of islands to the westward, there is a dangerous reef, already spoken of; it lies in 26° 7' north, and 127° 26' east; it bears 26' west, 15° north from the south point of the island, distant eight miles. Immediately round the point on the west side there is a shallow harbour, formed by coral reefs, but the entrance is narrow and intricate.

[Sidenote: South-western group.]

We stood over to the largest of the south-west group, on the east side of which there stands out a conical rock, behind which it was thought that a harbour might lie, but upon examination, it proved only fit for boats; it lies in 26° 11' north.

[Sidenote: Reef Island.]

Reef Island lies west by north, about two leagues from Napakiang Roads; on the north side the reefs stretch a great way, but the south is more clear.

Between Napakiang and the Sugar Loaf there is no place for ships to lie in safety; the bay immediately to the north was examined by Mr. Mayne, master of his Majesty's ship Alceste, when two shallow harbours were found.

[Sidenote: Tides.]

The flood runs to the northward and eastward, along shore, and the ebb in an opposite direction. The rise and fall is about nine feet perpendicular. High water at full and change IX.

[Sidenote: Variation of the compass.]

The variation of the compass, determined with great precision by the transit azimuth instrument, was 52' westerly.

The longitude of the Lyra's observatory at Napakiang by the mean of thirty-six lunar observations on both sides of the moon, is 127° 37' 28" east; by four chronometers, agreeing nearly, 127° 38' 30" east. The latitude is 26° 13' 39" north.

[Transcriber's Note: Crescent moons are denoted by [((or))]; a circle with a period therein is denoted by [(.)]]

OBSERVATIONS MADE AT NAPAKIANG OBSERVATORY, GREAT LOO-CHOO ISLAND.

Lunars with a Sextant. Lunars with a Sextant.

[(.)] West of [((*[Greek: a] Arietis, East of))]

25th September, 1816. 4th October, 1816

[(.)] [((127°. 38'. 15" East. *))] 127°. 31'. 00" East.

35 . 15 37 . 00
36 . 15 43 . 00
34 . 45 52 . 30
33 . 00 54 . 30
36 . 00 38 . 45
30 . 45 52 . 45
28 . 30 50 . 15
32 . 15 50 . 30
31 . 30 127°. 33'. 39" Mean 41 . 45
　　　　　　　　　　40 . 30

26th October, 1816. 34 . 15
　　　　　　　　　　43 . 15

[(.)] [((127 . 38 . 30 39 . 45
　　　　　39 . 45 ————————
　　　　　41 . 30 Mean by sextant 127 . 43. 20 * East of))]
　　　　　44 . 15
　　　　　44 . 30 Lunars by Circle.
　　　　　32 . 15 [(.)] West of [((
　　　　　33 . 00
　　　　　31 . 45 4th October, 1816
　　　　　31 . 15 [(.)] [((127°. 38'. 45"
　　　　　27 . 30 127° 36'. 16" Mean 32 . 30

Mean by sextant 127 . 34 . 58
　　　　[(.)] W. [((Mean 127 . 35 . 37 by circle.
　　Mean by sextant [(.)] west))] 127° 34'. 58"
　　　　　* East [((127 . 43 . 20

Mean longitude by sextant [(.) * D)] 127 . 39 . 9
by circle [(.)] * [((127 . 35 . 37

Mean longitude by 36 lunars 127 . 37 . 28
Longitude by chronometers 127 . 38 . 30 east of Greenwich.

LATITUDE OF NAPAKIANG.

By Meridian Altitudes of the Sun and Altitudes taken near Noon.
By meridian altitudes observed. By meridian altitudes deduced in the
usual way from sights taken near noon.
1816. 1816.
Sextant. 8th Oct. mean of 3 A.M.} 26°. 13'. 30" circle.
17th Oct. 26°. 13'. 43" and 3 P.M. }
20th Oct. 26 . 13 . 44 20th Oct. A.M.{ 26 . 13 . 46} sext.
{ 26 . 13 . 44}
Circle.
26th Oct. 26 . 13 . 29 20th Oct. P.M.{ 26 . 13 . 58}
{ 26 . 13 . 47} sext.
{ 26 . 13 . 57}
22d mean 2 A.M.& 2 P.M. 26 . 13 . 24} circle.
26th 3 P.M. 26 . 13 . 29}
Latitude by mean of 3 meridian altitudes 26°. 13'. 39" sextant and circle.
mean of 5 altitudes near noon 26 . 13 . 50 sextant.
mean of 3 do. do. 26 . 13 . 28 circle.

Mean latitude 26 . 13 . 39 north.
* * * * *

VARIATION OF THE COMPASS AT NAPAKIANG.
The declination of the magnetic meridian was ascertained with considerable precision by
means of the transit azimuth instrument: the needle seldom showed the same variation, as it
oscillated about ten minutes, but the mean position of the magnetic meridian was 52' 10" west of
the true. A coral reef was selected for the place of these observations, in order to avoid the
attraction arising from buildings, or from inequalities in the ground.
* * * * *

Variation observed on board by Walker's Azimuth Compass.
29th Sept. 1816, P.M. ship's head W. by S. variation by
1st azimuth 0°. 51'. 30" west.
2nd 0 . 53 . 30
3rd 1 . 17 . 30
Amplitude 1 . 15 . 00
30th A.M. 1st azimuth 0 . 55 . 30
2nd 0 . 34 . 15
3d Oct. A.M. ship's head E.N.E. 1st azimuth 0 . 37 . 00
2nd 0 . 48 . 00

Variation by mean of 7 azimuths and 1 amplitude 0 . 52 . 39 west.

TABLE OF OBSERVATIONS
MADE WITH
DR. WOLLASTON'S DIP SECTOR:
WITH AN ENGRAVING, AND A DESCRIPTION OF THE INSTRUMENT, AND
DIRECTIONS FOR ITS USE.
[Illustration: Wollaston's Dip Sector]
EXPLANATION OF THE DIP SECTOR,
AND
REMARKS ON THE OBSERVATIONS MADE WITH IT IN HIS MAJESTY'S
SLOOP LYRA.
In our tables for apparent dip of the visible horizon at different heights from the sea, as
calculated from the known curvature of the earth, allowance is made for the refraction of the
atmosphere, on a supposition of its being constant, but as it is known to vary, the tabular dip will
often be erroneous, and, consequently, altitudes taken under different states of the atmosphere,
will exhibit different instead of corresponding results.
It is foreign to the present purpose to shew what the causes are which have most effect in
raising or depressing the apparent horizon. It may be sufficient to mention, that changes in the

relative temperature of the air and the sea must produce changes in the refraction near the surface. Dr. Wollaston has published two papers in the Philosophical Transactions on this subject, in the volumes for 1800 and 1803, and to these I beg to refer the reader for precise information upon this very curious subject.

The object which this sector proposes to attain, is the actual admeasurement of the dip angle; that is, to ascertain how much the visible horizon is depressed below the horizontal plane passing through the eye of the observer. The instrument is so contrived as to measure double the dip angle twice over, so that we obtain four times the required dip, and one quarter of this angle is what must be applied to vertical angles, measured from that part of the horizon which has been observed.

Figure I. is the instrument seen in perspective, and Fig. II. is a plan of it with the telescope removed. In order to explain its use, let A and B (Fig. II.) represent the two reflecting glasses at right angles to the plane of the instrument, and also nearly at right angles to each other. It is clear that when the plane of the instrument is held vertically, an eye situated at E, and looking through the unsilvered part of the glass A at a distant point C, will at the same time see by joint reflection from both glasses, another distant point D at 180° from C; and D will appear to correspond with C, if a suitable motion be given to the index glass B by the tangent screw F.

The instrument may now be supposed to measure the arc CZD. If the points C and D be each three minutes farther from the zenith than 90°, the entire angle will then exceed 180° by double that quantity. The relative position of the glasses then corresponds to 180° 6', and the six minutes of excess would be shewn on the arc at F if there were no index error. But, by reason of the index error, the real quantity will not be known till a similar observation has been made with the instrument in an opposite direction.

If the instrument be now inverted, so that the unsilvered glass is uppermost, the arc intended to be measured is CND, or the sum of the distances of the points C and D from the Nadir instead of the Zenith, which of course falls short of 180° by as much as the former arc exceeded that quantity.

The difference of the two arcs is consequently twelve minutes, and if the index be now moved till the objects C and D appear to correspond, the amount of this double difference will be shewn by the *change of position* of the vernier.

Hence it is evidently unnecessary that the index error should be previously known, and even preferable that its amount should be such as to avoid the needless introduction of negative quantities by positions on different sides of zero.

In the preceding description, it is supposed that the eye is looking directly through the unsilvered glass at the horizon, and that it also perceives the opposite horizon after two reflections; but an inspection of the figure will shew that the observer's head would necessarily intercept the rays from the horizon behind him. To obviate this, both the direct and the reflected rays are received in coming from the unsilvered glass, (and after passing through the field-glass of the telescope) on a mirror placed at an angle of 45°, which reflects them to the eye. By this ingenious contrivance, the obstruction is removed, and the opposite points of the horizon may be both seen at one moment.

In practice, it is most convenient to direct the telescope to the same part of the horizon in both cases. Thus, if the east and west parts of the horizon be observed, and that the index glass be uppermost, and telescope pointing to the west, the observer is on the south side, and his face must be turned to the north. When the instrument is inverted, if the observer turn himself round at the same time, so as to face the south, then the telescope will be pointed as before to the west; but since the index glass is now undermost, the inferior arc will now be measured precisely as if his face were to the north, but with the advantage of the same lights seen in the erect position of the instrument.

In using this instrument at sea for the first time, considerable difficulty arises from the constant change in the plane of the instrument from the perpendicular position, in which it is absolutely necessary that it should be held, in order to obtain a correct observation. What at first appears to be a defect, however, is a real advantage, namely, that whenever it is held in the least degree out of the vertical plane, the two horizons (that seen direct, and the reflected one) cross each other, and it is only when the plane is vertical that the horizons can appear parallel.

The object is to get the two horizons to coincide exactly, and for this purpose it will often be necessary to have them of different shades. This is managed, as in the sextant, by means of the screw, which raises or lowers the telescope. When the telescope is brought nearer to the plane of the instrument, the reflected horizon becomes dark and distinct, but when screwed off it becomes fainter, and is not so well defined. Practice alone can teach the degree of intensity which is most favourable. In general it is best to have one horizon dark, and the other light; then bring them very nearly to coincide, and wait till the ship is steady, at which moment a slight touch of the tangent screw brings them exactly to cover one another. It will happen, of course, that when the coincidence is perfect, there is only one horizon to be seen, and a doubt remains whether all is right, but a slight motion of the instrument, by making the horizons cross each other, defines them at once.

It is advisable to take several observations, and the safest way is to take one first with the index glass uppermost, and then with the instrument inverted, after which to return to the first, and so on for two or three times each way.

In the pages which follow, there is given a table containing the result of all the observations made during this voyage, preceded by several sets of observations in the fullest detail. From the table it will be observed how seldom the dip, actually measured, agrees with that inferred from the mean refraction. Some of these experiments shew very remarkable differences, and point out the great utility of this instrument.

The practical navigator, particularly if he has been in hot climates, will recollect how discordant his observations for latitude always were, and how few even of the best observers agree in their determination of the latitude of the same place, simple as the observation is thought to be. The cause is quite clear; and though it equally affects altitudes taken for absolute time, the disagreement is less obvious, and it will often happen that a chronometer going extremely well appears to vary every day from inaccuracy in the observations. Thus it is, I think, generally admitted, that it is almost impossible to rate a chronometer from altitudes observed with the sea horizon. Nor is this difficulty removed by taking equal altitudes, because the refraction in all probability will be different at the two observations. With an artificial horizon, indeed, the changes in refraction are not felt, because, at a considerable elevation above the horizon, the changes are very trifling. But it often happens in practice, that the artificial horizon cannot be used, and we are then reduced to the sea horizon, where the changes of refraction are always the greatest. In the Yellow Sea, for instance, we had no opportunity of landing during all the time that the squadron was at anchor, till the day before we sailed. So that during nearly a fortnight that the ships were at anchor, the sea horizon was necessarily used. I need only to refer to the observations taken off the Pei-ho, viz. from No. 37 to 62, to shew how extremely fallacious the results must have been.

It is much to be wished that this excellent instrument should be brought into general use in navigation.

THE FOLLOWING EIGHT OBSERVATIONS ARE SET DOWN IN THE FULLEST DETAIL, IN ORDER TO SHEW THE METHOD USED IN RECORDING THEM.

No. 31.

YELLOW SEA.

July 23, 1816.—6 P.M.

Index uppermost. Instrument inverted.

$A + 8'. 10'' B - 7'. 10''$

8 . 05 7 . 10

8 . 00 7 . 10

Mean 8 . 05 Mean 7 . 10 B.

Mean + 8 . 05 A.

15 . 15

3 . 49 Dip.

3 . 50 Tabular.

1 Difference.

Height of the eye, 15 feet, 3 inches.

Parts of the horizon observed, WSW. and ENE.

Barometer 29 . 78 inches

Thermometer {Air 82°

{Sea 77°

Latitude 35° north.

Longitude 124° east.

Wind light from south; horizon uncommonly well defined and sharp; sky clear, and sea perfectly smooth.

No. 40.

OFF THE PEI-HO, YELLOW SEA.

July 29, 1816.—9 A.M.

Index uppermost. Instrument inverted.

A + 8'. 20" B - 11'. 40"

8 . 45 11 . 35

8 . 30 11 . 50

Mean 8 . 32 Mean 11 . 42 B.

Mean + 8 . 32 A.

---

4) 20 . 14

5 . 3 Dip.

3 . 50 Tabular.

1 . 13 Difference +

Height of the eye, 15 feet, 3 inches.

Parts of the horizon observed, NW. and SE.

The low land just visible in the NW. distant 12 or 14 miles.

Depth of the sea, 18 feet.

Barometer 29 . 60 inches.

Thermometer {Air 81°

{Sea 84°

Latitude 38°. 50' north.

Longitude 118°. 00' east.

There has been little wind this morning, after a very close night.

No. 43.

OFF THE PEI-HO, YELLOW SEA.

August 6, 1816.—1 P.M.

Index uppermost. Instrument inverted.

A + 7'. 48" B - 11'. 55"

7 . 48 11 . 45

7 . 55 11 . 45

Mean 7 . 50 Mean 11 . 48 B.

Mean + 7 . 50 A.

---

4) 19 . 38

---

4 . 54 Dip.

3 . 53 Tabular.

1 . 1 Difference +

Height of the eye, 15 feet, 6 inches.

Parts of the horizon observed, SW. by S. and NE. by N.

Depth of the sea, 29 feet.

Barometer - 29 . 64 inches.

Thermometer { Air 83-1/2°

{ Sea 81-1/2°

Latitude - 38° 50' north.

Longitude - 118° 00' east.

Moderate breeze from SE. by S.; rather hazy, but the horizon sharp and distinct.

No. 50.

OFF THE PEI-HO, YELLOW SEA.

August 8, 1816.—6.15. A.M.

Index uppermost. Instrument inverted.

A + 10'. 20" B - 12'. 50"

10 . 18 12 . 45

10 . 35 13 . 00

Mean 10 . 24, 3 Mean 12 . 51.7 B.

Mean + 10 . 24.3 A.

---

4) 23 . 16

5 . 49 Dip.

3 . 50 Tabular.

1 . 59 Difference +

Height of the eye, 15 feet, 3 inches.

Parts of the horizon observed, NNE. and SSW. clear of the land.

Depth of the sea, 26 feet.

Barometer 29 . 65 inches.

Thermometer { Air 69-1/2°

{ Sea 78°

Wind NNW. moderate.

Latitude - 38°. 50' north.

Longitude - 118°. 00' east.

Mem.—The top of the fort at the mouth of the river, is just visible at 30 feet from the surface of the water.

No. 53.

OFF THE PEI-HO, YELLOW SEA.

August 10, 1816.—6.10. A.M.

Index uppermost. Instrument inverted

A + 13'. 55" B - 7'. 30"

13 . 50 7 . 15

13 . 45 7 . 25

Mean 13 . 50 Mean 7 . 23.3 B.

Mean + 13 . 50 A.

4) 21 . 13.3

5 . 18.3 Dip.

2 . 20 Tabular.

2 . 58 Difference +

Height of the eye, 5 feet, 6 inches.

Depth of the water, 5 feet.

Parts of the horizon observed, N. by E. and S. by W. just clear of the land.

Barometer 29 . 69 inches. } On board His Majesty's ship Lyra,

Thermometer { Air 75° } distant three or four miles.

{ Sea 77° }

Wind WNW.

About one mile from the fort of Tung-coo, at the entrance of the Pei-ho river. *Note.*—Instrument readjusted.

No. 58.

OFF THE PEI-HO, YELLOW SEA.

August 10, 1816.—2 P.M.

Index uppermost. Instrument inverted.

A + 15'. 40" B - 8'. 50"

15 . 30 8 . 50

15 . 35 8 . 50

Mean 15 . 35 Mean 8 . 50 B.

Mean + 15 . 35 A.

4) 24 . 25 6 . 6.3 Dip. 3 . 50 Tabular. 2 . 16 Difference +

Height of the eye, 15 feet, 3 inches.

Parts of the horizon observed, N. by E. and S. by W.

Depth of the sea, 27 feet.

Barometer 29 . 68 inches.

Thermometer } Air 84°

} Sea 83°

Latitude 38° . 50' north.

Longitude 118° . 00' east.

No. 59.

OFF THE PEI-HO, YELLOW SEA.

August 10, 1816.—2. 15. P.M.

Index uppermost. Instrument inverted

A + 15'. 10" B - 7'. 50"

15 . 10 8 . 10

15 . 10 8 . 05

Mean 15 . 13.3 Mean 8 . 01.7 B.

Mean + 15 . 13.3 A.

4) 21 . 15

5 . 48.7 Dip.

3 . 50 Tabular.

1 . 59 Difference.

Height of the eye, 15 feet, 3 inches.

Parts of the horizon observed, NW. by N. and SE. by S.

Depth of the water, 27 feet.

Barometer 29 . 68 inches.

Thermometer { Air 84°

{ Sea 83°

Latitude 38°. 50' north.

Longitude 118°. 00' east.

The vessels in all parts of the horizon have an inverted image under them; this is very considerable, some having about a third of the sail, others only the hull.

No. 110.

OFF THE CAPE.

July 28, 1817.—2.30. P.M.

Index uppermost. Instrument inverted.

A + 6'. 35" B - 5'. 00"

6 . 35 4 . 55

6 . 40 5 . 00

Mean 6 . 36.7 Mean 4 . 58.3 B.

Mean + 6 . 36.7 A.

4) 11 . 35

2 . 53.7 Dip.

3 . 49 Tabular.

55 Difference -

Height of the eye, 15 feet.

Parts of the horizon observed, SE. and NW.

Thermometer { Air 64°

{ Sea 59°

Depth of the sea, 222 feet.

Latitude 34°. 57' south.

Longitude 20°. 15' east.

Cape Lagullus due north, distant 6 or 8 miles.

Calm all day; sky clear, and weather hazy.

On the 29th and 30th of July we were off the Cape, but the weather was so bad as to prevent any sights being taken.

[Transcriber's Note: The final column of each of the following tables is transcribed beneath the table.]

—+————+—+—————+——+————+————+——+———+—
——+———+ | |Height Dip. |Diff.|Then. |Differ.| | | | | | | of +——————+—+—
+—+—+—+—+ | | Long.|Sound-| No. Date. |eye.| Obs. |Tab.| + |- |Sea|Air| + | -
|Baro.| Lat. | East.| ings.| —+————+——+———+——+—+—+—+—+—+
+———+————+————+———+ |1816. |f. i|' " |' " | "| "| ° | ° | | | | ° ' | ° ' | feet |
18|June 16.|15 3|4 35.0|3 50|45| |83 |82-|1/2| |29.86| 5 11 S|106 3 | 60 | | | | | | | |
|1/2| | | | | | 19|June 16.|15 3|4 33.0|3 50|43| |83-|82 | 1-| |29.86| 5 05 S|106 10| 56
| | | | | | | |1/2|sh.|1/2| | | | | | | | | | | |{85| | | | | 20|June 16.|14 0|3 59 |3

41|18| |84-|{sh|1/2| |29.83| 5 05 S|106 10| 48 | | | | | | | |1/2|{95| | | | | | | | | |
| | | |{su| | | | | | 21|June 16.|14 |4 01 |3 41|20| |83 |81 | 2 | |29.85| 5 05 S|106 10|
57 | 22|June 27.|16 |4 21.0|3 56|25| |84 |82 | 2 | |29.81| 6 49 N|107 49| | 23 |June 28.|16
|4 22.2|3 56|26| |84 |82 | 2 | |29.80| 8 00 |108 10| | 24|July 3. |16 |4 08.2|3 56|12| |84-
|81 | 3-| |29.77|13 29 |112 59| | | | | | | | | |1/2| |1/2| | | | | 25|July 6. |16 |3 53 |3
56| | 3|84 |83-|1/4| |29.75|20 00 |114 | | | | | | | | |3/4| | | | | | 27|July 7. |15
3|4 3 |3 50|13| |85 |85 | | |29.79|21 11 |114 | | 28|July 8. |14 6|3 49 |3 45| 4| |84-|82 |
2-| |29.72| | | | | | | | | |1/2| |1/2| | | | | 29|July 16.|15 3|3 27 |3 50| |23|79 |79
| | |29.75|24 37 |118 56| | 30|July 21.|15 3|3 44 |3 50| | 6|77-|76 | 1-| |29.78|34 |124 |
270 | | | | | | | |1/2| |1/2| | | | | 31|July 23.|15 3|3 49 |3 50| | 1|77 |82 | |5
|29.78|35 |124 | | 32|July 23.|15 3|3 49 |3 50| | 1|77 |82 | |5 |29.78|35 |124 | | 33|July
23.|15 3|3 44 |3 50| | 6|77 |82 | |5 |29.78|35 |124 | | 35|July 27.|15 3|4 02 |3 50|12| |76
|76 | | |29.70|38 55 |118 50| 72 | 36|July 27.|13 |3 35 |3 33| 2| |76 |76 | | |29.70|38 55
|118 50| 78 | 37|July 28.|15 3|4 21 |3 50|31| |83 |84 | |1 |29.62|38 50 |118 00 20 |
38|July 28.|15 3|4 06 |3 50|16| |83 |84 | |1 |29.62|38 50 |118 00| 20 | —+————————+——
—+————————+————+—+——+————+————+————+————+————+————+————+————+—————+ Remarks.
—+—

——+ 18 |Weather hazy. The low land of Sumatra just visible. The land wind has | |been
blowing gently for about four hours. | 19 |East and west parts of the horizon observed. Coast of
Sumatra just | |visible. Hazy. The land-wind dying away. | 20 |The day has been extremely hot,
and almost a calm. The sea-breeze not yet | |set in, only a few light flaws. | 24 |A fresh breeze
from WNW. The sun set in fiery dirty red clouds. Weather | |squally, with occasional showers of
rain. Parts of the horizon observed | |east and west. | 25 |Weather remarkably fine; sky clear;
and a gentle breeze from the south. | |The sun set about five minutes after these observations
were taken. | |Parts of the horizon observed east and west. | 27 |The forenoon has been
extremely hot and oppressive. A rolling swell from | |the SW. | 28 |Parts of the horizon
observed SSW and NNE, the first clear to seaward, | | the other clear horizon, but the mainland
of China behind it, and | |various islands on each side of the NNE line. | 29 |Very hazy
weather: sky fiery. | 30 |Clear weather, with a light breeze from the eastward. Sun set behind a |
|low range of dark clouds: sky in that quarter was unusually red. A long | |swell from the
northward. | 31 |Wind light from south; horizon uncommonly well defined and sharp; sky |
|clear; and the sea perfectly smooth. These sights, and the two following, | |may be depended
on, I think, within ten seconds. | 32 |Circumstances similar to No. 31. | 33 |Parts of the
horizon observed were that immediately under the setting | |sun; viz. W 21° N, and the opposite
E 21° S, the sun being about 4° high. | |Day has been remarkably clear, although the wind has
been from the | |southward, which in these seas is said generally to bring fogs. | 35 |Weather
somewhat hazy; wind easterly. | 36 |Wind easterly. | 37 |These sights were taken while at
anchor off the mouth of the Pei-ho. The | |fort of Tung-coo, on the south bank of the river,
bearing W 50° N, distant| |about four or five miles. | —+————————————————————————
————————————+ | |Height Dip. |Diff. |Then. |Differ.| | | | | | of +————————————+————+-
+——+——+——+——+ | | Long.|Sound-| No. Date. |eye.| Obs. |Tab.| + |-|Sea|Air| + | -
|Baro.| Lat.| East.| ings.| —+————+————+————+——+————+——+-+-+——+—+———+
+———+————+————+————+ |1816. |f. i|'" |''|'|" |"| ° | ° | | | ° ' | ° ' | feet |
39|July 28.|15 3|3 46 |3 50| |4|82 |83-| 1-|29.61|38 50 |118 | 23 | | | | | | | | |1/2|
|1/2| | | | 40|July 29.|15 3|5 3 |3 50|1 13| |84 |81 | 3 | |29.60|38 50 |118 | 18 |
41|July 29.|15 3|4 00.9|3 50| 10| |84 |83 | 1 | |29.58|38.50 |118 | 20 | 42|Aug. 6. |15 3|5
09 |3 50|1 29| |80 |79 | 1 | |29.64|38 50 |118 | 22-| | | | | | | | | | | | | | | |1/2|
43|Aug. 6. |15 6|4 54 |3 53|1 1| |81-|83-| | 2 |29.64|38 50 |118 | 29 | | | | | | |
|1/2|1/2| | | | | 44|Aug. 6. |15 3|4 47 |3 50 57| |81-|83-| | 2 |29.64|38 50 |118 | 29
| | | | | | |1/2|1/2| | | | | 45|Aug. 6. |15 3|4 59 |3 50|1 9| |81-|83-| | 1-
|29.64|38 50 |118 | 29-| | | | | | |1/2|1/2| |1/2| | | 1/2| 46|Aug. 6. | 3 9|2 39 |1
54| 45| |81 |84-| 3-|29.62|38 50 |118 | 30 | | | | | | |1/2| |1/2| | | | 47|Aug. 6.
| 6 |3 26 |2 25|1 1| |81 |84-| 3-|29.62|38 50 |118 | 30-| | | | | | |1/2| |1/2| | |
1/2| 48|Aug. 6. |15 3|4 59.2|3 50|1 9| |82 |80 | 2 | |29.59|38 50 |118 | 30 | 49|Aug. 8.
|15 3|5 47 |3 50|1 57| |78 |69-| 8-| |29.65|38 50 |118 | 26 | | | | | | | |1/2|1/2| | |
| | 50|Aug. 8. |15 3|5 49 |3 59|1 59| |78 |69-| 8-| |29.65|38 50 |118 | 26 | | | | | |
|1/2|1/2| | | | | 51|Aug. 8. |15 3|5 47 |3 50|1 57| |77-|73 | 4-| |29.66|38 50 |118 | 24
| | | | | | |1/2| |1/2| | | | | 52|Aug. 9. |15 3|4 30.4|3 59| 40| |79-|75 | 4-|
|29.72|38 50 |118 | | | | | | | |1/2| |1/2| | | | | 53|Aug.10. | 5 6|5 18.3|2 20|2 58|
|77 |75 | 2 | |29.69|38 50 |118 | 5 | 54|Aug.10. | 5 6|4 28.3|2 20|2 8| | | | | | |38 50

72

|117 55| | 55|Aug.10. | 5 6|4 7 |2 20|1 47| |77 |75 | 2 | |29.69|38 50 |117 55| 12 |
56|Aug.10. | 5 6|3 55 |2 20|1 35| |77 |75 | 2 | |29.69|38 50 | 118 | 13 | —+————————+—
—+————+————+————+-+———+———+————+————+————+————————+————+————————+ Remarks.
—+

——+ 39|The day has been exceedingly close with little wind. | 40|There has been little wind this morning, after a very close night. | 41|Nearly calm, there being only a very light air from the SE.—Day sultry. | 42|Weather hazy; sky clear overhead; sea remarkably smooth; wind north. | 43|Moderate breeze from SE by S; rather hazy; but the horizon sharp and | |distinct. And this together with the four following observations, may be | |taken as very accurate, every circumstance being most favourable. | 45|Parts of the horizon observed E by N and W by S. | 46|Parts of the horizon observed SSE and NNW. Wind SE. | 47|Wind SE. | 48|Parts of the horizon observed E and W. The day, which has been remarkably | |fine, has resumed towards sunset a wild, stormy aspect. Wind fresh at SE. | 49|Parts of the horizon observed E by S and W by N. This morning unusually | |clear; so that when the sun's semi-diameter only was above the horizon, | |it was painful to look at him. The horizon has a rugged appearance. | 50|Parts of the horizon observed NNE and SSW. Wind NNW, moderate. | 51|Weather remarkably clear; horizon still rugged; wind NNW, moderate. | 52|This morning cloudy, and looks rainy but the air seems clear. Parts of the | |horizon observed NW by W and SE by E. | 53|Parts of the horizon observed N by E and S by W. Instrument readjusted. | |Wind WNW. | 54|Parts of the horizon observed WSW and ENE. Wind NW. These observations | |were taken close to the low land, near the mouth of the Pei-ho. The night | |had been cold, and the morning was still keen; but unfortunately there | |was no thermometer in the boat; I suppose, however, that the air was | |about 66° At the time these sights were taken, I observed a vessel bearing | |N by W, the lower half of whose sail was inverted. | 55|Wind NW. | 56|Wind NW. Parts of the horizon observed NW and SE. During these | |observations,(53, 54, 55, 56) the vessels near the land had more or less | |an inverted image under them. | —+————————————————
————————————————————————+

—+————————+————+————+————————+————+————————+————+————+————+——
——+————+ | |Height Dip. |Diff. |Then. |Differ.| | | | | | of +————————————+————+-
+———+———+———+-+ | | Long.|Sound-| No. Date. |eye.| Obs. |Tab.| | +-|Sea|Air| + | -
|Baro.| Lat.| East.| ings.| —+————————+————+————+-+-+————+——+———+——
+————+————+————+————+ |1816. |f. i|'"|'"|'"| '"|° |° | | |° '|° '| feet |
57|Aug. 10.|15 3| 5 37 |3 50|1 47| |78 |76-| 1-| |29.70|38 50 |118 | 26 | | | | | | |
|1/2|1/2| | | | | 58|Aug. 10.|15 3| 6 6 |3 50|2 16| |83 |84 | | 1 |29.68|38 50 |118 | 27
| 59|Aug. 10.|15 3| 5 49 |3 50|1 59| |83 |84 | | 1 |29.68|38 50 |118 | 27 | 60|Aug. 11.|15
3| 5 3 |3 50|1 13| |79 |76 | 3 | 2 |29.72|38 50 |118 | 26-| | | | | | | | | | | | | | 1/2|
61|Aug. 11.|15 3| 5 13 |3 50|1 23| |80 |79 | 1 | |29.73|38 50 |118 | 24 | 62|Aug. 12.| 16 |
4 52 |3 56| 56| |80 |79 | 1 | |29.79|38 50 |118 | 24 | 63|Aug. 12.|15 3| 4 35 |3 50| 45|
|81 |79-| 1-| |29.77|38 36 |117 56| 29-| | | | | | | |1/2|1/2| | | | 1/2| 64|Aug.
13.|16 | 4 4 |3 56| 8| |79 |78 | 1 | |29.80|38 31 |118 09| 42 | 65|Aug. 13.|16 | 4 6 |3 56|
10| |79 |78 | 1 | |29.80|38 31 |118 09| 42 | 66|Aug. 13.|16 | 4 20 |3 56| 24| |81 |83 | | 2
|29.80|38 21 |118 04| 44 | 67|Aug. 14.|15 3| 4 30 |3 30|1 | |78 |79 | | 1 |29.71|38 30
118 24	68	Aug. 14.	15 3	4 25	3 30	55		79-	80-		1	29.70	38 30	118 35	50			
			1/2	1/2				69	Aug. 15.	15 3	4 39	3 30	1 9		80	79	1		29.77	38 00
118 35	48	70	Aug. 15.	15 3	4 53	3 30	1 23		81-	79	2-		29.76	38 00	118 54	44
					1/2		1/2					71	Aug. 15.	15 3	5 4	3 30	1 34		82	79	3		29.70	37
54	118 56	40	72	Aug. 16.	15 3	4 43	3 30	1 13		81	76	5		29.17	37 38	118 57	39
73	Aug. 17.	15 3	4 38	3 30	1 8		80	79-	1/2		29.73	37 21	119 28	30							
1/2						74	Aug. 17.	14	4 29	3 41	48		81-	81	1/2		29.75	37 19	119 44	33
				|1/2|					75|Aug. 17.|15 3| 4 42 |3 30|1 12| |81-|82										
1/2	29.70	37 21	119 44	30							1/2					76	Aug. 18.	16	4 39	3 56
43		80	77	3		29.76	37 29	119 37	48	77	Aug. 20.	16	4 20	3 56	24		77	72	5
29.85	37 50	120 16		79	Aug. 21.	15 3	4 42	3 50	52		77	71	6		29.80	37 52	120
27| | 80|Aug. 21.| 4 | 2 37 |1 58| 39| |77 |79 | | 2 |29.80|37 52 |120 27| 60 | 81|Aug.
21.|15 3| 4 6 |3 50| 18| |77 |76 | 1 | |29.76| | | 60 | —+————————+————+————+————
+————+-+————+———+————+————+————————+————+————————+ Remarks. —+————————
————————————————————————————+

57|Weather very clear. Parts of the horizon observed ENE and WSW. | 58|Parts of the horizon observed N by E and S by W. | 59|The vessels in all parts of the horizon have an inverted image under them; | |this is very considerable, some having about one-third of the sail, others | |only the hull. | 60|Light wind from SE. Sky cloudy, somewhat hazy; but the horizon sharp and | |unbroken. | 61|The inversion of the vessels as conspicuous as before. Parts of the | |horizon

73

observed ESE and WNW. | 62 | A light breeze from the SE. Cloudy and close.—N.B. Instrument readjusted. | 63 | Part of the horizon observed N and S. | 64 | Part of the horizon observed E and W. A moderate breeze from the SW. Clear | | overhead; hazy in the horizon. | 65 | Parts of the horizon observed N and S. | 66 | Wind SE. Sky clear, and the horizon sharp. | 67 | Light breeze from ESE. Parts observed NE and SW. | 68 | Light breeze at ESE. Cloudy, with a haze in the horizon. Parts observed NE | | and SW. | 69 | Parts of the horizon observed E and W. Moderate breeze from ENE. | | Remarkably clear weather. | 70 | Steady moderate breeze at ENE. Very clear. Horizon sharp, and well defined.| 72 | Wind at East. Sky cloudy and rather hazy. | 73 | Light wind at SW. Hazy weather. | 74 | Light breeze from the Northward. Weather hazy. Parts of the horizon | | observed SE and NW. | 75 | Parts of the horizon observed NE by E and SW by W. | 76 | Moderate breeze from East. Parts of the horizon observed WNW and ESE. | 77 | The wind has been blowing hard for two days from NE; this evening it has | | lulled, and the weather has cleared off: there remains however a high | | swell. | 79 | Land-wind South. Fine clear morning. | 80 | Parts of the horizon observed SW by S and NE by N. | 81 | The inversions which were so conspicuous this morning have been entirely | | removed since the sea breeze set in. In some distant islands there is a | | slight inversion at the ends, but very trifling. |

feet	Baro.	Lat.	Height Long.	Dip. East.	Diff. Sound- ings.	Then. No.	Differ. Date.	eye.	Obs.	Tab.	Sea	Air	of
						1816.	f. i	' "	' "	' "	'	°	°			° '	° '
82	Aug. 21.	14	3 26	3 41	15	76	75	1		29.74			83	Aug. 21.	15 3	3 29	3 41	12	76	75	1	1	29.74			84	Aug. 22.	16	3 52	3 56		4	75	76	1		29.80		
85	Sept. 4.	12	3 46	3 25	21	81	83		2	29.86	36 10	126 30	56	86	Sept. 4.	12	3 42	3 25	17	81	83		2	29.86	36 8	126 35	56	87	Sept. 5.	15	3 47	3 49		2	79	80		1	29.80	35 40	126 17	88	Sept. 7.	15 3	3 33	3 41		8	74	80		6	29.84	34 32	126 34	89	Sept. 7.	15 3	3 27	3 41	14	74	80		6	29.84	34 32	126 34		1817.
90	Mar. 3.	14	3 57	3 41	16	82	84-	2-	29.74	2 18	102 20	1/2	1/2	91	Mar. 5.	14 8	4 49	3 46	1 3	83	85	2	29.73	3 40	100 35	92	Mar. 5.	14 8	4 50	3 46	1 4	83	85	2	29.73	165	93	Mar. 5.	14 8	4 53	3 46	1 7	94	Mar. 8.	14 8	4 33	3 46	47	84	84	29.86	5 12	100 14	120	a)	94	Mar. 8.	14 8	4 58	3 46	1 12	84	82-	1-	29.86	120	b)	1/2	1/2		Remarks.

——+ 82 | This and the following were observed towards sunset; they exhibit a | | considerable degree of refraction above what is usual. The sights on this | | morning in the same place gave upwards of 1' greater dip. | 83 | All other circumstances the same as in No. 82. | 84 | Fresh breeze from SE, with a remarkably clear sky. The horizon uncommonly | | sharp. | 85 | Wind moderate from WNW. Clear weather. | 86 | All other circumstances the same as in No. 85. Parts of the horizon | | observed SSW and NNE. | 87 | Parts of the horizon observed WNW and ESE. | 88 | The morning has been exceedingly hot before the breezes set in from sea at | | 11 A.M. | 89 | All other circumstances the same as in No. 89. | 90 | After a very hot day. | 91 | Parts of the horizon observed ESE and WNW. See further remarks under 93. | | Instruments readjusted. | 92 | Parts of the horizon observed NE and SW. All other circumstances as in No. | | 91. | 93 | Parts of the horizon observed SSE and NNW. These three observations (Nos. | | 91, 92, and 93) were made under the most favourable circumstances, and may | | be considered as shewing the accuracy which the instrument is capable of | | attaining. The sea was so perfectly smooth, that not the slightest motion | | could be detected. The horizon at all the parts observed was sharp, and | | better defined than I recollect to have seen it; and, what is not often the | | case, the opposite parts were alike in strength of light &c. The day has | | been hot, but not close, with a light breeze from the Southward. The dip is | | very great, but the observations were made with such care, that there can | | be no doubt of their accuracy. | 94 | There had been a light breeze from the North in the morning, but for an | a) | hour before these sights were taken it had been calm. | 94 | Nearly the same place as No. 94(a); but the other circumstances were | b) | changed, as the sea breeze at NW had set in about a quarter of an hour, | | whereas in the last instance it was calm. The above angles were taken with | | great care. The horizon sharp. Parts of the horizon observed NW and SE. | —+

		Height	Dip.	Diff.	Then.	Differ.						of			
			Long.	Sound-	No.	Date.	eye.	Obs.	Tab.	+	-	Sea	Air	+	-
Baro.	Lat.	East.	ings.												
					1817.	f. i	'"	'"	"'"	°	°			° '	° '	feet

95 | Mar. 19. | 14 8 | 3 51 | 3 46 | 5 | 80 | 82 | | 2 | 29.84 | | | | 96 | Mar. 19. | 14 8 | 3 48 | 3 46 |
2 | | 80 | 82 | | 2 | 29.78 | 13 30 | 89 30 | | 97 | Mar. 20. | 14 8 | 3 48 | 3 46 | 2 | | 79- | 82 | | 2-
29.83	14 30	89 15								1/2			1/2				98	Mar. 21.	14 8	3 48	3 46	2
80	82		2	29.84	15 00	89 00		99	Mar. 22.	14 8	3 39	3 46		7	79	79-
1/2	29.84	16 00	88 30								1/2					100	Mar. 23.	14 8	3 47	3 46
1		78-	79		1/2	29.80	17 00	88 00							1/2						101	Mar. 24.	14 8
3 53	3 46	7		78	80		2	29.78	17 30	88 15									South.		
102	July 22	15	3 36	3 49		13	71	72		1		34 0	26	400	103	July 24.	15	3 16	3
49		33	59	62		3		34 25	24 56	372	104	July 25.	15	3 36	3 49		13	62	63		1
	35 S	23 45	462	105	July 26.	15	3 30	3 49		19	58	60		2		35 S	23	462
106	July 26.	15	3 30	3 40		19	60	63		3		34 52	22 23	420	107	July 27.	15	2
55	3 49		54	56	59		3		35	21	24	108	July 27.	15	2 47	3 49		1 2	56	59		3
	35	21	240	109	July 28.	15	3 17	3 19		32	58	64		6		34 58	20 15	
110 | July 28. | 15 | 2 54 | 3 49 | | 55 | 59 | 64 | | 5 | | 34 57 | 20 15 | 222 | | | | |

Remarks. —

95 | The wind steady and moderate at NE; atmosphere clear; horizon well defined; | | a long swell from SW. This swell, which was not high, produced an obvious | | effect on the dip angle, as observed, the two horizons alternately | | separating and overlapping; this change was however so slight that I have | | not been able to measure it. | 96 | All other circumstances as in Nov. 95. Parts of the horizon observed NE | | and SW. | 97 | During the night there has been a light breeze from the East; at this | | moment it is freshening up a little. The atmosphere is clear; horizon | | sharp; a long low swell from SW, as yesterday. | 98 | It has been calm, or nearly so, during the night; occasionally a light air | | from SE and S. All circumstances favorable. | 99 | During the night there has been a light wind from SW. The weather is more | | hazy than when the wind was from the Eastward, and the horizon not so | | distinctly marked; but the above sights are good. There is still a swell | | from SW, which causes some little uncertainty as to the exact moment of | | taking the angle. | 100 | In the night there has been a light breeze from W by S. Weather hazy; but | | the horizon sharper than yesterday morning. | 101 | During the night almost calm; just now a light air from the NE. Parts of | | the horizon observed NE and SW. | 102 | Fine fair clear weather, but with so high a swell as to render the | | observation difficult. Wind light from N, after having been blowing fresh. | 103 | Light breezes from the North-eastward; smooth water, and a clear cool air; | | hazy about the land. The distance from the South cost of Africa was about | | 8 or 9 leagues. All circumstances seem favourable. No current; we have | | probably been too near shore for it. | 104 | Light breeze from the SW, with a long swell. Hazy weather. The wind has | | been from the West for 24 hours; at first blowing hard, but latterly | | moderate, the current setting us to the SW about a mile an hour. A very | | heavy dew falling this evening. Parts of the horizon observed East and | | West. | 105 | Moderate breeze from the NE; air hazy; long high swell from the Westward. | | From observations by stars and chronometers, it has been ascertained that | | there is not the least current. Distance from the South coast of Africa | | about 50 miles. A high range in sight to the Northward. Parts of the | | horizon observed North and South. | 106 | A light breeze from the NE; air hazy; a long swell from the Westward. | | About 50 miles distant from the land. | 107 | The wind has been moderate from the land all night; air hazy; weather raw; | | a very heavy dew falling all night. The land in sight to the Northward, | | distant about 40 miles, is inverted from one end to the other. | 108 | Parts of the horizon observed NNE and SSW. All other circumstances as in | No. 107. | 109 | Parts of the horizon observed NE and SW. Cape Lagullas North 2 or 3 | | leagues. A light breeze from the Eastward. Air hazy. | 110 | Parts of the horizon observed SE and NW. Cape Lagullas due North, distant | 6 or 8 miles. Calm all day; sky clear; and weather hazy. | | | N.B. On the 29th and 30th of July we were off the Cape, but the weather | | was so bad as to prevent any sights being taken. |

METEOROLOGICAL JOURNAL,
FROM JULY TO NOVEMBER 1816, WHILE THE SHIPS WERE IN THE YELLOW AND JAPAN SEAS.

| | | Thermom. | | | | | | | | | | | Hour. | Barom. | Air. | Sea. | Winds. |

Lat. | Long. | ———-+————+———+———+———+————+————+————+ 1 | | | | South |
| | *Sunday, July 14, 1816.* 2 | | | | SSW | | | 3 | | | | | | |The wind continued quite 4 | | | | |
| |light during the night, with 5 | | | | | | |one or two slight showers, but 6 | | | | | | |no
squalls. 7 | | | | | | | 8 |30i.01h| | | SW | | |About 8 A.M. the wind 9 | | | | | |hauled to
about SW, from 10 | | | | | |which quarter it blew a light 11 | | | | | | N | E |breeze.
Noon.|30 .01 | 83°| 84°| 22° 07'|115° 26'| ———+————+————+————+————+
+————-+ 1 | | | | | | 2 | | | | | Coast of | 3 | | | | | China. | 4 |29 .94 | | | | | 5 | | |
| | | 6 | | | | | 7 | | | | | 8 |29 .98 | | | | 9 | | | | | 10 | | | | | 11 | | | | | |
Mid.| | | | | | ————+———+———+———+———+————+
————————— 1 | | | | SW | | |*Monday, July 15, 1816.* 2 | | | | | | 3 | | | | |
|The same winds during the 4 | | | | | |night. 5 | | | | | | 6 | | | | | | 7 | | | | | |
8 | | | | | | | 9 | | | | | |Found that we had been 10 |29 .89 | | |SW by W| | |driven by a
current, 11 | | | | | N | E |setting about E by N, 2-1/2 Noon.|29 .89 | 82 | 83 | WNW |22
.43 | 117 .30 |miles an hour. ———+————+———+———+———+————+————+ 1 |
| | | West | | 2 | | | | | SE Coast | 3 | | | | | of China. |About 3 o'clock it became 4 | | | |
| |extremely hazy; the sun set 5 | | | | | in fiery clouds, and a blood 6 | | | | WSW | |red
tint was given to the low 7 | | | | |clouds all round the horizon. 8 |29 .76 | | | SW | | 9 | |
| | | 10 |29 .80 | | | | | 11 | | | | | | Mid.| | | | | | ————+———+———+————+
——+————+————+————————— 1 | | | | SW | | | 2 | | | |
		Tuesday, July 16, 1816. 3				WSW			4						During this day there has 5		
			been a moderate breeze from 6				West			the SSW, with a thick haze, 7				
	and dew at night. 8	29 .74			WSW			9						Soundings from 32 to 26 10		
SW			fathoms: dark fine sand. 11	29 .83				N	E	Noon.	29 .74	83			24 .37
118 .50	———+————+———+———+———+————+————+ 1					2	
	Straits of	We have seen no land all 3					Formosa,	day, having ran along nearly 4	
		China.	parallel with the coast 5					of about 30 or 40 about 6	29 .75			
Chusan, at the distance 7					leagues. 8	29 .78	80	79	SW					-1/2		9	
		10						11						Mid.|29 .76	80	79					|-1/2|	———+————
+———+———+———+————+—————————————— 1			
	2							*Wednesday, July 17, 1816.* 3							4	29 .74	80	80	SSW		The
weather is remarkably			-1/2			hazy, and there is a very 5						disagreeable sea
coming after 6	29 .76						us. 7					8	29 .80	82	81			9					
10	29 .81			SW			11	29 .80				N	E	Noon.	29 .81	82	80	SW by S	26 .1
122 .6	———+————+———+———+———+————+———+ 1	29 .80			SSW
2					Straits of	At night hazy with a heavy 3					Formosa,	dew; soundings 52
fathoms. 4	29 .76	82	81		China.	To-day we quitted the Straits 5	29 .76					of
Formosa, and stood towards 6					the Yellow Sea. Last evening 7	29 .76					we
were among a cluster of 8	29 .79	82	80	South		large islands near the coast 9				
of China, about two-thirds of 10					the way through the Straits 11						of
Formosa. Mid.	29 .80	81	80	S by W		———+————+———+———+———+
+————+—————————————— 1			SW			*Thursday, July 18, 1816.* 2
					3						The wind during all this day 4						has been from the South
5	29 .78					Westward. 6							From noon till midnight it 7					
continued fresh and steady, 8	29 .80	81	80	WSW			after which it lulled. 9				
Weather very hazy, and at 10	29 .86	1		SW			night a heavy dew falling. 11					N
Depth of water from 35 to Noon.	29 .80	81	79	SSW	26 .21		37 fathoms. ———+—
———+———+———+————+————+————+ 1			SW		2	29 .80				To the
northward	3				of the Straits	4	29 .80	81	80	SW by W	of Formosa.	5				
6	29 .76			SW		No land seen to-day, being 7					about 30 leagues off shore, 8
29 .76	81	79	SSW		to the Northward of the 9					Straits of Formosa. 10			
	11						Mid.						————+———+———+———+————+
+————————————— 1					*Friday, July 19, 1816.* 2						3
				4	29 .78	79	78	S by W			During this day there has 5						been a
moderate breeze from 6	29 .75					the SSW, with a thick haze 7						and dew at
night. 8	29 .78	78	78	SSW			9						Soundings from 32 to 26 10	29 .78	
SW			fathoms: fine dark sand. 11	29 .78				N	E	Noon.	29 .78	78	79	SW by
W	30 .54	123 .50	———+————+———+———+———+————+————+ 1				
2	29 .75				Off the Islands	3					of Chusan 30 or	4	29 .72	80	80	SSW	40
leagues.	5					We have seen no land this 6	29 .72					day, having ran along nearly
7						parallel with the coast about 8	29 .72	79	80	South		Chusan, at the distance
of 9					about 30 or 40 leagues. 10					11					Mid.	29 .74	80	79		
————+———+———+———+————+————+

76

—— 1 | | | |S by W | | |*Saturday, July 20, 1816.* 2 | | | | | | | 3 | | | | | |Light SSW winds, with thick 4 |29 .69 | 79 | 76 | | | |haze and dew at night. Regular 5 | | | | | |soundings 20 fathoms: mud and 6 |29 .70 | | | | | |black sand. 7 | | | | | | | 8 |29 .70 | 79 | 77 | South | | 9 | | |-1/2| | | | 10 |29 .72 | | | | | |11 |29 .70 | | | | N | E | Noon.|29 .70 | 80 | 78 |S by W |32 .35 |123 .50 | ——+———+——+——+——+—

——+———+———+ 1 | | | | | |To-day we are about halfway 2 |29 .70 | | |SW by W| Entering the |between the SE part of 3 | | | | |Yellow Sea. |Corea and the Chusan islands, 4 |29 .66 | 80 | 77 | WSW | |each being about 50 leagues 5 | | | | | |distant; the mouth of the 6 |29 .68 | | | | |great river Yang-tse-kiang is 7 | | | | | |nearly W 50 leagues, and the 8 |29 .66 | 79 | 77 |SW by W | |promontory of Shan-tung N by 9 | | | | |W 100 leagues. 10 | | | | | | 11 | | | | | | |Mid.|29 .69 | 78 | 77 | WSW | | ——+———+——+———+—

———————————————— 1 | | | | | | 2 | | | | |W by N | | |*Sunday, July 21, 1816.* 3 | | | |NNW | | | 4 | | | | | |The wind after noon yesterday 5 | | | | | | |freshened up towards sunset 6 | | | | | |from the WSW, and in the 7 | | | | | |night it hauled to the NW 8 |29 .76 | 75 | 76 |N by W | |gradually, and so to North; 9 | | | | | |about noon it became quite 10 |29 .78 | | | | |light as it drew to the 11 |29 .79 | | | N | E |northward. Noon.|29 .79 | 76 | 77 | North |33 .55 | 124 | | | |-1/2| | | | ——+—

——+———+———+———+———+The weather has become quite 1 |29 .78 | | | |clear since the change of the 2 |29 .80 | | | |Yellow Sea. |wind. 3 | | | | |4 |29 .78 | 77 | 77 | NNW | | | | |-1/2| | 5 | | | |Land in sight to-day about 6 |29 .79 | | |E by N | |East from us, supposed to be 7 | | | | | |the islands off the South end 8 |29 .79 | 77 | 77 | East | |of Corea. | | | |-1/2| | 9 | | | | | 10 | | | |E by S | | 11 | | | | | |Mid.| | | | SE | | ——+———+———+———+———+———+—

———————————— 1 | | | |SSE | | |*Monday, July 22, 1816.* 2 | | | | | | | 3 | | | | |In the night there was a 4 |9 .69 | 75 | 77 |S by W | | |breeze from the SSW with 5 | | | | | |very thick weather, and 6 |29 .72 | | | | |much lightning all round. 7 | | | | | 8 |29 .71 | 77 | 76 |SW by W | | 9 | | | | | | 10 |29 .71 | | SW | | 11 |29 .75 | | | N | E | Noon.|29 .75 | 78 | 77 | SSW |34 .44 |123 .55 | ——+———+———+——+———+——+—

——+———+ 1 | | | | | 2 |29 .74 | | | SW | Yellow Sea. |After noon it fell calm till 3 | | | | | |about 6 P.M. when there came 4 |29 .75 | 79 | 79 | Calm | |light breeze from the westward 5 | | | | |which hauled to north, and 6 |29 .73 | | | NNE | |about morning fell nearly calm. 7 | | | | 8 |29 .73 | 76 | 77 |N by E | |Regular soundings from 44 to 9 | | | | | |43 fathoms: mud. 10 | | | | | 11 | | | | | |Mid.|29 .74 | 75 | 76 | North | | ——

——+———+——+——+———+———+—

- 1 | | | |N by W | | |*Tuesday, July 23, 1816.* 2 | | | |West | | | 3 | | | | | 4 |29 .76 | 75 | 76 | Calm | | |About 8 this morning a 5 | | | | | |breeze sprung at South, which 6 | | | | | |lasted during the day, 7 | | | | | |freshening very gradually—sky 8 |29 .78 | 77 | 77 | SSE | | |clear. 9 | | | | 10 |29 .80 | | | SE | | |Regular soundings 43 11 | | | | N | E |fathoms: mud. Noon.|29 .80 | 79 | 78 | South |35 .06 |123 .06 | ——+———+——+—

+—— +———+———+———+———+ 1 | | | | | 2 |29 .79 | | | |Yellow Sea. | 3 | | | | | 4 |29 .79 | 81 | 78 | SSW | | 5 | | | | | |A moderate breeze from the 6 |29 .78 | | | | |Southward, and fine clear 7 | | | | | |weather. 8 |29 .76 | 78 | 77 | SE | | 9 | | | | | 10 | | | SSE | 11 | | | | | |Mid.|29 .77 | 77 | 76 |S by E | | ——+———+——+——+—

———————+———+———+———+ 1 | | | | SSE | | |*Wednesday, July 24, 1816.* 2 | | | | | 3 | | | | | |The wind during these 24 4 | | | | | |hours has become moderate 5 | | | | | |from the Southward.—Quite 6 | | | | | |clear, not the least 7 | | | | | |appearance of fog. 8 |29 .75 | 77 | 76 |SE by S | | | |-1/2| | 9 |29 .77 | | | | 10 |29 .82 | | |S by E | | 11 |29 .86 | | | NW | N | E Noon.|29 .88 | 75 | 78 |NW by W |36 .27 |123 .01 |A very curious assemblage ——+———+——+—

+———+———+———+of clouds passed over us at 1 | | | | |noon from the NW. 2 |29 .70 | | |E by S | Yellow Sea. | 3 | | | | | 4 |29 .69 | 76 | 74 |SE by E| 5 | | | | | 6 |29 .70 | | SSE | 7 | | | | | 8 |29 .70 | 75 | 72 |S by E | |Soundings 40, 38, and 37 9 | | | | |fathoms: brown mud. 10 | | |S by W | 11 | | | | | |Mid.| | | | | | ——+—

——+——+——+———+———+———+ 1 | | | SW | | 2 | | | | | |*Thursday, July 25, 1816.* 3 | | | | | | 4 |29 .70 | 70 | 71 | SSW | | |The wind during the night 5 | | | | | |hung to the SW, with rain 6 | | | | | |occasionally. 7 | | | | | 8 |29 .70 | 71 | 66 | Calm | | |After daybreak the 9 | | | WNW | | |weather cleared up, and the 10 |29 .70 | | |NW by W| | |breeze fell gradually as we 11 |29 .70 | | NW | N | E |rounded the NE point of the Noon.|29 .70 | 74 | 73 | |37 .32 |122 .37 |promontory of Shan-tung. ——+———+——+———+——+——+—

———+ 1 | | | | | 2 |29 .70 | | East |Nearly on the | 3 | | | |meridian of the | 4 |29 .66 | 77 | 72 | SE |NE point of | 5 | | | |Shan-tung | 6 |29 .66 | | | SSE |promontory, | 7

77

| | | | |Yellow Sea. |In the forenoon it felt 8 |29 .61 | 76 | 72 | | |calm, and towards sunset a 9 | | | | | |breeze sprung up from ESE 10 | | | | | |and SE which lasted during 11 | | | | | |the night. Mid |29 .61 | 75 | 75 |S by W | | ——+————+————+————+———— -+————+———————+————————————————————— 1 | | | |S by W | | *Friday, July 26, 1816.* 2 | | | | | | |3 | | | | South | | |As the day broke, the 4 |29 .61 | 74 | 72 | SSE | | |breeze which had been light 5 | | | | | | |during the night, freshened 6 | | | | | | |up, and the weather, hitherto 7 | | | | South | | |clear, became suddenly quite 8 |29. 61 | 74 | 72 | SSW | | |foggy; this however lasted 9 | | | | | | |only half an hour, and we 10 |29. 62 | | | | | |enjoyed during the day the 11 |29. 62 | | | | N | E |same fine clear weather, Noon.|29. 62 | 74 | 72 |S by W |38 .07 |122 .00 |with the exception indeed of ——+————+————+————+————+———————+————+————+————one thunder squall, which 1 | | | | SSW | |lasted only a few minutes, 2 |29. 62 | | | SW | |and passed over, going towards 3 | | | | | Yellow Sea. |the SE. 4 |29. 59 | 76 | 66 | WNW | | 5 | | | | | |N.B. This was the only 6 |29. 60 | | |SE by S| |instance of fog during the 7 | | | | SE | |six weeks that the ships were 8 |29. 60 | 73 | 68 | | |in the Yellow Sea. | |-1/2| | | 9 | | | | | | 10 | | | | | | 11 | | | | | | Mid.|29. 60 | 75 | 74 |SE by E| | ————+————+————+————+————+———————+————+————+———————— 1 | | | | South | | 2 | | | | | |*Saturday, July 27, 1816.* 3 | | | | | | | 4 | | | | SSE | | |During the whole of this 5 | | | | | | |day we had a fresh breeze 6 | | | | | | |from East and ESE, with dark 7 | | | | | | |cloudy weather. As we drew 8 |29. 69 | 77 | 77 | SE | | |across the Gulf of Petchelee | | |-1/2| | |we had the wind much stronger. 9 | | | | | | | 10 |29. 69 | | | East | | | 11 |29. 70 | | | | N | E | Noon.|29. 70 | 76 | 76 | ENE |38 .52 |117 .49 | ————+————+————+————+————+———————+————+————+ 1 | | | | | | 2 |29. 68 | | | E by S | | 3 | | | | | Yellow Sea. |We anchored at seven 4 |29. 61 | 76 | 77 |E by N | |o'clock in 3-1/2 fathoms water. 5 | | | | | | 6 |29. 61 | | | East | 7 | | | | | 8 |29. 80 | 77 | 82 |E by N | | 9 | | | | | |In the night it blew hard 10 |29. 84 | | |SE by E| |from the East, and at sunrise 11 | | | | | |we had a violent thunder Mid.| | | | | |storm. — ——+————+————+————+————+————+———————+————+

—— 1 | | | |SE by E| | *Sunday, July 28, 1816.* 2 | | | | | | | 3 | | | | | | |After the thunder storm had 4 |29 .70 | 80 | 80 |SE by S| |passed the weather cleared up, | | |-1/2| | |and became quite fine. 5 | | | | | | | 6 | | | | | | | 7 | | | | | | | 8 |29 .63 | 82 | 82 | SW | | | | |-1/2| | | | 9 | | | | | | 10 |29 .61 | | | | N | Noon.|29 .60 | 83 | 82 |W by N |38.52.42| | |-1/2 -1/2| | | ————+————+————+————+———————+————+————+————+ 1 | | | |N by E | | 2 |29 .60 | | | North | Pei-ho, |During the day the breeze 3 | | | | | Yellow Sea. |has been moderate, with fine 4 |29 .61 | 81 | 82 |E by S | | |clear weather. 5 | | | | SSE | | 6 |29 .62 | | |S by E | | 7 | | | | | | 8 | | | | | | 9 |29 .61 | 83 | 82 | South | | 10 | | | |S by E | | 11 | | | | | | Mid.|29 .60 | 80 | 82 | SW | | ————+————+————+————+————+———————+————+

- 1 | | | | SW | | 2 | | | | | |*Monday, July 29, 1816.* 3 | | | | WSW | | | 4 |29 .59 | 79 | 81 | NNW | | |Light breezes and cloudy | | |-1/2| | |weather. 5 | | | | | | | 6 | | | | | | 7 | | | | | | | 8 |29 .60 | 82 | 82 |E by N | | | 9 | | | | | | |Towards noon it fell calm. 10 | | | | | | | 11 |29 .62 | | | | N | E | Noon.|29 .60 | 82 | 84 | NE |38 .56 |118 .00 | ———— +————+————+————+————+———————+————+ 1 | | | | | 2 |29 .59 | | | SE |At anchor off the mouth of the 3 | | | | |Pei-ho river, Yellow Sea. 4 |29 .53 | 83 | 84 | ESE | | | | |-1/2| | 5 | | | | | | 6 |29 .55 | | | | 7 | | | | | | 8 |29 .55 | 82 | 82 | SE | |During the night a moderate | | |-1/2| | |breeze from the Eastward. 9 | | | | | | 10 | | | | | 11 | | | | | | Mid.|29 .63 | 80 | 82 |SE by E| | ————+————+————+————+———————+————+ 1 | | | | | |*Tuesday, July 30, 1816.* 2 | | | |SE by E| | 3 | | | | | |During this day there has 4 | | | | | | |been a light air from the 5 | | | | | |Eastward, and fine clear 6 | | | | East | | |weather. 7 | | | | | | | 8 |29 .50 | 82 | 82 | ENE | | | 9 | | | | | | 10 |29 .63 | | | | 11 |29 .63 | | | | | Noon.|29 .62 | 81 | |E by N | | | ——+————+————+————+———————+————+ —+ 1 | | | | | | 2 |29 .65 | | | |At anchor off | 3 | | | | |the mouth of the| 4 |29 .68 | 81 | 84 |SE by E|Pei-ho, Yellow | 5 | | | |Sea. | 6 | | | | 7 | | | | | 8 |29 .61 | 82 | 83 | | | | | |-1/2| | 9 | | | | | 10 | | | | | |At midnight it fell calm. 11 | | | | | | Mid.|29 .69 | 83 | 82 | Calm | | ————+————+————+————+————+———————+————+————+ ————————————————————————— 1 | | | | | | 2 | | | | | |*Wednesday, July 31, 1816.* 3 | | | | | | 4 | | | | |This morning there is a 5 | | | | | |light air from the eastward, 6 | | | | | |inclining to calm. 7 | | | | | | 8 |29 .62 | 88 | 82 | SW | | 9 | | | | | | 10 |29 .70 | | | | 11 | | | | | | Noon.|29 .70 | 84 | 85 | WNW | | | ——+————+————+————+———————+————+————+————+ 1 | | | | | 2 |29 .70 | | | ESE |At anchor off | 3 | | |the mouth of the| 4 |29 .61 | 83 | 86 SE |Pei-ho, Yellow | 5 | | | |Sea. | 6 |29 .71 | | | 7 | | | | | 8 |29 .72 | 82 | 82 | SSE | | | |-1/2| | | 9 | | | | |Towards night the

78

breeze 10 | | | | |freshened up from the SE. 11 | | | | | | Mid. | 29 .84 | 83 | 82 | South | |
| | | -1/2 | | | ——+———+———+———+———+———+———

——————————— 1 | | | | | | | *Thursday, August 1, 1816.* 2 | | | | | SW | | 3 | | | | | |
|During the night there has 4 | 29 .69 | 83 | 84 | West | | |been a fresh breeze from the 5 | | |
| | | |SW, with rain and lightning. 6 | | | | | | |7 | | | | | | 8 | 29 .70 | 81 | 82 |SW by S|
| | | | | -1/2| | | | 9 | | | | | | | 10 | 29 .69 | | | SSW | | |Towards noon it became more
11 | | | | | | | |moderate. Noon.| 29 .70 | 81 | 82 | SW by S| | | | | | -1/2| | | ——+———
——+———+———+———+———+———————+ 1 | | | | | | 2 | 29 .63 | | | |At anchor off
| 3 | | | | |the mouth of the| 4 | 29 .66 | 82 | 82 |S by E |Pei-ho, Yellow | 5 | | | | |Sea. | 6
| | | | SE | | 7 | | | | 8 | 29 .66 | 80 | 82 |S by E | |And at night it was very 9 | | | |
SSW | |squally, with rain. 10 | | | | | 11 | | | | | | Mid.| 29 .65 | 79 | 82 | SW | | ——
+————+————+————+————+———————+———

- 1 | | | | | | | 2 | | | |W by S | | |*Friday, August 2, 1816.* 3 | | | | | | | 4 | | | | | |
|During the whole of the night 5 | | | | | | |it rained. 6 | | | | | | | 7 | | | | | | 8 | 29 .62
| 78 | 82 | | | |Towards morning it blew fresh | -1/2| | | | |from the Westward. 9 | | | | |
| | 10 | | | | | | 11 | 29 .68 | | | SSW | | |Noon.| 29 .67 | 79 | 82 | | | | | | | -1/2| | |
|————+————+————+————+————————+ 1 | | | |S by W | | 2 | 29 .63
| | | SE |At anchor off |During the whole of the day 3 | | | | |the mouth of the| it has been
very hazy with 4 | 29 .68 | 78 | 83 | East |Pei-ho, Yellow |slight showers of rain. | -1/2| |
|Sea. | 5 | | | | | 6 | 29 .63 | | | | 7 | | | | | 8 | 29 .65 | 78 | 82 | SSE | | | | -1/2|
| | 9 | | | | |Midnight, fresh breezes and 10 | | | | |clear. 11 | | | | | | Mid.| 29 .70 | 79
| 82 | East | | ——+————+————+————+————+————+———

——————————— 1 | | | | | | |*Saturday, August 3, 1816.* 2 | | | |E by N | | | 3 | | | |
| | |Fresh breezes and cloudy 4 | 29 .72 | 77 | 81 | NE | | |weather. 5 | | | | | | | 6 | | | |
| | | 7 | | | | | | 8 | 29 .84 | 77 | 81 | ENE | | | -1/2| | | | | 9 | | | | | |Strong
breezes and cloudy, 10 | | | | | |with slight showers of rain 11 | 29 .84 | | | NE | | |at
intervals. Noon.| 29 .82 | 79 | 82 | | | | ——+————+————+————+————+————+———
————+ 1 | | | | | | 2 | 29 .80 | | | |At anchor off | 3 | | | | |the mouth of the| 4 | 29 .80
| 76 | 82 |NE by N |Pei-ho, Yellow | 5 | | | | |Sea. | 6 | 29 .84 | | | | |Towards evening it
cleared 7 | | | | | |up. 8 | 29 .90 | 76 | 80 | ENE | 9 | | | | | |A short swell from the NE.
10 | | | | | | 11 | | | | | |Moderate breezes and cloudy. Mid.| | 75 | 80 |NE by N | | | | |-
1/2| | | ——+————+————+————+————+———

——————————— 1 | | | | | | 2 | | | | North | | |*Sunday, August 4, 1816.* 3 | | | | | | | 4 |
| | | | |Light airs and fine weather. 5 | | | | | | 6 | | | NW | | | 7 | | | | | | 8 | 29
.69 | 78 | 80 | | | | 9 | | | | | | 10 | 29 .70 | | | | | 11 | 29 .70 | | | | | Noon | 29 .70
| 78 | 81 | West | | | | | -1/2| | | | ——+————+————+————+————+————+———
——————— + 1 | | | | NW | |Cloudy, with slight showers 2 | 29 .68 | | | WNW |At anchor off
|of rain at intervals. 3 | | | | |the mouth of the| 4 | 29 .68 | 78 | 81 | WSW |Pei-ho, Yellow |
5 | | | | |Sea. 6 | 29 .68 | | | | | 7 | | | | | 8 | 29 .68 | 78 | 80 | West | | 9 | | | | | |
10 | | | | | 11 | | | | | |Mid.| 29 .68 | 77 | 81 | SW | | ——+————+————+————+———
———+————+————+ *Monday,*
August 5, 1816. 2 | | | |W by S | | | 3 | | | | | | |Moderate breezes and cloudy. 4 | 29 .68 | 77
| 80 | WSW | | | 5 | | | | | | 6 | | | | | | | 7 | | | | | | 8 | 29 .68 | 78 | 80 |W by N |
| | | | -1/2| | | 9 | | | | | | 10 | 29 .69 | | | | |In the forenoon we had a 11 | | | | |
| slight shower. Noon.| 29 .68 | 78 | 81 | SW | | | ——+————+————+————+————
+————+————+ 1 | | | | | 2 | 29 .68 | | |W by S |At anchor off |Moderate breezes
and cloudy. 3 | | | | |the mouth of the| 4 | 29 .66 | 81 | 81 | WSW |Pei-ho, Yellow | | | |-
1/2| |Sea. | 5 | | | | | 6 | 29 .65 | | | | 7 | | | | | 8 | 29 .64 | 81 | 82 | | | 9 | | | |
| 10 | | | | |Light breezes and cloudy. 11 | | | | | Mid.| 29 .59 | | |W by S | | ——+——
——+————+————+————+————+————+——————— 1 |
| | | | | 2 | | | SW | |*Tuesday, August 6, 1816.* 3 | | | NE | | | 4 | 29 .65 | 71 | 79 |
North | | |Alight breeze from the SW. 5 | | | | | | 6 | | | | | | | |Towards 4 A.M. the wind
7 | | | | | |shifted round to NW, and 8 | 29 .64 | 73 | 77 | NNW | | |freshened up. | | | -
1/2| | | 9 | | | | | 10 | 29 .64 | | | | | 11 | | | | WSW | | |Noon.| 29 .63 | 76 | 81
|SW by W| | |Noon, a moderate breeze and | | | | | |fine weather. ——+————+————
+————+————+————————+ 1 | | | | | 2 | 29 .64 | 83 | 81 | SSE |At anchor off
| | | -1/2|-1/2| |the mouth of the| 3 | | | |Pei-ho, Yellow |After noon the breeze, which 4
| 29 .60 | 82 | 81 |Sea. |had hauled round to SE, 5 | | | | |freshened up considerably. 6
| 29 .62 | | | | 7 | | | |Towards sunset dark slaty 8 | 29 .66 | 79 | 82 | SE | |clouds
drew over us from the 9 | | | | |land, moving in a contrary 10 | | | | |direction from that
of the wind 11 | | | | |which we had. Mid.| 29 .66 | 80 | 81 |S by E | | ——+————+——
——+————+————+————+————————— 1 | | | | | |

79

Wednesday, August 7, 1816. 2				South			3							At sunrise it was moderate, 4	
	E by N			but about nine o'clock the 5							breeze freshened, and towards 6		
			noon blew fresh from the 7							Eastward. 8	29 .67	79	81	East		
1/2					9							10	29 .95						11								Noon.	30 .00	77	80	E
by N			———+————+————+————+————+————+————+ 1						2	30
.00				At anchor off	3				the mouth of the	4	29 .92	76	80	NE	Pei-ho, Yellow
Fresh breezes and cloudy. 5					Sea.	6	29 .82					Towards night it moderated. 7
				8	29 .81	73	78					-1/2			9					10					At midnight a
moderate breeze. 11							Mid.						———+————+————+————+————
———+————————+————————————————————————— 1						2							Thursday,
August 8, 1816. 3							4 |29 .65	71	78	North		|Moderate and cloudy. 5			
		6							7							8 |29 .66	73	77	NNW					|-1/2|		9			
		10	29 .67						11							Noon.	29 .68	76	81				Moderate and fine.
———+————+————+————+————+————+————+ 1					2	29 .66		
NNW	At anchor off	3				the mouth of the	4	29 .65	81			Pei-ho, Yellow			-
1/2			Sea.	5						6					7					8	29 .70	79	80	NE	9			
10					11					Light airs. Mid.	29 .71	77	79			———+————+————+——
—+————————+————+————————————————————————— 1				
Friday, August 9, 1816. 2				N by E			3						Light airs and cloudy. 4	29 .73
75	77	NW						-1/2			5						6							7					8	29 .74
76	79						-1/2				9					10						2 A.M. a moderate breeze 11	
				sprung up at NW. Noon.	29 .77	80	79	ESE						-1/2			———+——
———+————+————+————+————+————————+ 1					2	29 .76				At anchor off
3				the mouth of the	4	29 .70	79	77	SSE	Pei-ho, Yellow				-1/2		Sea.
5						6	29 .70					7					8	29 .70				Moderate breezes. 9			
10					11					Mid.	29 .70	76	78	NW		———+————+————+————+——
————+————+————————+ 1						2			
NW			Saturday, August 10, 1816 3							4			WNW			Moderate breezes and
clear. 5						6							7					8	29 .60	75	77	NW			9				
10	29 .70					11	29 .70					Calm and fine weather. Noon.	29 .70	81	79
Calm			———+————+————+————+————————+ 1					2	29
.69				At anchor off	3				the mouth of the	4	29 .67	79	78	SSE	Pei-ho,
Yellow				-1/2		Sea.	5					6	29 .65					7					8	29 .64	76	78
SW		9					10	29 .72					Moderate and cloudy. 11						Mid.	29 .74		
	———+————+————+————+————————+————+————————+—————————
————————— 1						2							Sunday, August 11, 1816. 3				SE			4	29 .70
75	78				5							6							7			SE by S		8	29 .70	76	79			
9						10	29 .75					11							Noon.	29 .74	79	80			———+——
———+————+————+————+————————+ Moderate and clear weather. 1					
2	29 .74			SE	Off the River	3					Pei-ho, Yellow	4	29 .72	79	78		Sea.	5
			6	29 .72				7					8	29 .72					9					10		75	79		
11						Mid.	29 .75				———+————+————+————+————————+————————+
———+————————————————————————— 1							2							Monday, August 12,
1816. 3							4		75	78	SE			Moderate breezes and cloudy. 5							6	
				7							8	29 .78	79	78			9						Moderate breezes from the
10								SE, with fine clear weather. 11						N	E	lightning at times. Noon.	29 .79
79	79	S by E	38 .38	117 .44	———+————+————+————+————+————+————
————+ 1					2	29 .79			Gulf of	3					Pe-che-lee.	4	29 .78	81	82	
5					Moderate and fine weather. 6	29 .78						7					8	29 .78	79	81
SE				-1/2			9					Moderate breezes and clear, 10						with lightning. 11
					Mid.	29 .80	79	80	SE by S				-1/2			———+————————+————+————+——
———+————+————————+ 1						2			
	Tuesday, August 13, 1816. 3				S by W			4							5						In the evening
we had fresh 6						breezes from the SE—sky 7						assuming a threatening 8
29 .79	89	79	SSW		appearance. Towards midnight 9						it moderated, at
which time it 10	29 .80					fell calm. 11							Noon.	29 .80	83	81	SE	38
.34	118 .08	———+————+————+————+————+————————+————+ 1					2
29 .74			Gulf of	3					Pe-che-lee.	4	29 .77	80	80	ESE				-1/2		
5					6	29 .80			SE	7					8	29 .79	79	78			9					10		
SE by S	11						Mid.				Calm		———+————+————————+————+————+——
———+————————+ 1						2			SE by S	
	Wednesday, August 14, 1816. 3				SE			4	29 .70	77	78	WSW			After midnight

80

a moderate 5 | | | | | |breeze sprung up from the SE. 6 |29 .71 | 79 | 78 | South | | | 7 | |
| | | | | 8 |29 .72 | 79 | 78 | SSE | | | 9 | | | | | | | 10 |29 .72 | | | | | |About 4 A.M. it
shifted 11 | | | | | | N | E |more to the Southward, and Noon.|29 .74 | 79 | 78 | |38 .29
|118.20 |remained so the rest of the day. | |-1/2| | | | ——+———+———+———
——+———+———+ Weather fine. 1 | | | | | | 2 |29 .71 | |S by E | Gulf of | 3 | |
| | Pe-che-lee. | 4 |29 .74 | 80 | 80 | | | 5 | | | | | 6 |29 .70 | | | | | 7 | | | | | 8 |29
.72 | 79 | 80 |E by N | | 9 | | | |E by S | 10 | | | | ESE | |At midnight the wind drew 11
| | | | | |round to the Eastward. Mid.|29 .75 | 76 | 79 |E by S | | ——+———+———+——
——+———+———+———+ ————————————————————— 1 | | | | | | 2 | |
| | | | |Thursday, August 15, 1816. 3 | | | | | | | 4 | | 76 | 79 | SE | | |Moderate and fine
weather. | | |-1/2| | | 5 | | | | | | | 6 | | | | | East | 7 | | | | | | 8 |29 .77 | 78 | 80
| | | 9 | | | | | 10 | | | | | | 11 |29 .79 | | | N | E |During the day the wind
Noon.|29 .78 | 78 | 81 | | 37.58 | 118.49 |remained at East and ENE, | |-1/2| | | |
| |blowing a moderate breeze. ——+———+———+———+———+———+———+ 1
| | | | | 2 |29 .76 | | | | Gulf of | 3 | | | | Pe-che-lee. | 4 |29 .74 | 80 | 82 | ENE | | 5
| | | | | 6 |29 .74 | | | | 7 | | | | |Towards night it freshened 8 |29 .76 | 78 | | | |up,
and remained quite steady. 9 | | | | | | 10 | | | | | 11 | | | | | Mid.|29 .86 | 77 | 80 | |
| ——+———+———+———+———+———+
————— 1 | | | | 2 | | | | |Friday, August 16, 1816. 3 | | | | | | 4 | | | | | |To-
day the wind continued at 5 | | | | | |East, the same as yesterday. 6 | | | | | | 7 | | | |
| | 8 |29 .79 | 79 | 81 |E by N | | 9 | | | | | | 10 | | |E by S | | 11 |29 .80 | | | |
N | E | Noon.|29 .80 | 79 | 81 |E by N | 37 .30| 118.57 | | |-1/2|-1/2| | | | ——+——
——+———+———+———+———+ 1 | | | |E by S | 2 |29 .74 | | | | Gulf of
| 3 | | | | Pe-che-lee. |In the evening it became 4 |29 .74 | 80 | 81 | ENE | |squally, with
rain. 5 | | | | | | 6 |29 .74 | | | | 7 | | | | | 8 |29 .74 | 79 | 80 SE by S| | | |-1/2| | |
| 9 | | | | |Towards midnight the wind 10 | | | | |hauled to the Southward. 11 | | | | | |
Mid.| | | |S by W | | ——+———+———+———+———+———+———+
——————————————— 1 | | | S by W| | 2 | | | | SSW | |Saturday, August 17,
1816. 3 | | | | | | 4 |29 .74 | 78 | 80 |SW by S| |To-day we have had a breeze | |-1/2| |
| | |from the SW. 5 | | | | | | 6 | | | | | | 7 |29 .74 | | | | | 8 | | | | | | 9 |29 .74
| 79 | 84 | SW | | |-1/2| | | | 10 | | | | | | 11 |29 .74 | | | N | E | Noon.|29 .75
| 81 | 81 | 37 .20| 119.33 | ——+———+———+———+———+ 1
				2	29 .74			Gulf of	3					Pe-che-lee.	During the afternoon the 4		
		wind shifted to the Eastward, 5					where it remained, and blew a 6	29 .70		
steady breeze. 7					8	29 .70	79	80	East	9					10					11		
		Mid.	29 .71	79	80	E by S		——+———+———+———+———+———+——
———+ ——————————————— 1						2			East			Sunday,
August 18, 1816. 3							4	29 .72	79	80	E by N			After midnight we had a		-
1/2				moderate breeze from the 5						Eastward, and at 4 A.M. it 6			
freshened up at ENE, where it 7				continued until the evening, at 8	29 .80	79
80				which time it shifted to the 9					SE, with rain. 10	29 .81					11	
	N	E	Noon.	29 .80	79	79	37 .47	119 .37			-1/2			——+———+———
+———+———+———+———+ 1				NE by E	2	29 .82				Gulf of
3				Pe-che-lee.	At eight it was nearly calm. 4	29 .88	78	79	ENE				-1/2	
5						About nine a breeze sprung 6	29 .82					up from the Eastward, 7		
SE by S		accompanied by rain. 8	29 .90	78	78	Calm		9						10	29 .98		
11						Mid.	29 .98	78	78	East		——+———+———+———+———+———
——+———+———+ 1						2				NNE	
Monday, August 19, 1816. 3							4							A light air. 5						6			
7						8	29 .98	78	78	ENE				-1/2	-1/2			9						10	29
.94					11	29 .92				N	E	Towards noon the breeze Noon.	29 .92	74	77
NE	37. 40	119.44	freshened up at North-easterly,			-1/2				where it continued all day,
and ——+———+———+———+———+———+———+blew rather fresh, with a
short 1					swell. 2	29 .92				3					Gulf of	4	29 .92	75	77		Pe-che-
lee.				-1/2		5			6	29 .94				7				8	29 .99	74	76	NE by
N|		|-1/2|		9						10					11						Mid.|					——+———
+———+———+———+———+———+ ——————————————————— 1			
	2							Tuesday, August 20, 1816. 3						4	29 .95	76	78	N by E	
During the night it blew a 5							steady fresh breeze from NNE, 6							in
which quarter it continued 7						all this day. 8	30 .00	76	77	NNE						-
1/2				The sky having a threatening 9						appearance. 10	30 .02						11	
		N	E	Noon.	30 .03	75			37 .46	120 .08	——+———+———+———+———+

+———+————+ 1 | | | | | |Towards the evening moderated. 2 |30 .00 | | | | | 3 | | |
| | Gulf of | 4 |29 .90 | 74 | 78 | | Pe-che-lee. | 5 | | | | | | 6 |29 .90 | | | | | 7 | | | | |
|Near midnight the wind came 8 |29 .90 | 74 | 77 |NE by N| |round to the SW, and blew a |
| | -1/2 | | |moderate breeze. 9 | | | | | | 10 | | | | | | 11 | | | | | Mid.| | | | | ———
+———+———+————+———+————+———+
- 1 | | | | SW | | |*Wednesday, August 21, 1816.* 2 | | | | | | | 3 | | | | | |The early part of
the day the 4 | | | | | | |wind has been moderate from the 5 | | | | SSW | | |Southward. 6 |
| | | | | | 7 | | | | | | 8 |29 .80 | 74 | 77 |S by W | | | 9 | | | | | | 10 | | | | | |
|About noon it died away, but 11 |29 .80 | | | | N | E |shortly after a breeze sprung Noon.|29
.80 | 79 | 77 | Calm | 37 .51| 120 .33| up from the Eastward, and blew ———+————+———
+———+———+————+————+pretty steady from that quarter 1 | | | | | | till the
evening, when it 2 |29 .78 | | | East | Gulf of |hauled round to the SE. 3 | | | | | Pe-che-lee.
| 4 |29 .76 | 76 | 77 | | 5 | | | | | 6 |29 .76 | | | | 7 | | | | | | 8 |29 .74 | 75 | 77
|SE by S| | 9 | | | | | 10 | | | | | 11 | | | | | Mid. |29 .82 | 74 | 73 |S by E | | | |-
1/2| | | ———+———+———+———+———+———+———
————— 1 | | | | | | | 2 | | | | | | |*Thursday, August 22, 1816.* 3 | | | | | | | 4 |29
.80 | | | | | 5 | | | | | | |During the early part of the 6 | | | | | | |day we had a moderate
breeze 7 | | | | | | |from the SE. 8 |29 .80 | 77 | 78 | | 9 | | | | | | | 10 |29 .80 | | | |
| | 11 | | | | | | Noon.|29 .74 | 80 | 78 | SE | | | ———+———+———+———+
+———+———+————+ 1 | | | | | 2 |29 .74 | | | | Off Cheatow, |After noon it hauled to
the 3 | | | | | Yellow Sea. |Southward. 4 |29 .74 | 78 | 78 | | 5 | | | | | | 6 |29 .72 | | | |
| 7 | | | | | | 8 |29 .72 | 77 | 78 | SSE | | 9 | | | | | 10 | | | | | 11 | | | | | Mid. | |
| | | | ———+———+———+———+———+———
————— 1 | | | | | | |*Friday, August 23, 1816.* 2 | | | | | | 3 | | | | | |During the
night the wind has 4 |29 .70 | 78 | 78 | NE | |been moderate, and steady 5 | | | | | |from
the Southward. 6 | | | | | 7 | | | | | 8 |29 .70 | 80 | 78 | | 9 | | | | | 10 | |
| | | | 11 | | | | | | Noon.|29 .72 | 81 | 78 | | | | | |-1/2 | | | ———+———+—
—+———+———+————+ 1 | | | | | 2 | | | |SE by E| At anchor in | In
the forenoon it veered to 3 | | | | | Cheatow Bay, |the NE, and towards night to 4 |29 .70 | 80
| 78 | SE | Yellow Sea. |the Southward. 5 | | | | | 6 |29 .68 | | | | 7 | | | | | 8 |29 .66
| 79 | 78 | Calm | | 9 | | | | | 10 | | | | | 11 | | | | | Mid.|29 .66 | 77 | 78 | South |
| ———+———+———+———+———+———
————— 1 | | | | | 2 | | | South | | |*Saturday, August 24, 1816.* 3 | | | | | | 4 |29 .70
| 77 | 78 | | |During the morning the wind 5 | | | | | |was steady from the Southward. 6
| | | | | | 7 | | | | | 8 |29 .68 | 78 | 78 | S by E| | | |-1/2 | | | | 9 | | | | | |
10 |29 .70 | | | | | 11 |29 .68 | | | | | Noon.|29 .68 | 79 | 78 | | | ———+———
+———+———+———+————+ 1 |29 .68 | | | | 2 |29 .66 | | | Che-a-tow,
| 3 |29 .66 | | | | Yellow Sea. | 4 |29 .66 | 79 | 78 | | |Towards night the wind hauled 5 |29
.64 | | | | |to the Eastward, blowing a 6 |29 .64 | | | |moderate breeze, and steady. 7 | | | |
| | 8 |29 .62 | 78 | 78 | East | | 9 | | | | | 10 | | | | | 11 | | | | | Mid.|29 .62 | 78 |
77 | E by S| | ———+———+———+———+———+———+———
————— 1 | | | | | | |*Sunday, August 25, 1816.* 2 | | | | E by S| | 3 | | | | |
| |The wind continued to blow 4 |29 .74 | | | | |from the NE quarter all the 5 | | | | | |
|forenoon. 6 | | | | | | 7 | | | | | 8 |29 .64 | 78 | 78 | N by E| | 9 | | | | | | 10 |
| | | NE | | 11 | | | | | | Noon.|29 .66 | 79 | 78 | | | ———+———+———+
+———+———+————+ 1 | | | | | 2 | | | NE | Che-a-tow, | 3 | | | | | Yellow
Sea. |In the afternoon it hauled 4 | | | | N by E| |more to the Northward. 5 | | | | | | 6 | |
| | E by S| 7 | | | | | 8 |29 .64 | 78 | 77 | | |At midnight it hauled to the | | |-1/2 | |
|SW, with fine clear weather. 9 | | | | |A heavy dew falling. 10 | | | | | | 11 | | | | |
Mid.| | | | | | ———+———+———+———+———+———+———
————— 1 | | | | | | 2 | | | | SW | | |*Monday, August 26, 1816.* 3 | | | | | |
| 4 |29 .56 | 77 | 77 | WNW | | |After midnight it continued | | |-1/2 | | |to blow a
moderate breeze from 5 | | | | | | |the SW. 6 | | | | | | 7 | | | | | 8 |29 .56 | 78 | 77
|W by N | | | | |-1/2 | | 9 | | | | | 10 | | | | | | 11 |29 .56 | | | | |
Noon.|29 .56 | 79 | 78 | | | |-1/2 | | | | ———+———+———+———+———+———
———+————+ 1 | | | | | |About 4 A.M. it shifted to 2 |29 .64 | | | | Che-a-tow, |the NW,
from which quarter it 3 | | | | | Yellow Sea. |blew the whole of the day. 4 |29 .52 | 79 | 78 |
NW | | | | |-1/2 | | 5 | | | | | | 6 |29 .52 | | | | 7 | | | | | 8 |29 .54 | 79 | 78 | | |
9 | | | | | 10 | | | | | 11 | | | | | Mid. |29 .56 | 78 | 78 | | | | |-1/2 | | | ———
+———+———+———+———+———+
- 1 | | | | | | |*Tuesday, August 27, 1816.* 2 | | | | NW | | 3 | | | | | |Towards noon the
wind hauled 4 |29 .58 | 77 | 77 | North | | |more to the Westward, with 5 | | | | | | |rain,

thunder, and lightning. 6 | | | | | | 7 | | | | | | 8 |29 .62 | | | | | | 9 | | | | | | 10 | |
| | | | | 11 | | | | | | | Noon.|29 .64 | 78 | 78 | | | | ——+———+———+———+———
——+———+———+———+ 1 | | | | | | 2 |29 .62 | | | |S by W | At anchor in | 3 | | | | | Oie-
hai-oie | 4 |29 .62 | 76 | 77 | | harbour, | 5 | | | | | Yellow Sea. | 6 |29 .62 | | | | | | 7 | | |
| | | 8 |29 .61 | 76 | 77 | NNE | |In the evening the wind came 9 | | | | | |to the NNE. 10
| | | | | | 11 | | | | | | Mid. |29 .64 | 75 | 77 | | ——+———+———+———+———
+———+———+———+—————————————————— 1 | | | | | | 2 | | | | |
|Wednesday, August 28, 1816. 3 | | | |NE by N | | 4 | | | | | | |To-day the wind has been 5 |
| | | | | |moderate and steady from the 6 | | | | | |North-eastward. 7 | | | | | | | 8 |29
.70 | 75 | 77 | | | 9 | | | | | | 10 |29 .72 | | | | | | 11 | | | | | | Noon.|29 .72 | 77 |
76 | | | | | |-1/2|-1/2| | | ——+———+———+———+———+
1 | | | | | | 2 | | |NE | Oie-hai-oie | 3 | | | | harbour, | 4 |29 .70 | 77 | 76 | ENE |
Yellow Sea. | | |-1/2| | | 5 | | | | | 6 | | | | | 7 | | | | | |Towards night the breeze 8
|29 .70 | 77 | 76 | NE | |freshened, and the sky became 9 | | | | | |cloudy, assuming a
threatening 10 | | | | | |appearance. 11 | | | | | | Mid. |29 .74 | 79 | 76 | | | ——+———
-+———+———+———+———+———+———— 1 | | |
| | | |Thursday, August 29, 1816. 2 | | | | | | | 3 | | | | | | |After midnight the wind hauled 4
|29 .78 | 77 | 76 |E by N | | |to the Eastward, blowing fresh, 5 | | | | | | |the weather still
looking very 6 | | | | | |black. 7 | | | | | | 8 |29 .78 | 78 | 76 |S by E | | |-1/2| |
| | 9 | | | | | | 10 |29 .80 | | | | | 11 | | | | | | Noon.|29 .80 | 81 | 77 | South | | |
——+———+———+———+———+———+———+ 1 | | | | | | 2 |29 .92 | | | |
Oie-hai-oie |After 4 it moderated, and the 3 | | | | | harbour, |weather cleared up and became
4 |29 .90 | 81 | 78 | SSE | Yellow Sea. |quite fine. 5 | | | | | | 6 | | | | | 7 | | | | |
|About 8 P.M. the wind came 8 |29 .92 | 78 | 77 | SW | |to the Southward. Towards 9 | | | |
| |midnight it drew round to the 10 | | | | | |SW, and then to South again. 11 | | | | | | Mid.
|29 .94 | 79 | 77 | | | ——+———+———+———+———+———+———
————————————————— 1 | | | | | | 2 | | | | | |Friday, August 30, 1816. 3 | | | |
| | 4 |29 .96 | 78 | 77 |S by W | | |All the forenoon the wind 5 | | | | | | |has been light
from the 6 | | | | | |Southward and SW. 7 | | | | | | 8 |29 .98 | 78 | 77 | SW | | | 9 | |
| | | | 10 |29 .98 | | | West | | | 11 | | | | | | N | E | Noon.|29 .96 | 80 | 76 | Calm |37
.58 |122 .58 |About noon it fell calm. ——+———+———+———+———+———
——+ 1 | | | | | 2 |29 .94 | |Calm | Yellow Sea. | 3 | | | | | 4 |29 .92 | 80 | 81 |
NNE | | 5 | | | | | |At 2 a breeze sprung up from 6 |29 .90 | | | | |the NE, with small
drizzling 7 | | | | | |rain, and thick weather. 8 |29 .90 | 79 | 79 | ENE | | 9 | | | | | | 10 | |
| | | | 11 | | | | | | Mid. | | | | | | ——+———+———+———+———+———+———
———+————————————————— 1 | | | | | | 2 | | | | | |Saturday, August 31,
1816. 3 | | | | | | 4 | | | | | | 5 |29 .90 | 79 | 79 |W by N | | |After midnight a light
breeze 6 | | | | | | |from the Eastward, inclining 7 | | | | | | |to calm. 8 |29 .92 | 80 | 79 | |
| 9 | | | | | | 10 |29 .94 | | | | | 11 | | | | | | N | E | Noon.|29 .96 | 80 | 79 |NW by
N |37 .55 |123 .37 |About noon a breeze sprung up ——+———+———+———+———
+———+———+from the Westward; weather 1 | | | | | |cloudy. 2 |29 .94 | | | NW |
Yellow Sea. | 3 | | | | | | 4 |29 .94 | 80 | 79 | | | | |-1/2| | | 5 | | | | | |In the
afternoon it died away 6 |29 .92 | | | | |quite light. 7 | | | | | | 8 |29 .92 | 79 | 79 | Calm | |
| | |-1/2| | 9 | | | | | | 10 | | | | |Towards midnight a moderate 11 | | | | | |breeze
from the Northward. Mid. | | | | NW | | ——+———+———+———+———+———+———
————————————————— 1 | | | |NE by N | | 2 | | | | |
|Sunday, September 1, 1816. 3 | | | | | | | 4 | | | | | 5 |29 .90 | 76 | 78 | N by E | |
|During this day there has been 6 | | | | | |a steady breeze at North and 7 | | | | |
|North by East. 8 |29 .90 | 76 | 76 | | | 9 | | | | | | 10 |29 .92 | | | | | 11 | | | | N
| E | Noon.|29 .90 | 76 | 76 | |37 .45 | 124 .48| ——+———+———+———+———+——
——+———+ 1 | | | | North | 2 |29 .98 | | | | Yellow Sea. |Towards night the wind 3
| | | | | |freshened up. 4 | | | | | | 5 | | | | | | 6 |29 .98 | | | | | 7 | | | | | | 8 |29 .98 |
75 | 75 | | | 9 | | | | | 10 | | | | | | 11 | | | | | | Mid. | | | | | | ——+———+———+———
+———+———+———+————————————————— 1 | | | | |
Monday, September 2, 1816. 2							3						About 2 A.M. the wind shifted 4		
			to the Eastward, where it 5						freshened. 6	29.82	78	79				7			
	8	29.82	80	79			9						10	29.82					11				N	E
Noon.	29.82	81	80	NW by N	36 .45	124 .51	——+———+———+———+———
+————+———+	S by W	West Coast of	2	29.96				Corea.	3			
	In the afternoon it freshened 4	29.98	80	80	SSE		and shifted to the Southward, 5
		|accompanied by a slight shower 6	29.98				|of rain. 7						8	30.04	80
80 |S by W		9						10						11						Mid.				South		——+———

83

—+——+——+——+————+————+——————————————————————— 1 | |
| | | | |*Tuesday, September 3, 1816.* 2 | | | | | | | 3 | 30.02 | | | South | | | 4 | | | | | | | 5 |
| | | | | |The wind during all the night 6 | | | | | | |has been steady from the 7 | | | | |
|Southward, and remained so all 8 | 30.04 | 77 | 79 |S by W | | |day until the evening, when it
9 | | | | | | |shifted to the Westward. 10 | 30.04 | | | SSW | | | 11 | | | | | | | Noon.|
30.00 | 79 | 78 | |36 .18 |126 .09 | ——+————+————+————+————+————+————
—+ 1 | | | | | | 2 | 29.98 | | | SW | | 3 | | | | WSW | | 4 | 29.95 | 81 | 78 | West |
|About sunset it fell calm. 5 | | | | | | 6 | 29.94 | | | | | 7 | | | | | | | 8 | 29.92 | 80 | 77 |
Calm | | 9 | | | | | | 10 | | | | | | 11 | | | | | | Mid.| | | | | | ——+————+————+————
-+————+————+————+————
|*Wednesday, September 4, 1816.* 2 | | | | Calm | | | 3 | | | | | | |It continued calm all night. 4 |
| | | | 5 | | | | | | 6 |29 .95 | 78 | 78 | | | | 7 | | | | | | | 8 | 29 .95 | 79 | 78 | West
| | |About 8 A.M. a light breeze 9 | | | | | | |from the Westward. 10 |29 .95 | | | | | | 11 |
| | | | N | E | Noon.|29 .92 | 80 | 82 | NW |36 .13 | 126 .34| ——+————+————+————
+————+————+————————+At noon it freshened, hauling 1 | | | | | |from W to NW. 2
|29 .85 | | | West | West Coast of | 3 | | | | |Corea. | 4 | 29 .84 | 81 | 82 | WSW | | 5 | |
| | | | 6 |29 .84 | | | | | 7 | | | | | | 8 |29 .84 | 79 | 80 |N by E | |Towards night the wind
shifted 9 | | | | | |to the Northward, and 10 | | | | | |continued to blow steady. 11 | | | | N
| | Mid. | | | | | | ——+————+————+————+————+————+————
——————————— 1 | | | | | | 2 | | | N | | |*Thursday, September 5, 1816.* 3 | | |
| | | 4 | | | | | | 5 | | | | | | 6 |29 .82 | 78 | 79 | | | | |-1/2|-1/2| | | 7 | | |
| | |About 7 it fell calm. 8 | 29 .82 | 80 | 79 | Calm | | | | |-1/2| | | | 9 | | | | | | 10
|29 .82 | | | | | 11 | | | | N | E | Noon.|29 .82 | 80 | 80 | WNW |36 .05 |126 .42
|Towards noon a breeze sprung | | |-1/2| | | |up from WNW, with fine clear ——+————
+————+————+————+————————+weather. 1 | | | | | | 2 |29 .82 | | | WNW | |
3 | | | | 4 |29 .80 | 80 | 79 | | 5 | | | 6 |29 .80 | | | | | 7 | | | | 8 |29 .80 |
80 | 79 | | | 9 | | | | |Towards midnight the wind came 10 | | | | | |to the Northward. 11
| | | | | | Mid. | | | | | | ——+————+————+————+————+————+————
——————————— 1 | | | | | |*Friday, September 6, 1816.* 2 | | | | | | | 3 |
| | |N by E | | | 4 | | | | | |The most part of this day the 5 | | | | | |wind has been
from the 6 |29 .86 | 78 | 78 | NNE | |Northward, blowing a steady | |-1/2| | |
|moderate breeze. 7 | | | | | | 8 |29 .86 | 79 | 78 | | 9 | | | | | 10 |29 .88 | | | |
| 11 | | | | N | E | Noon.|29 .88 | 79 | 78 | |35 .17 |126 .24| | |-1/2| | | | ——+——
——+————+————+————+————————+ 1 | | | |North | | 2 |29 .89 | | | | West
Coast of | 3 | | | | | Corea. | 4 |29 .90 | 79 | 77 | | |Towards night the wind drew | | |-
1/2| | Corea. |round to ENE, and became quite 5 | | | |N by E | |light. 6 |29 .90 | | | | | 7
| | | | | 8 |29 .88 | 77 | 74 | ENE | |At midnight it fell calm. | |-1/2| | | 9 | | | | |
10 | | | | | 11 | | | | Calm | | Mid. | | | | | | ——+————+————+————+————+——
——+————+————————————— 1 | | | |NNW | | |*Saturday,*
September 7, 1816. 2 | | | | | | | 3 | | | | | |After midnight a light breeze 4 | | | | | |
|sprung up from NNW. 5 | | | | | | 6 |29 .82 | | |N by E | | |About 4 it hauled round to
NE, 7 | | | | | | |and at noon it was at North. 8 |29 .82 | 76 | 75 | | | | 9 | | | |ENE | | |
10 |29 .82 | | | | | 11 | | | | | N. | E. | Noon |29 .88 | 79 | 78 | |34 .32 |125 .50 | | |-
1/2| | | | ——+————+————+————+————————+ 1 | | | | N | | 2
|29 .80 | | | | 3 | | | | NNE | |At 2 the wind shifted to NE, 4 |29 .82 | 80 | 72 | Calm |
|and by 4 it fell calm. 5 | | | | 6 | | | | |Towards 8 P.M. a breeze sprung 7 | | | | | |up
from the Northward, and 8 |29 .82 |78 | 82 | N | |continued so the remainder of 9 | | | |
|the night. 10 | | | | | 11 | | | Calm | | Mid. | | | | | | ——+————+————+————
+————+————+————+————————————— 1 | | | | NNW | |
|*Sunday, September 8, 1816.* 2 | | | | | | | 3 | | | | North | | |Shortly after midnight it fell 4 | |
| | | | |calm; this did not last above 5 | | | | Calm | | |half an hour, before a breeze 6 | | | |
NNW | | |sprung up from the Northward, 7 | | | | | |which continued so all day. In 8 | 29
.86 | 74 | 70 | North | | |the night a heavy dew fell; and 9 | | | | | | |much lightning was
observed in 10 |29 .82 | | | | |the NE quarter. 11 | | | | | N | E | Noon |29 .81 | 78 | 71
| |34.22.30|126 .03| ——+————+————+————+————————+————+————+ 1 | | |
|N by E | | 2 |29 .80 | | | |Moored in | 3 | | | | |Murray's Sound, | 4 |29 .80 | 76 | 70 |
|among the | 5 | | | |islands which | 6 |29 .80 | | | |lie off the SW | 7 | | | |extreme of
| 8 |29 .79 | 74 | 70 | NNE |Corea. | 9 | | | | | 10 | | | | | | 11 | | | | | | Mid. | | | |
|————+————-+————+————+————————+————+————+————
——————— 1 | | |N by W | | 2 | | | | | |*Monday, September 9, 1816.* 3 | | | | | | 4 | | |
| | |In the forenoon the wind came 5 | | | | | |to NW, and continued so all 6 |29 .78 | 74 |
70 | | | |day, with a steady moderate 7 | | | | | |breeze, and fine clear weather. 8 |29 .78 |

84

76 | 70 | NNW | | | 9 | | | | | | | 10 | | | | | | | 11 | 29 .80 | | | | N | E | Noon | 29 .80
| 75 | 78 | | 34.22.30 | 126 .03 | ——+———+———+———+———+———+
1 | | | | | 2 | | | NW | | 3 | | | | | | 4 | 29 .80 | 74 | 71 | NNW | | A heavy dew fell
during the 5 | | | | | | night. 6 | | | | | | | 7 | | | | | 8 | 29 .78 | 74 | 70 | | | 9 | | | | | |
10 | | | | | | 11 | | | | | | Mid. | 29 .78 | 73 | 69 | | | ———+———+———+———+
——+———+———+ —————————————————— 1 | | | | | | | Tuesday,
September 10, 1816. 2 | | | | | | | 3 | | | | | | | The breeze continued at NW 4 | 29 .76 | 72 |
68 | NW | | | until the afternoon, when it 5 | | | | | | | drew round to the Northward, 6 | | |
| | | | and freshened up from that 7 | | | | | | | quarter, looking threatening 8 | 29 .76 | 73 | 68
| | | | and squally. 9 | | | | | | | 10 | 29. 77 | | | | | | 11 | 29. 76 | 73 | 68 | | | N | E |
Noon. | | | | | 34 .19 | 126 .05 | ——+———+———+———+———+———+
+ 1 | | | | | | 2 | 29. 74 | 72 | 68 | North | Got under weigh | 3 | | | | | from Murray's | 4
| 29. 78 | 76 | 80 | N by W | Sound, and stood | Midnight, strong breezes with 5 | 29. 90 | | | | to
the Southward | occasional showers of rain, and 6 | 29. 90 | | | | into the Japan | a very high
irregular swell from 7 | | | | | Sea. Saw | the NE. This seems to be the 8 | 29. 74 | 76 | 80 |
| Quelpaert. | NE monsoon, which sets in to 9 | | | | | the Northward much earlier than 10 |
| | | | | in lower latitudes. 11 | | | | | | Mid. | 29. 76 | 76 | 80 | North | | ——+———
+———+———+———+———+ ——————+———+ —————— 1 | | | |
| | *Wednesday, September 11, 1816.* 2 | | | | | | | 3 | | | | | | To-day we have had a strong 4 |
| | | | | breeze from the N by W, with 5 | | | | | | a high irregular swell setting 6 | | | |
| | after us. In the afternoon the 7 | | | | | | wind hauled round to NW. 8 | 29. 73 | 80 | 80
| N by W | | | | | -1/2 | | | 9 | | | | | | 10 | 29. 72 | | | | | | 11 | | | | | N | E |
Noon. | 29. 71 | 81 | 83 | NNW | 31 .41 | 126 .44 | ——+———+———+———+———+
——+———+———+ 1 | | | | 2 | 29. 71 | | | | Japan Sea. | 3 | | | | | 4 | 29. 71 | 82 | 82
| NW | | 5 | | | | | Towards midnight it 6 | 29. 71 | | | | | moderated: weather cloudy. 7 | |
| | | 8 | 29. 73 | 79 | 82 | | | | | -1/2 | | | 9 | | | | | 10 | | | | | | 11 | | | | |
Mid. | 29. 80 | | | North | | ——+———+———+———+———+———+———+
————————————————— 1 | | | | | | | *Thursday, September 12, 1816.* 2 | | | | North
| | | 3 | | | | | | During the night the wind 4 | | | | | | shifted to the Northward, with 5 |
| | | | a moderate breeze, and fine 6 | 29 .74 | 80 | 82 | | | clear weather. 7 | 29. 75 | | | |
| | 8 | 29. 75 | 82 | 82 | | | | | -1/2 | | | | 9 | | | | | 10 | | | | | | 11 | | | | | N
| E | Noon. | 29 75 | 82 | 83 | 29. 38 | 127 .56 | | -1/2 | | | | ——+———+———+——
——+———+———+ 1 | | | | | In the afternoon it became 2 | | | | | Japan
Sea. | squally, with a heavy shower 3 | | | | | of rain. 4 | 29. 70 | 83 | 83 | N by E | | 5 | | |
| NE by N | | This wind, though not fixed, 6 | 29. 72 | | | NE | | has much the appearance of 7
| | | | | | the monsoon. 8 | 29. 78 | 83 | 83 | | 9 | | | | | Latitude by Polaris 30° 3 min. 10
| | | | | 30 in. at 2 h. 57 min. A.M. 11 | | | | | 13th. Mid. | 29. 78 | 82 | 82 | | | | -1/2|
| | | ——+———+———+———+———+———+
————————— 1 | | | | | | *Friday, September 13, 1816.* 2 | | | | | | The wind continued at NE,
3 | | | | | with a steady fresh breeze; 4 | | | | | | which towards noon freshened 5 | | | |
| | considerably, and a swell got 6 | 29. 72 | | | N by E | | up from the NE. At noon 7 | | |
| | | observed in 27° 48' N latitude. 8 | 29. 70 | 83 | 84 | | | stormy 2° 30' it became dark 9 |
| | | | | and in the NE, and the signal 10 | 29. 70 | | | | | being made to shorten sail, we 11
| 29. 76 | | | | N | E | brought the ship under the main Noon. | 29. 78 | 84 | 84 | 27 .48 | 128
.20 | topsail and foresail, and made ——+———+———+———+———+
—+preparations for a gale. At 4 1 | 29. 60 | | | NE | we saw the Loo-choo Islands SW 2 | 29.
74 | | | | Off Sulphur | by S 20 miles. At 5 the wind 3 | 29. 75 | | | | Island, Japan | shifted
from N to NE, and the 4 | 29. 80 | | | | Sea. | mountainous swell which we had 5 | 29. 90 | | |
| | experienced during the day 6 | 29. 95 | | | | rose still higher. The wind did 7 | 29. 94 | | | |
| not blow fresh except in short 8 | | | | | rainy squalls. After 8 P.M. it 9 | | | | | blew at
times very fresh, and 10 | | | | | also in the night, but when the 11 | | | | | moon got up it
became clear. Mid. | 29. 52 | | | | | ——+———+———+———+
—+—————————————— 1 | | | | | | *Saturday, September 14, 1816.* 2 | | | |
| | | 3 | | | | | | During the night the wind 4 | | | | | | shifted from NE to NW, and 5 | |
| | | | continued to blow fresh with a 6 | 29 .52 | | | | | high irregular swell. 7 | | | | | |
8 | 29 .52 | 83 | 82 | NW | | | | | -1/2 | | | 9 | 29 .54 | | | | | 10 | 29 .54 | | | NW by
W | | | 11 | 29 .56 | | | | N | E | Noon. | 29 .60 | 83 | 82 | 27 .44 | 127 .35 | ——+———+
+———+———+———+———+ 1 | 29 .58 | | | | | 2 | 29 .60 | | | | Off Loo-
Choo, | Towards evening it became 3 | 29 .64 | | | | Japan Sea. | moderate and clear. 4 | 29 .52 |
83 | 82 | NW by N | | 5 | 29 .54 | | | | | 6 | 29 .66 | | | NW | | 7 | | | | | 8 | 29 .70 | 82 |
82 | NW by N | | 9 | | | | | In the night fine clear 10 | | | | | weather. 11 | | | | | | Mid.
| 29 .74 | 81 | | NW | | ——+———+———+———+———+———+———+

———————————————— 1 | | | | | | 2 | | | | | | *Sunday, September 15, 1816.* 3 | |
| | | | 4 | | | | | |A moderate breeze from NNW, 5 | | | | | |with a clear sky; the swell
6 |29 .80 | | | NNW | | |much less, though still 7 | | | | | |considerable. 8 |29 .78 | 80
|83 | | | | 9 | | | | | | 10 |29 .76 | | | | | 11 |29 .71 | | |NW by N| N | E | Noon.|29
.75 | 83 |84 | |26 .44 |127 .32 | ——+————+————+————+————+————+————+—
+ 1 | | | | | | 2 |29 .75 | | | Off Loo-Choo, | 3 | | | | | | Japan Sea. | 4 |29 .75 | 83 | 88
|N by W | | | | |-1/2 | | | 5 | | | | | |Towards night the wind veered 6 |29 .75 | | | | |to
NNE. 7 | | | | | | 8 |29 .80 | 81 |North | | | |-1/2 | | | 9 | | | | | | 10 |29 .81 | | |
NNE | | 11 | | | | | | Mid. |29 .80 | 81 | 84 |NE by N| | ——+————+————+————+——
——+————+————+————————————————— 1 | | | | | | | *Saturday,*
September 16, 1816. 2 | | | | | | | 3 | | | | | |The wind continued at NNE. 4 | | | | | | | 5
| | | | | | |About 4 A.M. we had several 6 |29 .84 | | | NNE | | |showers of rain, but soon 7
| | | | | | |cleared off. 8 |29 .84 | 81 | 83 |N by E | | | 9 | | | | | | 10 |29 .90 | | | | |
11 | | | | N | E |About noon the breeze Noon.|29 .90 | 82 | 83 | |26.13.39 |127
.38 | freshened. ——+————+————+————+————+————+————+————+ 1 | | | | | | 2
|29 .80 | | | At anchor in | 3 | | | | | Napakiang | 4 |29 .80 | 82 | 83 | NE |harbour,
Great |In the afternoon we had a 5 | | | | |Loo-choo Island.|shower. 6 |29 .80 | | | | | 7 |
| | | | 8 |29 .80 | 80 | 83 | | | |-1/2 |-1/2 | | | 9 | | | | | 10 | | | | | |Midnight, clear
weather, with 11 | | | | | |lightning in the SW. Mid.| 2 9.8 | 80 | | | | ——+————+————
+————+————+————+————————————————————— 1 | | | | | | |
2 | | | | | | |*Tuesday, September 17, 1816.* 3 | | | | | | | 4 | | | | | |The wind continued at
NE, with 5 | | | | | |a moderate breeze. At 4 there 6 | | | | | |was a slight shower of rain
7 | | | | | |but it cleared up again in a 8 |29 .79 | 81 | 82 |NE by E| | short time. | |-1/2|
| | | 9 | | | | | | 10 |29 .82 | | | | | 11 | | | | | | Noon.|29 .82 | 83 | 82 | E by N |
| | ——+————+————+————+————+————+————+ 1 | | | | | | 2 |29 .78 | |
| Moored in |After noon the wind shifted 3 | | | | | Napakiang |to the Eastward: squally with
4 |29 .77 | 82 | 82 | | harbour. |showers of rain. 5 | | | | | 6 |29 .78 | | | | 7 | | | | | |
8 |29 .80 | 81 | 82 |ESE | 9 | | | | | 10 | | | | |Midnight, clear: moderate 11 | | | | |
|weather. Mid.|29 .78 | 81 | 82 |E by N | | ——+————+————+————+————+————+
+————————+————————————————— 1 | | | | | | *Wednesday, September 18,*
1816. 2 | | | ENE | | | 3 | | | | |To-day the wind has been at NNE. 4 | | | | | | | 5 |
| | | | | | 6 | | | | | |After 4 A.M. we had several 7 | | | | | |showers of rain. 8 |29 .72 |
80 | 82 |NE by E| | | |-1/2 | | | 9 | | | | | | 10 |29 .75 | | | | | 11 | | | |
|Towards noon the breeze Noon.|29 .75 | 82 | 82 | ENE | | |freshened. | | |-1/2 | | | —
——+————+————+————+————+————————————————+ 1 | | | | | 2 |29 .70 | | | |
Napakiang | 3 | | | | | harbour. | 4 |29 .72 | 82 | 82 |NE by E| | | |-1/2 | | | 5 | | | | |
| 6 |29 .74 | | | | 7 | | | | | | 8 | | 82 |82 | NE | 9 | | | | |At night squally, with rain.
10 | | | | | | 11 | | | | | | Mid. |29 .72 | | | NNE | | ——+————+————+————+——
——+————+————————————————————— 1 | | | | | | 2 | | | | |
Thursday, September 19, 1816. 3						4						After midnight it continued to 5	
		|rain, with occasional squalls. 6						7						8 |29 .63	81 |82	NNE
|As the day advanced it cleared 9					|up. 10 |29 .62					11					
Noon.	29 .62	82	83				At noon quite moderate.		-1/2				——+————+————
+————+————————+————+————————+ 1					2 |29 .50				3				|In the
evening it looked very 4	29 .58	82	83	NE		black all round, and fell calm.			-1/2	
About 7 a breeze sprung up from 5						the Eastward, and it commenced 6	29 .56		
Calm		lightning. About 8 the wind 7					shifted to SSE, and freshened, 8	29 .54		
East		with squalls. 9					10	29 .54			SSE		Towards midnight heavy squalls, 11
				with rain: thunder and Mid.	29 .54					lightning. ——+————+————+————+
+————————+————————+————————+ 1							*Friday,*
September 20, 1816. 2						3					|After midnight the same 4					|squally
weather continued. As 5						the day advanced it cleared up. 6					7					
8	29 .60	80	83	SSE		In the afternoon it became		-1/2				squally, with slight
showers 9						of rain. Towards evening it 10						looked very black all round.
11 |29 .62					Noon.|29 .63	84	83	S by E			|-1/2 |-1/2			——+————
———+————+————————+————————+————+ 1						2					Napakiang	3		
	harbour.	4 |29 .63			SSE	5				|It seems probable that this 6 |29 .64			
is the breaking up of the 7					monsoon. We were so completely 8	29 .69	82	82	E
by S		sheltered by the land, that we			-1/2		did not feel the wind much; 9						but
it was evidently blowing 10					|hard outside. 11						Mid.|29 .69	81	82		
——+————+————+————+————+————+————————————————
———— 1 | | | | | | 2 | | | | | | |*Saturday, September 21, 1816.* 3 | | | | | | 4 |29 .68 | |

| | | |During the day the wind has 5 | | | | | | |been South-easterly, with 6 | | | | |
|occasional squalls and showers 7 | | | | | | |of rain, and lightning. 8 | 29 .69 | 80 | 82 | SE | |
| 9 | | | | | | |In the forenoon the wind 10 | 29 .70 | | | | | |hauled to the Eastward, and 11
| | | | | | |cleared up. Noon. | 29 .70 | 83 | 83 | E by S | | | |-1/2| | | | ——+———
+———+———+———+———+————————+ 1 | | | | | 2 | 29 .70 | | | ESE | 3 | | | |
| | 4 | 29 .70 | 83 | 83 | | | | |-1/2|-1/2| | | 5 | | | | | | | 6 | 29 .70 | | |E by S | 7 | | | |
| | 8 | 29 .70 | 81 | 82 | | | | |-1/2| | | | 9 | | | | | | |10 | | | | | |11 | | | | | | Mid. | 29
.70 | 80 | 82 | | | ——+————+————+————+————+————+————+————
————————————————— 1 | | | | | | | 2 | | | | | |*Sunday, September 22, 1816.* 3 | | | | | |
| 4 | | | | | | |After midnight squally, with 5 | | | | | | |rain and lightning. 6 | | | | | | | 7 |
| | | | | | 8 | 29 .70 | 81 | 82 | ENE | | | |About 7 the wind hauled to the 9 | | | | | | |ENE,
and cleared up, and 10 | 29 .70 | | | | | |continued fine all day. 11 | | | | | | | Noon. | 29 .70 |
83 | 82 | E by N | | | ——+————+————+————+————+————+————+ 1 | | | |
| | 2 | | | | | |Napakiang | 3 | | | | |harbour. | 4 | 29 .68 | 82 | 82 | ENE | 5 | | | | | |
6 | 29 .66 | | | | | 7 | | | | | | | 8 | 29 .66 | 81 | 82 | | | | |-1/2| | | 9 | | | | | |10 | | |
| | | 11 | | | | | | Mid. | 29 .66 | | | | | ——+————+————+————+————+————
+———————+————————————————— 1 | | | | | | |*Monday, September 23, 1816.* 2
| | | | | | 3 | | | | |To-day the wind has been about 4 | | | | | | |NE; squally at times,
with 5 | | | | | | |showers of rain, and every 6 | | | | | |appearance of approaching bad 7 |
| | | | |weather. 8 | 29 .62 | 80 | 82 |NE by E| | 9 | | | | | |10 | 29 .62 | | | | | |11
| | | | | | Noon. | 29 .62 | 81 | 82 | | | | ——+————+————+————+————+————
+————————+ 1 | | | | | | | 2 | 29 .60 | | | ENE | | | 3 | | | | | | | 4 | 29 .58 | 81 | 82 | |
| | | |-1/2|-1/2| | | 5 | | | | | |During all this day the 6 | 29 .50 | | | | |barometer
continued falling, 7 | | | | | | |in the evening it had reached 8 | 29 .50 | | |NE by N| |
|29.50. The wind in the early 9 | | | | | |part of the night hauled to 10 | | | | | | |NNE,
and towards morning to 11 | | | | | | |the Northward. Mid. | | | | | | | ——+————+——
—+————+————+————+—————————————— 1 | | | | |
|*Tuesday, September 24, 1816.* 2 | | | | NNE | | | 3 | | | | | | |In the night the wind has been 4
| | | |NE by N| | |about NNE. About 4 A.M. it 5 | | | | | |began to blow very fresh, with
6 | 29 .43 | | | | | |squalls. 7 | | | | | | | 8 | 29 .42 | | | | | 9 | | | | | | |10 | | | | |
|About noon the wind shifted 11 | | | | | | |to NNW, and increased in Noon. | 29 .40 | 81 |
81 | | | |-1/2| | | ——+————+————+————+————+————+————+————
—+ 1 | | | | | | 2 | 29 .40 | | | NNW | Napakiang |During the afternoon it blew 3 | | | | |
harbour. |hard, and gradually shifted to 4 | 29 .44 | 81 | 81 | | |the North-westward, with fresh
| | |-1/2| | |squalls of short duration. At 5 | 29 .50 | | | |3 30 P.M. the mercury began 6 | 29
.55 | | |NW by N| |to rise, and continued rising 7 | 29 .56 | | | | |very rapidly. 8 | 29 .63 | 79
| 81 | | | 9 | 29 .65 | | | |The weather at sunset assumed 10 | | | | |a very stormy
appearance. 11 | | | | | | Mid. | 29 .66 | 78 | 80 | NW | | | | |-1/2| | | ——+————+————+
——+————+————+————+————————————— 1 | | | | |
| 2 | | | | | |_Wednesday, September 25, 1816. 3 | | | | | | | 4 | | | | | |Shortly after
midnight it 5 | | | | | |cleared up and moderated. 6 | 29 .72 | | |NW by W| 7 | | | |
8 | 29 .80 | 78 | 80 | NW | | | 9 | | | | | | |10 | 29 .86 | | | | | |11 | | | | | | Noon. | 29
.86 | 79 | 80 | | | | ——+————+————+————+————+————+————+ 1 | | | | |
|During the day it has been 2 | 29 .84 | | | |blowing a steady moderate 3 | | | | |breeze
from the NW. 4 | 29 .84 | 78 | 80 |NW by W| | | |-1/2| | | 5 | | | | | | | 6 | 29 .86 | | |
NW | | 7 | | | | | | | 8 | 29 .92 | 77 | 79 | | | |-1/2|-1/2| | | 9 | | | | | |10 | | | |
|Midnight, moderate and cloudy. 11 | | | | | | Mid. | 29 .95 | 77 | 78 |NW by N| | ——+——
———+————+————+————+————+————————————————— 1 |
| | | | |*Thursday, September 26, 1816.* 2 | | | | | | 3 | | | | | | |The wind continued about
NNW 4 | | | | | |all day, blowing a moderate 5 | | | | | |breeze, with fine weather. 6 | 29
.96 | | |NNW | | | 7 | | | | | | | 8 | 29 .96 | 78 | 80 | | | 9 | | | | | |10 | 29 .99 | | |
| | 11 | | | | | | Noon. | 30 .00 | 79 | 81 |NW by W| | | | |-1/2| | | ——+————
-+————+————+————+————+ 2 | 30.00 | | | Napakiang | 3 | |
| | | harbour. | 4 | 29 .99 | 83 | 81 | |8 P.M. it fell calm. | | |-1/2| | 5 | | | | | | | 6 | 29
.99 | | | Calm | | 7 | | | | | 8 | 29 .99 | 79 | 81 | | 9 | | | | | |10 | | | | |Towards
midnight a light 11 | | | | |breeze sprung up from NNE. Mid. | 29 .99 | 79 | 80 | NNE | | |
| |-1/2| | ——+————+————+————+————+————+————————
————————————— 1 | | | | | | 2 | | | NNE | | |Friday, September 27, 1816. 3 | | | |
| | 4 | | | | | | |After midnight the wind died 5 | | | | | |away. 6 | 29 .99 | 70 | | Calm |
| | 7 | | | | | | 8 | 29 .99 | 76 | 81 | | 9 | | | | | |10 | 29 .99 | | | | |Towards
noon a breeze sprung 11 | 29 .99 | | | | |up from the Northward. Noon. | 29 .99 | 80 | 81 |
North | | | | | |-1/2| | | ——+————+————+————+————+————+————+ 1

87

| | | | | 2 |29 .98 | | | | | 3 | | | | | |In the afternoon it shifted to 4 |29 .96 | 79 | 80 | ENE | |ENE. | | |-1/2| | 5 | | | | | | 6 |29 .96 | | | | | 7 | | | | | | 8 |29 .94 | 78 | 80 | NE | 9 | | | | | | 10 | | | | | |Midnight, calm and cloudy 11 | | | | | | |weather. Mid.|29 .94 | 77 | 79 | Calm | | ————+————+————+————+————+————

———————————————— 1 | | | | | | |*Saturday, September 28, 1816.* 2 | | | | | | | 3 | | | | | |All the early part of the 4 | | | | | | |morning it was quite calm. 5 | | | | | | | 6 | | | | | | 7 | | | | | | | 8 |29 .90 | 76 | 79 | Calm | | | | |-1/2| | | | 9 | | | | | | 10 | | | | | |About 8 A.M. a breeze sprung 11 |29 .94 | | | | | |up about ESE; in the afternoon Noon.|29 .94 | 81 | 81 | | | |it hauled round to East. | |-1/2|-1/2| | | | ————+———————+————+————+————+————+————— + 1 | | | | | | 2 |29 .90 | | | |ESE | Napakiang | 3 | | | | |harbour. | 4 |29 .92 | 81 | 81 | | 5 | |-1/2| | | 6 |29 .90 | | | | 7 | | | | 8 |29 .90 | 80 | 81 | East | 9 | | |-1/2| | | 10 | | | | |Midnight, the breeze shifted 11 | | | | | |to NE, and was moderate. Mid.|29 .90 | 76 | 79 | NE | | ————+———————+————+———— +———————+————+————+————+———————————— 1 | | | | | | | 2 | | | | | |*Sunday, September 29, 1816.* 3 | | | | | | | 4 |29 .90 | 75 | 79 | NE | |During this day the wind 5 | | | | | |shifted occasionally from NE to 6 | | | | | |ENE, blowing a moderate breeze, 7 | | | | | |with fine clear weather. 8 |29 .90 | 80 | 81 | | | | 9 | | | | | 10 |29 .92 | | |ENE | | | 11 | | | | | | |Noon.|29 .92 | 82 | 81 | | | ———————+————+———————+————+———————+————+————————————+ 1 | | | | | | 2 |29 .94 | |NE by E| | 3 | | | | | | 4 |29 .94 | 81 | 81 | | | 5 | | | | | | 6 |29 .95 | | | |Towards night it became cloudy. 7 | | | | | | 8 |29 .95 | 80 | 80 | NE | | | | |-1/2| | 9 | | | | | | 10 | | | | | | 11 | | | | | | Mid.|29 .95 | 78 | 80 | | | ————+———————+————+————+————+———————+———————+————————— + ———————————————— 1 | | | | | | | 2 | | | |NE by E| | |*Monday, September 30, 1816.* 3 | | | | | | 4 | | | | | | |During the forenoon the wind 5 | | | | | |has been light from the NE. 6 |29 .96 | 79 | 80 | | | |-1/2| | 7 | | | | | 8 |29 .96 | | | 9 | | | | | |Towards noon it freshened up. 10 |29 .97 | | | | | 11 |29 .98 | | | | | Noon.|29 .98 | 82 | 81 | | | | ————+———————+————+————+———————+————+———————+———————+ 1 | | | |NE by N| | 2 |29 .91 | | | | Napkiang | 3 | | | | |harbour. | 4 |29 .96 | 81 | 81 | | | | |-1/2| | | 5 | | | | | | 6 |29 .95 | | | | 7 | | | | | | 8 |29 .95 | 80 | 80 | | | | | |-1/2| | 9 | | | | | 10 | | | | | | 11 | | | | | |Midnight, cloudy weather. Mid.| | | | | | — ————+———————+————+————+———————+————+———————+———————— — 1 | | | | | | 2 | | | | | |*Tuesday, October 1, 1816.* 3 | | | | | | 4 | | | | | |After midnight the wind drew 5 | | | | | |more to the Eastward, and the 6 |29 .95 | | | | |sky became very black all 7 | | | | | |round: squally, with rain at 8 |30 .02 | 79 | 80 | East | | |intervals. | |-1/2| | | | 9 | | | | | |We got under weigh at daylight, 10 |30 .07 | | | | | |and proceeded along shore to 11 | | | | |N | E |the Northward. Noon.|30 .07 | 80 | 80 | ESE | 26 .34| 127 .38 | | |-1/2| | | ————+———————+————+————+————+——— ————+ 1 |30 .00 | | | | 2 |29 .94 | | | |Sugar Loaf |The wind continued to the 3 | | | |Point. N .24° E.|Eastward. 4 |29 .94 | 79 | 80 |E by S | | | |-1/2|-1/2| | 5 | | | | | | 6 |29 .94 | | | | 7 | | | | 8 |29 .94 | 78 | 80 | | 9 | | | | 10 | | | | | 11 | | | | | Mid.|29 .92 | | | | ————+———————+————+————+———————+————+———————+————————— ———————————————— 1 | | | | | | |*Wednesday, October 2, 1816.* 2 | | | | | | | 3 | | | | | 4 |29 .91 | | | | |The whole of this day the wind 5 | | | | | |has been from the Eastward, 6 | | | | | |blowing a moderate breeze, 7 | | | | | |with fine weather. 8 |29 .91 | 78 | 80 |E by S | | 9 | | | | | | 10 |29 .94 | | | | | 11 |29 .96 | | | |N | E | Noon.|29 .96 | 79 | 80 | | 26 .25| 127 .38| ————+———————+————+———————+————+———————+————+———————— +———————+ 1 | | | | 2 |29 .92 | | | 3 | | | | 4 |29 .89 | 80 | 81 | East | |Towards night cloudy weather. 5 | | | | | | 6 |29 .88 | | | | 7 | | | | | 8 |29 .99 | 79 | 81 | | | | |-1/2| | 9 | | | | | 10 | | | | | 11 | | | | | Mid.|29 .90 | | | | ———— +————————+————+————+————+———————+————+————————— - 1 | | | | | | 2 | | | | | |*Thursday, October 3, 1816.* 3 | | | | | 4 | | | | |During the night the wind 5 | | | | |shifted to NE by E. 6 | | | | | 7 | | | | |Towards noon it shifted to 8 |29 .87 | 78 | 81 |NE by E| |East, and in the evening to 9 | | | |ENE again. 10 |29 .87 | | | | 11 | | | | | Noon.|29 .87 | 81 | 81 |E by S | | | |-1/2| | ————+———————+————+—— ——+————+————————+————+————————— + 1 | | | | | 2 | | | |East | Napaking | 3 | | | | |harbour. | 4 |20 .86 | 80 | 81 | | 5 | | | | | | 6 | | | |ENE | 7 | | | | | 8 |29 .86 | 78 | 81 | | 9 | | | | | 10 | | | | | 11 | | | | | Mid.|29 .86 | 78 | 80 |E by N | | — ———+————————+————+————+————+———————+————+————————— ——— 1 | | | | | |*Friday, October 4, 1816.* 2 | | | | | | 3 | | | | | | 4 | | | | | |To-day we had a light breeze 5 | | | | | |from the NE, until the 6 | | | | | |afternoon, when it shifted to 7 | | | | | |SE by E, but only remained a 8 |29 .87 | 78 | 81 | NE | |short time, coming back to NE 9 | | | | | |again, where it continued until 10 | | | | | |near midnight,

88

when it fell 11 | | | | | |calm. Noon.|29.87 | 79 | 84 | | | | | | |-1/2| | | | ——+——
—+——+————+————+—+——————+ 1 | | | | | | 2 |29 .86 | | | ENE |
Napakiang | 3 | | | | | |harbour. | 4 |29 .86 | 79 | 80 |SE by E| | | | |-1/2| | | 5 | | | | |
| 6 |29 .85 | | | | | | 7 | | | | | | 8 |29 .85 | 79 | 80 | NE | | 9 | | | | | | 10 | | | | | | 11 |
| | | | | Mid.|29 .85 | | | | | ——+————+—+——+————+
+————————————————————— 1 | | | | | |*Saturday, October 5, 1816.* 2 | | | | | | |
3 | | | | | | | 4 | | | | | |In the morning a breeze sprung 5 | | | | | |up from the
Eastward, where it 6 | | | | | | |remained until noon; then 7 | | | | | | |shifted to NE, and
continued 8 |29 .86 | 78 | 80 | E by N| | |to blow from that quarter all | | | -1/2| | | |the
rest of the day. 9 | | | | | | | 10 |29 .87 | | | | | | 11 |29 .87 | | | | | | Noon.|29 .85 | 81 |
81 |NE by E| | | | ——+————+——+——————+————+ 1 | | | | | |
2 |29 .84 | | | | | 3 | | | | | | 4 |29 .82 | 81 | 81 | N by E| | | | -1/2| | | 5 | | | | | | 6
|29 .82 | | | NE | | 7 | | | | | | 8 |29 .83 | 79 | | 9 | | | | | | 10 | | | | | | 11 | | |
| | | Mid.|29 .83 | 78 | 80 | | | | | | -1/2| | | ——+————+——+——+——+
-+————+———————————————— 1 | | | | | | | 2 | | | | | | |*Sunday,*
October 6, 1816. 3 | | | | | | | 4 | | | | | |The early part of the day from 5 | | | | | | |wind
has been moderate from the 6 | | | | | | |NE. 7 | | | | | | | 8 |29 .83 | 78 | 80 |NE by N|
| | | | -1/2|-1/2| | | 9 | | | | | | 10 |29 .84 | | | | | | 11 | | | | | |About noon the
wind shifted to Noon.|29 .84 | 80 | 81 | North | | |the Northward. ——+————+——+
+————+————————+——————+ 1 | | | | | | 2 | | | | | Napakiang | 3 | | | | |
harbour. | 4 |29 .83 | | | | |At night it came back to NE, 5 | | | | | |with rain. 6 | | | | | | 7
| | | | | | 8 |29 .83 | 79 | 80 | NE | | | | -1/2|-1/2| | 9 | | | | | | 10 | | | | | | 11 | | |
| | | Mid. |29 .86 | | | NNE | | ——+————+——+——+————+——+
—+—————————————————————— 1 | | | | | | | 2 | | | |NE by E| | |*Monday,*
October 7, 1816. 3 | | | | | | | 4 | | | | | | 5 | | | | | |After midnight the wind 6 | | | |
| |continued at NE by E, with 7 | | | | | |showers of rain. 8 |29 .80 | 78 | 80 | North | | |
9 | | | | | | 10 | | | | | | 11 |29 .94 | | | | |Noon.|29 .95 | 79 | 80 |N by E | | | |
|-1/2|-1/2| | | ——+————+——+——+————+——————+ 1 | | | | |
2 |29 .92 | | | N by E| |At 4 A.M. the wind came to 3 | | | | |north, and the weather
cleared 4 |29 .93 | 79 | 80 | | |up: it blew a fresh breeze from 5 | | | | |that quarter all day.
6 | | | | | | 7 | | | | | | 8 |29 .93 | 78 | 80 | | | | -1/2| | | 9 | | | | |Towards
midnight it moderated. 10 | | | | | | 11 | | | | | | Mid.|29 .96 | 78 | 79 | | | | -1/2|-1/2|
| | ——+————+——+——+————+—————+
————————— 1 | | | | | |*Tuesday, October 8, 1816.* 2 | | | | | | | 3 | | | | | | | 4 | | | |
|To-day we have had a moderate 5 | | | | | |breeze at NE by N. 6 | | | | | | 7 | | | | |
| 8 |30 .00 | 78 | 79 |NE by N| | |Squally at times. | | | -1/2| | | 9 | | | | | | 10 |30 .02
| | | | | | 11 | | | | | | Noon.|30 .02 | 78 | 79 | NNE | | | | | -1/2| | | ——+———
—+——+————+————+——————+ 1 | | | | | | 2 |30 .00 | | | | Napakiang |
3 | | | | harbour. | 4 |30 .00 | 78 | 79 |NE by N| | | | -1/2| | | 5 | | | | | |Towards
midnight fine clear 6 | | | | | |weather. 7 | | | | | | 8 |30 .00 | 76 | 78 | | | 9 | | | | | | 10
| | | | | | 11 | | | | | | Mid. |30 00 | 75 | 78 | | | ——+————+——+——+
+————+————+———————————————— 1 | | | | | | | 2 | | | | |
|*Wednesday, October 9, 1816.* 3 | | | | | | | 4 | | | | | |During the morning a moderate 5 | |
| | | |breeze from NE by E. 6 |30 .00 | | |NE by E| | | 7 | | | | | |About 6 A.M. we
got underweigh, 8 |30 .04 | 75 | 78 | | | |and stood to the Northward. | | | -1/2| | | 9 | | |
| | | | 10 |30 .10 | | | ENE | | 11 |30 .10 | | | | N | E | Noon.|30 .10 | 77 | 78 | | 26
.34| 127 .26 | | | -1/2| | | ——+————+——+——————+————+
1 | | | | | | 2 |30 .06 | | | | | 3 | | | | |In the afternoon the wind 4 |30 .00 | 78 | 78 |
East | |shifted to the Eastward, and 5 | | | | |continued so the remainder of 6 |30 .06 | | |
| |the day. 7 | | | | | | 8 |30 .13 | 77 | 78 | E by S| | 9 | | | | | |At night, cloudy weather.
10 | | | | | | 11 | | | | | | Mid.| | | | | | ——+————+——+——+————+——+
+————+————————————————— 1 | | | | | | |*Thursday, October 10, 1816.* 2
| | | | | | | 3 | | | | | | 4 | | | | | | 5 | | | | | |During this day the wind has 6 |30
.00 | | | |been moderate from the 7 | | | | | |Eastward. 8 |30 .00 | 77 | 79 | ESE | |
| |-1/2| | | 9 | | | | | | 10 |30 .01 | | | | | | 11 | | | | East | N | E | Noon.|30 .01 |
78 | 79 | E by N| 26 .50| 127 .50| ——+————+——+————+————+——+
—+ 1 | | | | | 2 |29 .98 | | | ENE | Off the Great | 3 | | | | |Loo-choo Island.| 4 |29
.98 | 79 | 79 | | | | | -1/2| | 5 | | | | | | 6 |29 .98 | | | NE | | 7 | | | | |At night
fine clear weather. 8 |29 .98 | | | | | 9 | | | | | | 10 | | | | | | 11 | | | | | | Mid.|29 .96 |
78 | 79 | | | ——+————+——+——+————+——+
————————— 1 | | | | | | 2 | | | NE | | |*Friday, October 11, 1816.* 3 | | | | | | | 4
| | | | | | 5 | | | | | |After midnight the wind 6 |29 .98 | | | | | |shifted from NE to

89

SE, with a 7 | | | | | |light air. 8 |29 .97 | 78 | 79 | SE | | | 9 | | | | | | | 10 |29 .97 | | |
| | | |Ten A.M. it fell calm. 11 | | | | | | N | E | Noon.|29 .97 | 80 | 80 | | 26 .42| 127 .53| —
——+———————+———————+————+———————+———————+———————+1 | | | | | | 2 |29 .96 | | | Off
Port | 3 | | | | | |Melville. | 4 |29 .96 | 80 | 80 | West | | 5 | | | | |In the afternoon a
breeze 6 | 29 .96 | | | N by E| |sprung up from the Westward; 7 | | | | | |about 8 it looked
very dark all 8 | 29 .94 | | | NNE | |round, and shortly afterwards 9 | | | | | |began to blow
fresh from N by 10 | | | | | |E, and continued so all night. 11 | 30 .00 | | | | | Mid.| | | | | |
———————+———————+————+————+———————+———————+———————+

——————— 1 | | | | | | |Saturday, October 12, 1816. 2 | | | |NE by E| | 3 | | | | NE | |
|During the night the wind came 4 | | | | | | |to NE with a fresh breeze, and 5 | | | | |
|rain at intervals. 6 | 30 .30 | | | | | | 7 | | | | | | 8 | 30 .26 | 76 | 79 | | | 9 | | | | | |
10 | 30 .22 | | | | | | 11 | 30 .22 | | | N | E | Noon.| 30 .22 | 76 | 79 | |25 .33 |127 .50 |
———————+———————+————+————+———————+———————+———————+1 | | | | | | 2 | 30 .20 | | |
|Off Loo-choo. | 3 | | | | | |In the afternoon a swell got up 4 | 30 .20 | 76 | 79 | ENE |
| from the NE; the wind 5 | | | | | |moderated, and drew round to 6 | 30 .30 | | | | |ENE. 7
| | | | | | 8 | 30 .34 | 76 | 79 | | | 9 | | | | | |Midnight, fresh breezes and 10 | | | | |
|cloudy. 11 | | | | | | Mid.| 30 .20 | | | | | ———————+———————+————+————+———————+
+————+———————+————————————————— 1 | | | | ENE | | | 2 | | | | | | |Sunday,
October 13, 1816. 3 | | | | | | | 4 | | | | | |After midnight it became quite 5 | | | | | |
|moderate, with rain at times. 6 | 30 .10 | | | | | | 7 | | | | | | 8 | 30 .06 | 75 | 78 | | | | 9
| | | | | | 10 | 30 .04 | | | | | |In the forenoon it fell calm. 11 | | | | | | N | E | Noon.| 30
.04 | 75 | 78 | Calm | 27 .00 |128 .03 | | |-1/2| | | | ———————+———————+————+————+
-+———————+———————+1 | | | | | | 2 | 30 .00 | | | | | 3 | | | | | | |During the afternoon a
breeze 4 | 30 .00 | 75 | 78 | NE | |sprung up at NE. 5 | | | -1/2| | 5 | | | | | 6 | 30 .00 |
| | | | 7 | | | | |Towards midnight it freshened 8 | 30 .02 | 75 | 78 |NE by E|
|considerably. 9 | | | | | 10 | | | | | | 11 | | | | | | Mid.| 30 .02 | | | | | ———+———————
+————+————+———————+————+———————————————————————— 1 | | | |
| | | 2 | | | |NE by N| | |Monday, October 14, 1816. 3 | | | | | | | 4 | | | | | | |After
midnight the wind 5 | | | | | | |moderated. 6 | | | | | | | 7 | | | | | | | 8 | 30 .04 | 75 | 79
| | | |About 8 A.M. it fell nearly | | |-1/2| | | |calm, but shortly after it 9 | | | | | |
|freshened at NNE. 10 | 30 .02 | | | | | | 11 | | | | | N | E | Noon.| 30 .00 | 75 | 79 | NNE
|26 .36 |127 .56 | ———————+———————+————+————+———————+———————+1 | | | |
2 | 29 .94 | | | North |Off Loo-choo. | 3 | | | | | | 4 | 29 .97 | 75 | 79 | NNW | | | -1/2|
| | | 5 | | | | |Towards midnight the wind 6 | 29 .98 | | | | |shifted to NNW, and
continued 7 | | | | | |to blow fresh. 8 | 30 .02 | 75 | 79 | N by W| | 9 | | | | | | 10 | | | |
| 11 | | | | | | Mid.| 30 .18 | | | NNW | | ———————+———————+————+————+———————
+————+———————————————————— 1 | | | | | | | 2 | | | | | | |Tuesday,
October 15, 1816. 3 | | | | | | 4 | | | | | |During this day the wind has 5 | | | | | |been
from the N by W, blowing 6 | | | | | |a fresh breeze, with occasional 7 | | | | | |squalls. 8
|30 .10 | | 78 |N by W| | | 9 | | | | | 10 | 30 .10 | | | | | | 11 | | | | | N | E |
Noon.|30 .10 | 74 | 78 | North |26 .02 |127 .35 | | |-1/2| | | | ———————+———————+————+
——+———————+———————+1 | | | | | | 2 | 30 .08 | | | | | 3 | | | | | | 4 | 30 .08 |
74 | 78 | | |At midnight it moderated. | |-1/2| | | 5 | | | | North | | 6 | 30 .08 | | | | | | 7
| | | | | | 8 | 30 .10 | 74 |79 | | | | -1/2| | | 9 | | | | | | 10 | | | | | | 11 | | | | | | |
Mid.| | | | | | ———————+———————+————+————+———————+
——————— 1 | | | | | | |Wednesday, October 16, 1816. 2 | | | | | | 3 | | | | | |
4 | | | | | |During the night the wind drew 6 | | | | | |round to N by E, with a 7 | | | | |
| |moderate breeze. About 7 A.M. 8 | 30 .20 | 73 | 77 |N by E| | |we weighed and stood to
the 9 | | | | | |NW, shortly after the breeze 10 | 30 .20 | | | | |freshened, with squalls; at
11 | | | | | N | E |2 P.M. anchored in Napakiang Noon.| 30 .10 | 74 | 77 | |26 .11 |127 .30
|harbour. | | |-1/2| | | ———————+———————+————+————+———————+———————+1 |
| | | | 2 | 30 .00 | | | |Off Loo-choo. | 3 | | | | | 4 | 30 .00 | 74 | 77 | | 5 | | | | |
6 | 30 .00 | | | |Towards midnight the breeze 7 | | | | |freshened. 8 | 30 .00 | 74 | 77 | N
by W| | 9 | | | | | 10 | | | | | | 11 | | | | | | Mid.| | | | | | ———————+————+————+
——+———————+————+———————+————————————————————— 1 | | | | | | 2 | |
| | | | |Thursday, October 17, 1816. 3 | | | | | | | 4 | | | | | | | 5 | | | | | |The whole of
this day we have 6 | | | | | |had a breeze from the NNE, with 7 | | | | | |fine clear
weather. 8 | 30 .00 | 71 | 76 | NNE | | | 9 | | | | | | | 10 | 30 .00 | | | | | | 11 | | | | | | |
Noon.| 30 .00 | 75 | 77 | | | | ———————+———————+————+————+———————+
1 | | | | | | 2 | 30 .00 | | | |NE by N| Napakiang | 3 | | | | |harbour. | 4 | 30 .00 | 75 | 77 |
| 5 | | | | | 6 | 30 .01 | | | | | 7 | | | | | | 8 | 30 .02 | 75 | 76 | | | | |-1/2| | 9 | |
| | | 10 | | | | | 11 | | | | | | Mid.| 30 .00 | | | | | ———————+————+————+————+

90

—+———+———+————————————————— 1 | | | | | | |Friday, October
18, 1816. 2 | | | | | | | 3 | | | | | |The wind continued about NE by 4 | | | | | |N. 5 | |
| | | | | 6 | | | | | | 7 | | | | | | 8 |30 .00 | 73 | 76 |NE by N| | | | |-1/2| | | | | 9 |
| | | | | 10 |30 .00 | | E by N | | 11 | | | | | | Noon.|30 .02 | 74 | 75 | | |
|Towards noon it came to the | | |-1/2| | | |eastward with a moderate ———+———+————
+———+———+———+————+———+breeze. 1 | | | | | | 2 |30 .02 | | | | Moored in | 3 |
| | | | Napakiang | 4 | | | | | harbour. | 5 | | | | | 6 |30 .00 | | |NE by E| |At night it
shifted to the NE. 7 | | | | | | 8 |30 .00 | 71 | 75 | NE | | 9 | | | | | | 10 | | | | | 11 | |
| | | | Mid.| | | | | | ——+———+———+———+———+———+———+
——————————————————— 1 | | | | NE | | | 2 | | | | | | |Saturday, October 19, 1816. 3 |
| | | | | 4 | | | | | 5 | | | | | | 6 | | | | | | 7 | | | | | | 8 |29 .98 | | | | |
|During all this day the wind 9 | | | | | |has been moderate and steady 10 | | | | | | |at
NE, with fine clear weather. 11 | | | | | | | Noon.|29 .98 |76 | 76 | | | | ——+———+———
—+———+———+———+———+ 1 | | | | NE | 2 | | | | | | 3 | | | | | | 4 |29
.98 |73 | 75 | | | 5 | | | | | | 6 |29 .98 | | | | | 7 | | | | | | 8 |29 .98 |73 | 75 | | | 9 | | |
| | | 10 | | | | | | 11 | | | | | Mid.| | | | | ——+———+———+———+———+—
——+———+———+ 1 | | | | | | |Sunday, October 20,
1816. 2 | | | | | | 3 | | | | | | 4 | | | | | | 5 | | | | | | 6 | | | | | | 7 | | | | | |
| 8 |29 .98 | 72 | 75 | NE | | |The breeze still continues at | | | | | | 9 | | | | | | |NE,
with the same fine clear 10 |29 .98 | | | | |weather as yesterday. 11 | | | | | | | Noon.|29
.98 | 73 | 75 | | | | |-1/2|-1/2| | | | ——+———+———+———+———+———+
———+ 1 | | | | | | 2 |29 .98 | | | | Napakiang | 3 | | | | | harbour. | 4 |29 .98 | 73 |75
| | | 5 | | | | | | 6 |29 .98 | | | | | 7 | | | | | | 8 |29 .98 | 72 |75 |NE by N| | |-1/2| |
| | 9 | | | | | | 10 | | | | | | 11 | | | | | Mid.| | | | | ——+———+———+———+—
——+———+ 1 | | | | | | 2 | | | |
| |Monday, October 21, 1816. 3 | | | | | | 4 | | | | | |After midnight the wind 5 | | | | | |
|shifted to the N by E, with a 6 | | | | | |moderate breeze. 7 | | | | | | 8 |30 .00 | 73 |
75 |N by E | 9 | | | | | | 10 |30 .00 | | | | | 11 | | | | | | Noon.|30 .00 | 74 | 75
| | | ——+———+———+———+———+———+———+ 1 | | | | | 2 | | | | |
3 | | | | | 4 |30 .00 | 73 |75 | | 5 | | | | | | 6 |30 .00 | | | | | 7 | | | | |Towards
night it fell almost 8 |30 .04 | 72 | 74 | NNE | |calm. | | |-1/2| | 9 | | | | | | 10 | | | |
| 11 | | | | | | Mid.| | | | | ——+———+———+———+———+———+
+———————————————————— 1 | | | | NNE | | | |Tuesday, October 22, 1816. 2 | | | |
| | | 3 | | | | | |After midnight the breeze 4 | | | | | |freshened up at NNE, and 5 | | |
| | | |continued so all day, with 6 | | | | | |fine clear weather. 7 | | | | | | 8 |30 .06 | 72
| 74 | | | | | |-1/2| | | 9 | | | | | | 10 | | | | | | 11 |30 .06 | | | | | Noon.|30
.06 | 73 | 75 |NE by N| | | |-1/2| | | | ——+———+———+———+———+———+
-+——————+ 1 | | | | | 2 |30 .00 | | | Napakiang | 3 | | | | | harbour. | 4 |30 .08 | 73
| 74 | | | | |-1/2| | 5 | | | | | 6 |30 .08 | | | | | 7 | | | | | | 8 |30 .08 | 72 | 74 | |
| | |-1/2| | | 9 | | | | | | 10 | | | | | | 11 | | | | | Mid.| | | | | ——+———+———
—+———+———+———+ 1 | | | |NE
by N| | | 2 | | | | | | |Wednesday, October 23, 1816. 3 | | | | | | | 4 | | | | | | |The wind
continued steady at 5 | | | | | |NNE, with the same fine weather 6 | | | | | | |as yesterday.
7 | | | | | | 8 |30 .08 | 73 |75 | NNE | | | 9 | | | | | | | 10 |30 .10 | | | | | | 11 | | | |
| | | | Noon.|30 .10 | 74 |75 | | | | ——+———+———+———+———+———+
—+ 1 | | | | | 2 |30 .10 | | | | 3 | | | | | 4 |30 .10 | 73 |74 |N by E | | 5 | | | | | |
6 |30 .12 | | | | | 7 | | | | | | 8 |30 .12 | 72 | 73 | | | 7 | | |-1/2| | 9 | | | | | 10 | |
| | | | 11 | | | | | Mid.| | | | | ——+———+———+———+———+———+
———+ 1 | | | | | | |Thursday, October 24, 1816. 2 | | | |
| | 3 | | | | | |After midnight we had a 4 | | | | | |moderate breeze at NNE. 5 | | | |
| | | 6 | | | | | | 7 | | | | | | 8 |30 .04 | | |N by E | | 9 | | | | | |Towards noon it
shifted to 10 | | | | | | |north, and freshened up in 11 | | | | | |that quarter. Noon.|30 .00
| 72 | 75 | | | ——+———+———+———+———+———+———+ 1 | | | | | | 2
|29 .99 | | |North | Napakiang | 3 | | | | harbour. |After noon we had a slight 4 |29 .98 |
| | | |shower of rain, but soon after 5 | | | | | |it cleared up. 6 |29 .98 | 72 | 74 | | | |-
1/2| | 7 | | | | | 8 | | | | | 9 | | | | | | 10 | | | | | | 11 | | | | | | Mid.| | | | | |
——+———+———+———+———+———+———+ 1 | | | | | | 2 | | | | | | |North | | |Friday, October 25, 1816. 3 | | | | | | 4 | | | |
| |At daylight the breeze 5 | | | | | |freshened. 6 |30 .05 | | | | | 7 | | | | | | 8 |30
.08 | 74 | 75 | | | | | | | | 9 | | | | | |At 9 the weather became 10 |30 .00 | | | | |
|squally, with a shower of rain. 11 | | | | | | | Noon.|30 .00 | | | | | ——+———+———
+———+———+———+ 1 | | | | | | 2 |30 .00 | | | NNW | | 3 | | | | |

91

|After noon the wind hauled 4 |30 .00 | 74 | 74 | | |to NNW, and continued to blow | |-
1/2 |-1/2 | | |a fresh breeze all day. 5 | | | | | | 6 | | | | | | 7 | | | | | 8 |29 .96 | 73 | 74
| | | 9 | | | | | | 10 | | | | | | 11 | | | | | | Mid.| | | | | ——+———+———+——
+———+———+———+ | | | | | | | 1 | | | | NNW | |
|*Saturday, October 26, 1816.* 2 | | | | | | 3 | | | | | |During this day the wind has 4 | | | |
| | |been at north, blowing a fresh 5 | | | | | |breeze, with occasional 6 | | | | | | |squalls.
7 | | | | | | 8 |30 .04 | 74 | 74 | North | | | | |-1/2 | | | 9 | | | | | | 10 | | | |
| 11 | | | | | | | Noon.|30 .00 | 74 |75 | | | ——+———+——+———+———+———
———+———+ 1 | | | | | | 2 |29 .99 | | | | Napakiang | 3 | | | | | harbour. | 4 |29 .98 |
| 74 | | | 5 | | | | | |Towards midnight it moderated. 6 |29 .98 | | | | | 7 | | | | | 8 | | |
74 | | | 9 | | | | | | 10 | | | | | | 11 | | | | | | Mid.| | | | | ——+———+——
———+———+ 1 | | | | | | | 2 | |
| | Calm | | |*Sunday, October 27, 1816.* 3 | | | | | | 4 | | | | | |After midnight it fell calm.
5 | | | | | | 6 |30 .05 | | | | | 7 | | | | | | 8 |30 .08 | 68 |73 | NNE | | | 9 | | | |
| |About 9 A.M. a breeze sprung up 10 |30 .00 | | | | | |from NNE. Weighed and stood out
11 | | | | | | |of the harbour. Noon.|30 .00 | 70 | 74 |N by E | | | ——+———+———+
+———+———+———+———+ 1 | | | | | 2 |30 .00 | | | | 3 | | | | | 4 |30 .00
| 71 |74 | NNE | | 5 | | | | | | 6 | | | | | | 7 | | | | | 8 |29 .96 | 72 |74 | | |Towards
night the breeze 9 | | | | | |freshened. 10 | | | | | 11 | | | | | | Mid.| | | | | ——+—
———+———+———+———+———+———+ 1 |
———+———+———+ | | | NNW | | |*Monday, October 28, 1816.* 2 | | | | | | 3 | | | | | |During all this day the
wind 4 | | | | | | |has been at NNE, blowing a 5 | | | | | |steady fresh breeze. 6 | | | | |
| 7 | | | | | | 8 |30 .10 | 72 | 77 | North | | | |-1/2 | | | | 9 | | | | | | 10 |30 .08 |
| | | | 11 | | | | | N | E | Noon.| | | | |24 .41 |126 . 00| ——+———+———+
+———+———+———+ 1 | | | | | 2 |29 .99 | | | | Japan Sea. | 3 | | | | | 4
|29 .98 |74 | 79 | | 5 | | | | | 6 |30 .00 | | | 7 | | | |Towards night it shifted to
NE. 8 |30 .05 | 74 | 79 | | | 9 | |-1/2 | | | | | | | | 10 | | | | | | 11 | | | | | Mid. | |
			——+———+———+———+———+———+———+ 1						2				Calm			*Tuesday, October 29, 1816.* 3						4
				The wind has been from the NE, 5						and a swell rising from that 6			
		quarter. 7						8	30 .02	76	79	NNE				-1/2				9				
10	30 .02					11					N	E	Noon.	30 .02	76	79	N by E	23 .24	124 .01
	-1/2				——+———+———+———+———+ 1					2
29 .95				3				4	29 .99	76	79	NNE		5				6	30 .00			
Towards night the sky 7						assumed a threatening 8	30 .00	76	79			appearance.
9					10					11					Mid.					——+———+———+———+———
———+———+———+ 1			NNW	
Wednesday, October 30, 1816. 2						3						During the night the wind 4			
	shifted to the Northward, and 5						continued to blow fresh, with 6						a
heavy swell. Saw the islands 7						of Botel-Tobago-Zima, and 8	30 .50	72	77
North			Formosa.		-1/2			9					10	30 .30					11	30 .00				N
E	Noon.	29 .92			24 .41	126 .00	——+———+———+———+———+
+———+ 1					2	30 .50				3					4	30 .85	74	79			5			
6	31 .10				7					Towards night it shifted to NE. 8	31 .00	74	79					-
1/2			9					10					11					Mid.					——+———+———
+———+———+———+ 1				
2					*Thursday, October 31, 1816.* 3					4					Passed Formosa, and
entered 5						the China sea. 6						7						8					9			
10					11					Noon.					——+———+———+———+
+———+———+ 1					2					3					4					5					6
		7					8					9					10					11					Mid.|				—
——+———+———+———+———+———+———+
———

**ABSTRACT OF THE LYRA'S VOYAGE, FROM LEAVING ENGLAND TILL
HER RETURN;**
SHEWING
THE DISTANCE BETWEEN THE DIFFERENT PLACES AT WHICH SHE
TOUCHED, AND THE TIME TAKEN IN PERFORMING EACH PASSAGE.
ABSTRACT
OF THE
VOYAGES OF HIS MAJESTY'S SHIP LYRA,
In 1816 and 1817.

The Lyra, in the short space of twenty months, viz. from the 9th of February 1816, to the 14th of October 1817, visited Madeira, the Cape, Java, Macao, the Yellow Sea, the West Coast of Corea, the Great Loo-choo Island, Canton, Manilla, Prince of Wales's Island, Calcutta, Madras, the Mauritius, and St. Helena; having run, in direct courses, a distance of 11,940 nautic leagues, or 41,490 statute miles.

An abstract of the various passages, from place to place, during this voyage, illustrated by brief remarks on the particular circumstances of each, will probably be considered interesting.
* * * * *

[Sidenote: England to Madeira and Cape, 2520 leagues.]
1.
Sailed through the Needles passage on the 9th of February, 1816.
Arrived at Madeira, 18th of February 9 days
Crossed the equator in longitude 25° 20' west, 4th March 15
Reached the Cape of Good Hope, 14th April 41

———

From England to the Cape, in 9 weeks, 2 days, or 65 days.

This is not a very good passage, considering that we carried the north-east trade wind to the latitude of 4° north, and longitude 23° west, where we got the south-east trade, without any interval of calms.
* * * * *

2.
[Sidenote: Cape to Java, 1800 leagues.]
Sailed from the Cape on the 26th April 1816.
Arrived at Anjier Point, Java, 7th June. 42 days. —— Six weeks.
After leaving the Cape we had strong westerly winds, with which we ran the longitude down, in the parallel of 38° and 39° south, till in longitude 57° east, where the weather being very stormy, we hauled to the north-east till in 35° south latitude, and then ran east till in 90° east, when we steered to the east-north-east, and crossed the tropic in 102° east, which was probably too far west. The south-east trade hung far to the eastward, and made it difficult to fetch Java Head, which had we not succeeded in doing at first, might have caused considerable delay, as the wind still blew out of the Straits of Sunda.
* * * * *

3.
[Sidenote: Java to China, 600 leagues.]
Sailed from Anjier Point, Java, on the 12th June, 1816.
Reached Gaspar Straits on the 17th June 1816 5 days.
Arrived off Macao, 8th July 21

———

From Java to Macao in 3 weeks 5 days, or 26 days.

This passage was unusually bad, it being nearly a week before we reached Gaspar Straits, an ordinary run of one day: in the south part of the China sea the south-west monsoon was very light. An American brig, which sailed only one day before us from Anjier Point, carried the breeze along with her, and reached Macao twelve days before us.
* * * * *

4.
[Sidenote: Ladrone Islands to the Yellow Sea, 520 leagues.]
Sailed from the Ladrone Islands off Macao, on the 13th July 1816.
Rounded the promontory of Shantung and entered the
Yellow Sea, 25th July 12 days.
From thence to the anchorage off the Pei-ho
or Pekin River, 27th July 2

———

Macao to Pekin River, in 2 weeks, or 14 days.

This voyage can be compared only with that of the Lion on the occasion of the former embassy. The Lion was nearly three weeks, exclusive of the time at anchor at Chusan. We had fine weather and steady south-west winds, with very heavy dews at night. When nearly abreast of the south point of Corea, the wind became variable from the south-east and southward. In the Yellow Sea we had easterly winds and no fogs.
* * * * *

5.
[Sidenote: Pei-ho to Oei-hai-oei in the Yellow Sea, 90 leagues.]

Sailed from the anchorage off the Pei-ho on the 11th August, 1816.

Arrived at Cheatow Bay, after having coasted from the anchorage along the south side of the Gulf of Pe-che-lee, 22d August 11 days.

From thence to the harbour of Oei-hai-oei, 23d August 1

———

From Pekin River to harbour of Oei-hai-oei, 1 week 5 days, or 12 days.

In this cruise round the Gulf of Pe-che-lee we had constant easterly winds, which obliged us to tide the whole way. It blew a gale of wind on the 19th from the north-east, with a high short sea. With this exception, and a fresh breeze on the 3d and 6th, the weather was uniformly fine during our stay in the Yellow Sea, and we never experienced any fogs.

* * * * *

6.

[Sidenote: Yellow Sea to Corea, 40 leagues.]

Sailed from Oei-hai-oei, in China, on the 29th August, 1816.

Made the islands off the coast of Corea, 1st September 3 days.

Running along the coast of Corea till the 10th September 9

———

12 days.

On the coast of Corea the winds were mostly from the northward, and the weather uniformly fine, with heavy dews at night.

* * * * *

7.

[Sidenote: Corea to Loo-choo, 240 leagues.]

From the south-west end of Corea to the Great Loo-choo Island, on the 14th September, 1816, 4 days.

From Corea to the Great Loo-choo Island we had northeasterly and northerly winds, with one gale from the northward.

* * * * *

8.

[Sidenote: Loo-choo to China, 320 leagues.]

From Loo-choo to Lintin, off Canton.

27th October to the 2d November, 1816 6 days.

As the north-east monsoon was blowing fresh, this quick passage was to be expected.

* * * * *

9.

[Sidenote: China to Manilla, 200 leagues.]

From Lemma Islands to Manilla. 2d February to the 5th February, 1817 3 days.

A good passage for this season of the year.

* * * * *

10.

[Sidenote: Manilla to Penang, 600 leagues.]

From Manilla to Prince of Wales's Island. 21st February to 8th March, 1817 15 days.

In the north-east monsoon this is somewhat under the average passage.

* * * * *

11.

[Sidenote: Penang to Bengal, 400 leagues.]

From Prince of Wales's Island to Saugor Roads, Bengal. 13th March to the 27th March, 1817 14 days.

The average at this season is twenty-one days, consequently this passage is very good. At this season of the year the north-east monsoon has entirely ceased in the centre of the Bay of Bengal; so that a ship which steers well out between the Nicobars and Andamans need not apprehend northerly winds; whereas in the north-eastern parts of the bay, the monsoon still blows faintly, with long intervals of calm. A merchant brig, reputed a good sailer, left Prince of Wales's Island 6 days before us, and followed the inner route, while we went outside, and arrived 10 days before her at Calcutta.

* * * * *

12.

[Sidenote: Calcutta to Madras, 300 leagues.]

Sand Heads off Calcutta to Madras, against the south-west monsoon.

From 19th April to the 7th May, 1817 18-1/2 days.

Three weeks is said to be a good passage. We beat down as far as the latitude 11° north, and longitude 87° east, before we hauled across. We had fine weather all the way.

* * * * *

13.

[Sidenote: Madras to Mauritius, 1140 leagues.]

From Madras to the Mauritius.

1st June to the 1st July, 1817 30 days.

We were driven by the south-west monsoon as far as longitude 92° east, before crossing the equator; here we had a constant high swell. We were much baffled, and did not get the steady south-east trade till in 7° south, and longitude 88° east. The average passage is between five and six weeks at this season of the year.

* * * * *

14.

[Sidenote: Mauritius to rounding the Cape, 800 leagues.]

From Mauritius to making the land of Africa, about Algoa Bay.

8th July to the 22d July, 1817 14 days.

Thence to rounding the Cape on the 30th July 8

———

Mauritius till round the Cape, 3 weeks 1 day, or 22 days.

The average from the Mauritius to rounding the Cape, is twenty-eight days; on this occasion we kept close in-shore: we had no current, and though in the depth of winter, the weather was invariably fine, and the water smooth. At night a breeze generally blew off shore. There was a heavy dew every night.

* * * * *

15.

[Sidenote: Cape to St. Helena, 570 leagues.]

From off the Cape to St. Helena on the 11th August 12 days.

Mauritius to the Cape (see above) 22 days.

———

From Mauritius to St. Helena in 4 weeks 6 days, or 34 days.

[Sidenote: Mauritius to St. Helena, 1370 leagues.]

This is an excellent passage. It appears to be a great object in making a passage from India to England, to pass the Cape without going in; for it is often easy to round the Cape and go to St. Helena, when it is difficult and tedious either to go to Simon's or Table Bay, and much delay is produced by the difficulty of getting out of the former anchorage.

* * * * *

16.

[Sidenote: St. Helena to Ireland, 1800 leagues.]

From St. Helena to Bantry Bay in Ireland.

Sailed from St. Helena on the 14th August, 1817.

Arrived off Bantry Bay, 14th October, 1817 61 days.

This passage was unusually long, owing to a succession of hard gales from north-east to south-east, which we encountered in latitude 47° north, longitude 13° west, beginning on the 27th of September, and continuing, with little intermission, till the 8th of October; after which period the weather became fine, but the wind hung constantly to the eastward, so as to render it difficult to fetch Ireland.

GEOLOGICAL MEMORANDUM; BEING A DESCRIPTION OF THE SPECIMENS OF ROCKS COLLECTED AT MACAO AND THE LADRONE ISLANDS, AND ON THE SHORES OF THE YELLOW SEA, THE WEST COAST OF COREA, AND THE GREAT LOO-CHOO ISLAND.

GEOLOGICAL MEMORANDUM.

It is greatly to be regretted, that, during this voyage, our means of gaining information on this interesting subject were so limited. In China we were restrained, sometimes by the jealousy of the Chinese, and sometimes by an apprehension on our part of giving offence, or of exciting suspicion, by following up enquiries, the nature of which it was impossible to explain when interrogated by the inhabitants. On the coast of Corea, the still greater jealousy of the natives rendered it impossible to prosecute geological investigations beyond the beach. Both in China and on the coast of Corea our stay at each place was very short, and our time being often necessarily occupied by avocations foreign to such enquiries, many opportunities were lost merely for want of time. Even at the Great Loo-choo Island, where we remained much longer, our researches were confined to a coast which offered nothing interesting.

Having therefore nothing of a general or striking nature to offer to the scientific world on this subject, I shall merely give an account of the specimens collected at the various places which we touched at during this voyage, accompanied by brief explanations from memorandums made on the spot.

The geologist will be struck with the resemblance which the rocks in this remote quarter of the globe bear to those with which he has been familiarly acquainted.

SPECIMENS FROM CHINA.

MACAO.

1. Granite, composed of white quartz, porcelain clay, and greenish steatite, with veins of white quartz intersecting each other.

2. Fine-grained granite, composed of yellowish feldspar, white quartz, and black mica. Quartz dykes of great magnitude traverse the granite which forms this peninsula.

HONG-KONG, ONE OF THE LADRONE ISLANDS, OFF MACAO.

3. Lead-coloured compact quartz rock, with imbedded crystals of flesh-coloured feldspar.

GREAT LEMMA, ONE OF THE LADRONE ISLANDS, OFF MACAO.

4. Coarse-grained granite, with distinct crystals of feldspar.

SOUTHERN SHORE OF THE YELLOW SEA.

CHE-A-TOW.

5. Fine-grained gneiss, composed of white quartz, white feldspar, and black mica, with a vein containing hornblend and crystals of feldspar.

6. The strata are here very much contorted; the cliffs at some places being folded up like webs of cloth.

7. Granular primitive lime-stone, containing greenish steatite.

8. Quartz rock, alternating with gneiss.

9. A specimen containing amorphous pieces of iron.

CUNG-CUNG-CHEEN ISLANDS.

10. Very fine-grained gneiss, composed of white quartz, flesh-coloured feldspar, and black mica.

11. Coarser variety of the same.

12. Compact blueish-grey feldspar, with grains of quartz.

OEI-HAI-OEI.

13. Gneiss, composed of yellowish feldspar, white quartz, and black mica.

LUNG-CUNG-TAO ISLANDS.

14. Coarser variety of the rock described above.

WEST COAST OF COREA.

From an Island in Latitude 37° 45' North.

1. Compact stratified pale-pink lime-stone; variegated in colour; strata highly inclined.

2. Very compact slaty light-grey rock; strata inclined at an angle of 75°, dipping towards the north-east.

3. Dark olive steatitic rock, containing fragments of granular marble.

4. Very fine-grained greenish hornblend rock.

5. Vine-grained purplish slate; the strata highly inclined.

6. Greenish-grey slate, containing crystals of white feldspar and specks of hornblend: strata highly inclined, dipping towards the north-east.

SPECIMENS FROM HUTTON'S ISLAND, COAST OF COREA.

Latitude 36° 10' north, longitude 126° 13' east.

The following note is taken from the narrative at page 8.

We found the north-east end composed of a fine-grained granite[19]; the middle of the island of a brittle micaceous schistus of a deep blue colour[20]; the strata are nearly horizontal, but dip a little to the south-west. This body of strata is cut across by a granite dyke[21], at some places forty feet wide, at others not above ten; the strata in the vicinity of the dyke are broken and bent in a remarkable manner: this dislocation and contortion does not extend far from the walls of the dyke, though veins of granite branch out from it to a great distance, varying in width from three feet to the hundredth part of an inch: the dyke is visible from the top of the cliff to the water's edge, but does not re-appear on the corresponding cliff of an island opposite to it, though distant only thirty yards. This island is composed of the same schistus, and is cut in a vertical direction by a whin dyke[22], four feet wide, the planes of whose sides lie north-east and south-west, being at right angles to those of the great granite dyke in the neighbourhood, which run south-east and north-west. The strata contiguous to the whin dyke are a good deal twisted and broken, but not in the same degree as at their contact with the granite dyke. The whin dyke is formed of five layers or sets of prisms laid across in the usual way.

Beyond the small island cut by the whin dyke, at the distance of only forty or fifty feet, we came to an island rising abruptly out of the sea, and presenting a high rugged cliff of breccia[23], fronting that on which the granite dyke is so conspicuous: the junction of this rock with the schistus cut by the granite and the whin would have been interesting; but although we must have been at times within a few yards of it, the actual contact was every where hid by the sea.

The whole of the south-west end of this island is formed of breccia, being an assemblage of angular and water-worn pieces of schistus, quartz, and some other rocks, the whole having the appearance of a great shingle beach and cliffs. The fragments of the schistus in this rock are similar to that which forms the cliff first spoken of. (Specimen 8.)

The theory which presented itself to us on the spot was, that the lower part of the great mass of strata which now forms the centre of the island was formerly at the bottom of the ocean; and that the western part, now a firm breccia, had been a beach of shingle produced by the action of the waves on the upper strata, which may have formed a coast above the sea: the granite of the eastern end of the island had been forced into its present situation from beneath the strata, with sufficient violence to dislocate and contort the beds nearest to it, and to inject the liquid granite into the rents formed by the heaving action of the strata as they were raised up. It is natural to suppose that the ragged edges of the strata forming the sides of these cracks would be subjected to a grinding action, from which the strata more remote might be exempted; and in this way we may account for the extraordinary twisting, and separation of masses along the whole course of the granite dyke. In the dyke, as well as in the veins which branch from it, there are numerous insulated portions of schistus. That this last was softened, seems to follow from the frequent instances which occur of its being bent back upon itself without producing cracks. The same heat, generated by the melted granite in the neighbourhood, and which appears to have been just sufficient to soften the schistus, may be supposed to have reduced the shingle beach to a state of semi fusion by the aid of some flux contained in the sand scattered amongst the fragments. We could not discover any circumstance by which the relative antiquity of the two dykes mentioned above could be inferred.

The junction of the granite and schistus above described, resembles very much the well known junction at the Lowrin mountain, in Galloway, described by my father, Sir James Hall, in the 7th vol. of the Edinburgh Transactions. It is also very like the junctions at the Cape of Good Hope, described in the same volume. The same theory has been found to explain them all.

Specimen 7. Fine-grained granite, composed of white quartz, white feldspar, and olive-green mica. This rock (7) forms the eastern end of the island; the schistus next described (8) the centre, and the breccia mentioned immediately afterwards (9) the western end.

8. Fine-grained compact micaceous schistus: some of the specimens appear to contain plumbago. The strata lie north-west and south-east, dipping only a few degrees from the horizontal line.

9. Breccia, composed of angular and contorted fragments of micaceous schistus, and angular pieces of feldspar and quartz. This rock forms the western end of Hutton's Island[24]: it rises in high rugged cliffs. The angular pieces of schistus are of a similar rock to that described above (8).

10. Dyke, porphyritic granite, composed of white quartz, white feldspar, and bronze-coloured mica. This dyke cuts across the schistus last mentioned, in a direction north-east and south-west. It is nearly vertical, and varies in breadth from nine to forty feet, with numerous ramifications.

11. Dyke of compact whin stone. This dyke is composed of five layers of prisms, whose length is at right angles to the walls of the dyke. It is nearly vertical. Its direction north and south, and is about five feet thick.

MAIN LAND OF COREA.

12. Lead-coloured, fine-grained, micaceous schistus. From the main land of Corea, latitude 36° 10' north, longitude 126° 48' east. The strata lie north-west and south-east, and are nearly vertical; the natives objected to our examining the cliffs, though distant less than a quarter of a mile from the beach.

ANOTHER ISLAND OFF THE COAST OF COREA.

Latitude 34° 23' north, longitude 126° east.

13. Decomposing fine-grained rock; composed of flesh-coloured feldspar, white quartz, and porcelain clay.

ANOTHER ISLAND NEAR THE ABOVE.

14. Rock composed of white feldspar and quartz. The strata of this rock were very much contorted.

This rock is the most general of any in this range of islands, at least as far as we had opportunities of examining them. The islands on this coast are very numerous; they lie in great clusters along a line of three degrees and a half of latitude. The islands vary in length from five or six miles to as many yards, and are of all forms. We saw none that were remarkably high, and none which seemed volcanic. As our stay on the coast was only nine days, and as the ships were almost always under weigh except at night, it was quite impossible to make any careful or valuable geological observations. It offers a splendid field to future voyagers.

GREAT LOO-CHOO ISLAND.

1. Grey stratified lime-stone without shells. This specimen was taken from the north end of the island, where the ranges of hills were mostly composed of it: the strata being highly inclined. The hills rise to the height of four or five hundred feet, and present nothing interesting.

2. Fawn-coloured, cellular, granular lime-stone. The cliffs at Napakiang are composed of this rock; it also appears to stretch along the whole of the south-west and south parts of the coast. In the narrative, this rock has been erroneously called coral. These cliffs are curiously hollowed out into horizontal caves, which have all the appearance of having been worn by the dashing of the waves; but as it is obvious, that in their present situation the sea can never have reached the face of the cliffs, it seems probable that the whole coast may have been raised up, by a gentle movement, without dislocating the strata, or disturbing the horizontal position, in which it seems probable that these caves were formed.

The variety of coralines which girt the shores of this island was very great, and large collections were made, as well of these as of the numerous zoophites which filled up every part of the reefs below high-water mark. This collection, of which unfortunately no duplicates were kept, was afterwards lost.

SULPHUR ISLAND

Lies in latitude 27° 5' north, and longitude 128° 25' east. An accurate representation of it is given as a frontispiece.

We attempted to land, but the surf broke every where so high against the rock that this was impossible. There is a crater on the left side with white smoke issuing from it; this has a strong sulphuric smell. The sides of the crater are stratified. The south end of the island is about four or five hundred feet high, and is formed of a dark dingy red rock distinctly stratified; at several places it is cut vertically by great dykes, which being more durable than the strata which they intersect, stand out from the face of the cliffs to a considerable distance.

FOOTNOTES:
[Footnote 19: Specimen 7, infra.]
[Footnote 20: Specimen 8.]
[Footnote 21: Specimen 10.]
[Footnote 22: Specimen 11, infra.]
[Footnote 23: Specimen 9.]
[Footnote 24: The island above described was so named by Captain Maxwell, in compliment to the memory of the distinguished philosopher whose theory has been used to explain the curious phenomena which it exhibits.]

END OF THE APPENDIX.
VOCABULARY OF THE LANGUAGE SPOKEN AT THE GREAT LOO-CHOO ISLAND, IN THE JAPAN SEA.
COMPILED BY HERBERT JOHN CLIFFORD, ESQ. LIEUTENANT, ROYAL NAVY.
IN TWO PARTS.
OBSERVATIONS ON THE LOO-CHOO LANGUAGE.

Of the grammar of this language I pretend to little knowledge, but the following observations upon some points may perhaps be worth attending to. The most striking circumstance, is the frequent use of the words *noo* and *ka*; the former of which seems to signify *of*, or the *'s* of the English language, as will appear in *choo noo ka*, a man's skin, or the skin of a man; *oóshee noo stínnoo*, the bullock's horn, or the horn of the bullock; and in *moo noo kee saw'teeyoong*, to dig potatoes out of the ground, or, literally, potatoes of the earth to dig out.

Ka, it will be observed, is used to denote skin, and also seems to signify a receiver or enclosure, as is expressed in the words *meézee ka*, a well of water, *meézee* being water, and *ka*, the place containing the water; and in *ya ka saut eéchoong*, to go out of a place, *ka* in this instance expressing the enclosure, *ya* you, and *sawt eéchoong* to go out from, as *eéchoong* signifies to go.

The adjective is for the most part placed before the substantive, as *teeshoóee íckkeega*, an old man; *wúsa ya*, a mean house; and *wóckka innágo*, a young woman.

There is little variety in the termination of the verb, the tenses being expressed by other means. I have throughout the vocabulary considered the termination *oong* to denote the infinitive, and have translated it as such, even when the sense points to another mood, merely to preserve consistency; there are, however, a few exceptions to this, and some of the verbs will be found to terminate in *ang,ing, awng, ong,* and *ung.* Those ending in *oong* seem generally to make the participle terminate in *ee,* as *wóckkayoong,* to separate, makes the participle *wóckkatee,* separated. The negative termination of the verb is generally *nang* or *rang,* as *noómang,* not to drink, is the negative of *noómoong,* to drink; *meérang,* the negative of *meéoong,* to see; and *noóboorang,* the negative of *noóbooyoong,* to climb or ascend. *Na* is also used as a negative, *coónsoona,* not to rub out, being the negative of *coónshoong,* to rub out.

Nang, nárang, and *náshee* are negatives used with a substantive, and are always placed after it, as *koómoo nang,* no clouds; *meézee nárang,* no water; and *feéjee náshee,* no beard.

Some peculiarities will be found by referring to the following words: deaf; the sole of the foot; head-ache; palm of the hand; the toe; and the wrist.

PART I.

VOCABULARY OF ENGLISH AND LOO-CHOO WORDS ALPHABETICALLY ARRANGED, WITH NOTES, AND OCCASIONAL REFERENCES TO THE SENTENCES IN THE SECOND PART.

VOCABULARY OF THE LOO-CHOO LANGUAGE.

Note on the orthography used in the following vocabulary.—The sounds in the Loo-Choo words are expressed by the letters which in English correspond nearest to those sounds. There are no mute vowels. The letter *a* is invariably sounded as in the English word *far.* The emphasis is marked by an accent over the last vowel of the accented syllable. *Ee* and *oo,* whether accented or not, always express one syllable.

English. Loo-Choo.
    Above, or the top of a thing Wee.
Alive Itch-it´chee.
Alive, to be It´ch-chawng.
All (every one) Eénea, or I´gnea
                    (Italian gn[25].)
All drink, every one drinks I´gnea noódung.
Anchor Eéki.
Angry Neétsa.
Ankle Shánna go oóshee.
Answer, to Aree ga aányoong.
Arm Teénoo.
Arrow Eéa.
Awake, to Oóking.
Awaking Oócatee.
Bad Neésha.
Bad man Yáwna moon, or Yánna choo.
Bad building Wása ya.
Bailer of a canoe Yoo-toóee.
Baize, red Moóshung.
Bake, to I´rreechang.
Bake bread, to Quáshee soókooyoong.
Bamboo-cane Dákee.
Bamboo (instrument of punishment) Boóchee.
Basket Teéroo.
Beads Támma.
Beard Feéjee.
Beardless Feéjee náshee.
Beat, to Soó-go-yoong.
——, as the heart Nácoo-choong.
—— on the gong Tánna óchoong (lit. to
                    play on the gong.)
—— to, with the bamboo Chíbbee oótchoong.
Bed Coócha.
Bell St´chee-gánnee.
Belly Wátta.
Belly, big Wátta mágesa.
Below, or the bottom of a thing Stcha.
Bend to, a thing Támmeeoong.
Bird Hótoo.

Birdcage Hótoo-coo.
Bishop at chess (lit. priest) B[=o]dsee, or B[=o]dzee[26].
Bite to, as a dog Coóyoong[27].
Bitter Injássa.
Black Korósa.
Bleed, to, (lit. to draw blood) Chee-hoóga-choong.
Blind Meégua.
Blind man Akee meégua.
Block Kooroóma.
Blood Chee[28].
Blow up, to, or light a fire Foó-tchoong.
Blowing (through a musical instrument) Gácoo.
Blue (colour) Táma-eeroo.
Blue (light colour) Meéz-eeroo.
Blunt Chírrarung.
Blush (lit. red) Akássa.
Boat Tímma, or Sabánnee,
Boat, the bottom of a Nakámma.
Boil, to Tájeeing.
Book Sheémootsee[29].
Bone Coótsee.
Bonnet, or head-dress worn by the natives Hat´chee Mat´chee.
Both alike, or all the same Neéchawng, or Yoónoomoong.
Bow to, to a person passing Deéshoong.
Bow Yoómee.
Bow, to pull a Yoómee feétchoong.
Bower Tánnan.
Boy (lit. a man child) Ic´kkeega wárrabee.
Brass Cheéjackko, or Toong.
Bread Quáshee.
Bread-basket, or tray Quáshee boong.
Breadth Hábba.
Break, to, a stick Oóyoong[30].
——————— a tea-cup Wy´oong.
Breakers Námee.
Breast Moónee.
Breathe, to It´chee shoong[31].
Bridge Háshee[32].
Bring here Moot´chee coo.
Bring fire here Feetoótee coo.
Brinjal (an Indian vegetable) Nasíbbee.
Broke Oótee, Chírreetee.
Brother Weékee.
Bucket Tágoo.
Bull Woo Oóshee.
Burn, to Yáddee, or A´kka.
Butterfly Habároo.
Button Hogánnee, or kánnee.
By and by A´tookára[33].
Cake, a sweet flowered Magía quáshee.
Calf Oóshee gua.
Calf of the leg Koónda.
Candle Daw.
Candlestick Soócoo[34].
Candle and stick together Daw´secoo.
Cannon I´shee-beéa.
Cap Cammoódee, Maw´tsee.
Carpenter's black line box Stínseeboo.
[35]Carry to, or take away Moótchee eéchoong.
——————, a basket on the head Téeroo kámmeetong[35].
——————, a child in the arms Dáchoong.
——————, with a bar on the shoulders[35] Katam´meeoong.

100

Carrying a basket on the arm Téeroo tenakíkakíttee.
Cask Soócoo.
Castle Eegoósecoo, or Gooseécoo.
Cat Mía, or My´a (Chinese).
Cat, to mew as a Náchoong deéoong.
Catch, to Kaoótoochung.
Catch, to, a butterfly Kabároo skéhdang.
Chair Ee (Chinese).
Charcoal Chácheejing.
Cheeks Hoo.
Cheese (literally cow's milk and fat) Oóshee noo[36] chee quátee.
Chessmen Choónjee.
Child (infant) Wórrabee.
Child, male (literally man-child) I´ckkeega wórrabee.
Child, female (literally woman-child) Innágo wórrabee.
Children Qua.
Chin Oootoóga.
Chin, the beard of the (lit. lower beard) Stcha feéjee.
Chopsticks Fáshay, or May´shung.
Climb, to, a pine-tree Mátsee kee noóbooyoong.
Cloth, or clothes Ching.
Cloth, red Akássa nónoo.
Clouds Koómoo.
Cock Toóee.
Cocoa-nut tree Nash´ikee.
Cocoa-nuts Náee.
Cold Feésa.
Cold water Feézeeroo Meézee.
Colours Eéroo eéroo.
Come, to Choong[37].
Come here Cung coo.
Come, to, down a hill Oódeeyoong.
———— on board Choó-oong.
Coming up from below Nooboóteecoo.
Compass Kárahigh, or Kássee toóee[38].
Conk shell Neénya goóroo.
Cool Seedásha.
Copper Acoógannee.
Coral Oóroo
Cover, to, over with sand Sínna sheeóstang.
Cough, to Sáck-quee.
Count, to Oohaw´koo-oong[39].
Country A´whfee.
Cow Mee Oóshee.
Crab Gaánnee.
Crab, to crawl as a Hóyoong.
Creep, to Haw´yoong.
Crow, to O´tayoong.
Crow Gárrasee.
Cry, to Nachoong.
Curlew U´nguainan.
Cut, to Cheéoong, or feéoong, or
                              feéjoong.
Dance Oodoóee, or Makátta.
Dark Coórasing.
Daughter Innágo oóngua, or úngua.
Day (at Napakiang) Nit´chee[40].
—— (in the north of the island) I´sheeree.
—— after to-morrow Asáttee.
—— the following Asá tínnacha.
Daylight Heéroo.
Dead Sheénoong, or gang.

Deaf (literally, ear not to hear) Mímmee chee karung.
Deep Fookássa.
Deity (the Indian God Boudha) Boósa (Chinese).
Dice Sheégo roócoo.
Dice, to play with Sheégo roócoo ochoong.
Die, to Níntoong.
Dig, to, up the ground Oóchoong.
——, potatoes Moo noo kee saúteeyoong.
Directly (by and by) Atookar´ree, or Atookára.
Dive, to, under water Seénoong.
Dog Ing.
Dog barks I´nnoo nachoong.
Don't stir (said to a person rising to Wfay´sa[41].
  depart)
Door Hasbírree.
Draw, to, a picture Eé-katchoong[42].
———— blood Chee na by´oong.
Dress, to Ching cheéoong.
Drink Noómoo.
Drink, to Noómoong[43].
———— wine Sack´kee noómoong.
——, not to, wine Sack´kee noómang.
Drop, to, a thing Oocheérooshoong.
Drunk Weétee[44].
——, to get Weéoong.
Dry, to Karacháoong.
————, powder Eénshoo foóshoong.
Dung, cow, for manure Oóshee noo coósoo.
Duck, a tame A´feeroo.
Eagle Hack´ka.
Ear Mímmee.
——, left Feéjeeree noo mímmee.
——, right Meéjeree noo mímmee.
Ears, to pull the Mímmee feéoong, or feétchoong.
Earth Jee.
East Fingássee.
Eat, to Kámoong[45].
——, I Moónoo kámoong.
——, to, boiled rice Méeshee kámoong, or kánoung.
Eggs Coóga.
Eight [46]Kwat´chee, or fat´chee
                    (Loo-Choo); Eeyat´see
                    (Japan.)
Eighteen Kwat´chee joo, or fat´chee joo.
Eighty Hapáck coo, or Habbáck coo.
Elbow Teénoo feéjee.
Eleven Too.
Empty, to, or pour out Hárashoong.
Ends of a thing Yoókoo.
Every thing A´dee-coódee[47]?
Exchange, to, fans Káyra.
Exclamation of surprise Yeéah, or Cheé-oo-oo.
———————————— I´yi-yi-yi-yi.
Expression of respect, or salutation Taw.
———————— thanks in returning How.
  any thing
Eye Mee.
Eyebrows Maí-oh.
Eyelashes Matsídjee.
Eyes, to open the Mee hoóra choong.
——, closing the Neebóoee.
Face Steéra, or Skeéra[48].

102

Fall, to Taw´shoong, or Taw´ring[49].
Fan O´jee.
——, to, one's self O´jeeshoong.
——, to offer a O´jee kára.
Fat Quaítee.
Father Shoo.
Feathers of a fowl Toóee noo han´nee.
Female Mee.
Fence of bamboo Dack´kee gat´chee.
Fiddle Neéshing.
————, to play on the Feétchoong (lit. to pull.)
———— strings Cheéroo.
Fifteen Goónjoo.
Fifty Gooshácoo, or gooyácoo.
Fill, to I´ddeecoong.
Find, to Toómatung[50].
Finger Eébee.
————, fore Choo sháshee.
————, little Eébeegwaw.
————, middle Nack´ka eébee.
———— ring Nanna shee.
———— nail Thímmee.
Fire Fee.
——, to put out Fee cha-chee.
——, to, a gun Narashoong.
Fish Eeo[51].
——, a small Coosa eeo.
———————— blueish Tamung eeo.
——, a large red Matchee eeo.
——, the back of a Kánjee.
——, the fin of a Hannay.
——, the gills of a Ajee.
——, the head of a Chee-boo-soo.
——, the tail of a Dzoo.
——, to catch Eéo kákeeoong.
—— hook and line Cheéna.
—— spear Eéo stit´chee.
Five Goo (Loo-Choo); Ittítsee
(Japan)[52].
—— sided figure Roo-ka-coo.
Flag Háta.
Flail[53] Coóra ma baw[53].
Flesh Shíshee.
Flesh, no Shíshee ning.
Flower, a red, the name of A´ckka hanna.
Flower of a plant Fánna.
Flute, to play on the Hánshaw.
Fly Háyeh.
Fly, to, as a bird Toóbeeoong.
Foot Shánna.
——, the sole of the Shánna watta (lit. belly of
the foot).
——, of a bird Físha.
Forehead Fitcháyeh.
Forty Speéakoo, or Sábacoo.
Four [54]Shee (Loo-Choo); Eéots see,
or joo (Japan).
Four-sided figure Sícca Coódair.
Fourteen Sheénjoo.
Friend Eedoóshee.
Frog A´tta beétsee.
Full Meetchíttee.

——, half Ham´boong.

Get up Tá-tee.

Girdle O´bee.

Girl Tack´kee.

Give, to Queéoong[55].

Glass Kágung.

Go, to Eéchoong[56].

——, away Haddee.

——, in a boat Tímma ki eéchoong.

Go, to, fast Háyee sit´choong.

——, up a hill Noóbooyoong (lit. to climb,).

—, not to, up a hill Noóboorang.

—, to, slow Yaw´na eéchoong.

——, on shore Amáki eéchoong, or moódoeéong.

Goat Feéja.

——, he Woo Feéja.

——, she Mee Feéja.

Going down below Oórittee coo.

Gold Ching.

Good (for eating) Mása.

—— (proper) Choorása.

—— man Yoókachoo, or Eéchoo.

—— bye (taking leave) Wóckkatee.

—— for nothing Máconárang.

——, not Worroósa.

Grand-children Soong mága.

Grass Goosit´chee, or Coosá.

——, to cut Coosá cheéoong.

Grasshopper Sheéto, or Sáyeh.

Grave Háka.

Greybeard Feéjee sheerájee.

Great coat (made of straw, worn also New.
  by the Chinese)

Great man (Chinese Tajin) A´jee, or Páychin.

—— many Oowhóko.

Green O´sa.

Grind, to, the teeth Ha gíssee gíssee.

Groaning Doónee.

Hair Kurrázzee[57].

Hammer Goóshung.

—— of a stone-cutter Oónoo.

Hand Kee[58].

——, right Meéjeeree.

——, left Feéjeeree.

Handkerchief Tee-sádjee[59].

Handsome Choorása.

Harp San´gshing.

Hat, worn by the natives Kássa.

———————————— English Kamoóree.

Have not got Nang[60], or Nárang.

—————————— water Meézee[61] nárang.

Head, human Boósee.

Head-ache (lit. sick head) Seeboóroo yádong.

Head, of a bird Tseeboóroo.

Hear, to Sit´choong, or Skit´choong.

——, I Moónoo sit´choong[62].

——, I cannot (or understand) Sit´cheerang, or
                              Sit´cheekárang.

Heart Nácoo.

Heaven Ting.

——, praying to Ting oóneewhfa[63].

Heavy Boósa.

Heel of the foot Shánna-a-roo.

Here Coo.

Hide, to, or cover (lit. cannot see) Meérang.

—— of a bullock Oóshee noo ka.

Him (a third person) A´ree (meéchay)[64].

Hips Gammácoo.

Hissing Seésee.

Hoe Quáya.

Hold, to take, of a person Kat´sameéoong.

Holding a thing (a butterfly) Meecháwree[65].

    (Letting a thing escape) Oótoo Batch[65].

Hole A´nna.

—— to make in the ground A´nna hoóyoong.

—— in the jeeshee, or urn Mee hoojíttee[66].

Hoop of a cask Obee[67]

Horn of a bullock Oóshee noo stínnoo.

Horse Ma[68] (Chinese).

Hot A´tteesa.

Hour Twit´chee[69].

House Ya, or Kat´chee.

House where salt is made Máshoo ya.

Hundred Sing.

Hungry Yása.

I, or me (a first person) Wang[70] (choóee).

Jar, a large earthen Kámee.

——, its top or cover Hoóta.

Inch, one Eésing.

Inches, ten; Eesháckkoo.

Infant Wórrabee.

Ink Sim´mee.

Inkstand Sim´mee shee.

Inside Oóchee.

——, or soft of bread Mee.

Iron Títzee.

Jump, to Móyoong.

Key Quaw.

Kick, to, with the foot King.

Kid (lit. small goat) Feéja água.

Kill, to Sheémoong, or Koórashoong[71]

——, birds Hótoo eéchung.

——, by the fire of a gun Doogaítee sheénoung.

King, or monarch Kówung (Chinese).

King's palace Oogoós-coo.

Kiss, to, (lit. kissing the mouth) Coóchee spoótee[72].

Kiss Sheemir´ree.

Knee Stínsee.

Kneel, to Shúmma git´cheeoong.

Kneeling Shúmma git´chee.

Knife, crooked, for cutting grass Eeránna.

——, small (a penknife) Seégo.

Knight, at chess Samoóree.

Knot Coónja coótchee.

——, to tie a Coónjoong.

Knuckles Foóshee.

Lacker, to Noóyoong.

Ladder Háshee.

Lake, or light purple Coonmoóla sat´chee.

Land, or shore Amáki.

Lantern Tíndoo.

———, folding Cháwching.

Lantern, glass Támma-doóroo.

Large Weésa.

105

Laugh, to Wárrayoong.
Laughing Wárratee.
Lead (metal) Meéjee kan´nee.
Leaf (of a tree) Wha.
———, green (lit. the leaf of a tree) Kee noo wha.
———, withered (lit. a dried leaf) Kárree wha.
Lean (not fat) Yaítee.
———, to, against a thing Yookátatoong[73].
Learning, or studying Cootooba[74].
Let, to, fall a thing Nágeeoong.
Letter, or character Jee.
———, to seal a Ing sit´choong.
———, to write a Jee kátchoong.
Letting go a thing O´too batch.[75]
Loo-Choo song Loóchoo, or Doóchoo oóta.
Lift, to, a thing Moóchoong.
Light, not dark (daylight) Feéroo, or Heéroo.
———, not heavy Gása.
———, to, a pipe Sheéoong.
Lips Seéba.
Lip, lower Stit´cha seéba.
—, upper Quaw seéba.
—, the beard on the lower Coofeéjee.
Liquor Sac´kkeedia, or Sam´tchoo
                                    (Chinese).
Live, or reside, to Sim´matong[76].
Lizard U´ndlecha.
Look, or see, to Meéoong, or Meéing[77].
———, to, at, or see the sun Teéda meéing.
———, at a distance Han´na-rat´chee.
Look, to, closely Teétsheeoong.
Looking-glass Kágung.
Long, or length Nagása.
Lose, to Oótoochung.
Make, to, clothes Ching náwyoong[78].
Make, a noise Hábbeecoong.
Make, a rope Cheéna oótchoong[79].
Make, salt Máshoo tátchoong.
Make, sugar Sáta skóyoong[80].
Make, a tea-pot Tácoo soókooyoong[80].
Making a false step Koonsínda dakat´chee.
Male Woo.
Mallet, wooden Cheé-chee.
Man (homo) Choo.
Man (vir) I´ckkeega[81].
Man, medical I´shsha.
Man, of rank Páychin, or Quángning
                                    (Chinese).
Man, short Injása.
Man, sick I´ckkeega yádong.
Man, the skin of a Choo-noo-ka.
Man, small Feecoósa.
Mast of a ship, or boat Hásseeda.
Mat Mooshoóroo, or Hátung.
Match, or fire-stick used in the temples Kaw[82].
Me, or I Wang.
Meal, 1st (at sunrise) Stim´mee teémoong.
Meal, 2nd (two hours after) A´ssa bung.
Meal, 3rd (at noon) Feéra moómoong.
———, 4th (at sunset) Yoó bung.
Measure, to Gáwjee háckkiyoong.
Melon Toóqua.

106

Men, a great many Oowhóko Ickkeega.
Mew, to, as a cat Nachoong deeoong.
Midday, or noon Teéda mátchoo.
Milk Chee.
——, to draw Chee háyoong.
Million Chaw.
Mine Coóra wa moong.
Mixed Bátee.
Moon, the Stchay.
——, or month, one It´chee stit´chee, or
       gwaútsee[83].
——, full Oostit´chee, or Mároo.
——, half Mécasit´chee.
Monkey Sároo.
More Gnáfing.
Morrow A´cha.
Mother Um´ma.
Mud Doóroo.
Musical instrument, to play on a Koótoo feétchoong.
Mustachios Wa feéjee.
Nail to hang things on Coójee.
Naked Harráka.
Name Na.
——, my Wa na.
——, your Ya na.
——, his A´rree ga na.
Navel Whoósoo[84].
Neck Coóbee.
——, short (lit. no neck) Coóbee nang[85].
Needle Háyee skíttee.
Net, fishing Sheébee.
Night Yoóroo.
——, one It´chee yoóroo.
Nine Coo[86] (Loo-Choo), Koónitsee
       (Japan).
Nineteen Coónjoo.
Ninety Coohácoo, or Queeshácoo.
Nipples Chee.
No Oóngba, or Oomba[87].
Nod, to Nájeechoong.
North Cheéta.
Nose Hónna.
Nostrils Hónnakee.
Octagon Hacac´koo.
Offer, to Ozágadee.
——, wine Ozágadee sac´kkee.
——, more, or again Mátta ozágadee.
Old Teeshoóee.
—— man Teeshoóee ic´kkeega.
Olives Kárang.
One It´chee (Loo-Choo), Teétesee,
       or ta (Japan[88].)
Onions Dehchaw.
Open, to, or unlock A´keeoong[89].
Open it Akírree[2].
Orange, fruit Koóneeboo.
——, the rind of an Koóneeboo noo ka.
——, divisions Mee.
——, the seed of an Tánee.
Overturn, to, or upset Koóroobáshoong.
Outside Foóca.
——, of bread (lit. skin) Ka.

Paddle of a canoe Wayácoo.
Paint, to Oóroo[90] sheenoóstang.
Palanquin chair Kágoo.
Palm of the hand (lit. belly of the hand) Tee noo wátta[91].
Pant, to Eétchee hoótoong.
Panting Eétchee.
Paper of any kind Kábee.
Path Yamána meetchee.
Paupaw apple Wangshoóee.
Pawns at chess Toómoo.
Pencil Hoódee.
Perspiration Ac´kkaddee[92].
Pepper pod Quáda coósha.
Pick up any thing, to Moóchoong.
Picture Keé-ee, or Kackkeé-ee.
Pig Boóta.
Pin worn in the hair of boys Jeépha, or Jeéwa.
—— flower head worn by men Kam´mashíshee.
——, ladle head, do. Oósheethúshee.
Pinch, to Kátcheemeéoong[93].
Pine, the wild Adánnee.
——, leaves of the Wha.
——, fruit of the Adánnee nay.
—— tree Mátesee kee.
Pipe Shírree.
——, the mouth-piece of a Quee coótchee.
——, wooden part of a Saw.
——, bowl of a Sárra.
——, case of a Shírree bookoóroo.
Pitchfork Feéra.
Pivot on which the scull of a boat traverses Jeéco[94].
Place Skáta.
Plank of a boat Fánna[95].
Plant Mee boósha.
Plantain, leaf of a Woo noo fa.
Play, to, at chess Choónjee óchoong.
——, with dice Sheégo roócoo óchoong.
——, on a musical instrument Koótoo feétchoong[96].
——, on the flute Hánshaw.
——, on the violin Feétchoong.
Pleased Oósha.
Plough Sit´chee.
————, to Sit´choong.
Point, to, with the finger Noóchoong.
Potatoes, sweet Moo, or Moóndee.
Pour in, to I´rreeing.
—— out, to Cheéjoong.
Pouring Cheéjee.
Praying to the Deity Boósa, or Bósa meéwhfa[97].
———— to Heaven Ting oóneewhfa.
Powder Eéenshoo.
————, to dry or air Eénshoo foóshoong.
Pregnant Kássee jeétawng.
Press, to, or squeeze Sheétskeeoong.
Prick, to, with a knife Hoogáshoong[98].
Pricking Yátee.
Prickly pear bush Cooroójee.
Priest (Bonzes of China) Bódzee.
————, the silk dress of a Eéchoo coóroom.
————, the cotton dress of a Básha coóroom.
————, the belt of silk of a Quára.
Pull, to, or draw out Injat´chee.

————, out of the ground Noójoong.

————, a person Feétchoong, or fit´choong.

Purple Moóla sat´chee.

Push, to, with the hand Koóroo báshoong[99].

Put, to, a thing above or upright I´sheeoong.

————, up a thing above, high Injáshoong.

————, on the hat Kánjoong.

————, or lay a thing down Oócheeking.

————, a thing in I´ttee.

—————————— under Kásseemeéoong.

————, on clothes Ching cheéoong.

————, out fire Fee cháchee.

————, a ring on the finger Eébee gánnee sáshoong.

Quack, to, like a duck Náchoong.

Quarrel, to Títskoong.

Queen, also at chess Oónajerra.

Quick Háyee.

Quick, to be Yoohǎoong

Rain A´mee.

————, to A´mee foóyoong.

————, heavy Sheejeékoo foóyoong.

————, lightly Koókoo foóyong.

Rainbow Noo-oójee.

Rat A´ck-a-sa.

Read, to Yoómoong, or Yoóno-oong.

Red Akása.

Rind of a shaddock Pow noo ka.

———— an orange Koóneeboo noo ka.

———— (lit. skin) Ka.

Ribbon, silk Eéchoo.

Ribs Sáwkee.

Rice Coómee.

————, boiled U´mbang, or bang, or
                              oómbang[100].

Ride, to, a horse Man´ayoong.

Right, in writing characters Kátchee yánjee.

Ring Coósayee.

———— for the finger Eébee gánnee.

————, to put on a Eébee gánnee sáshoong.

Rise, to, from a chair Tátchoong.

Road Meéchee.

Rock See, or Weésa is´hee.

Root (bulb) Weé-ee.

Rope Chínna.

————, to make Chínna oóchoong.

Rough Soóroo soóroo.

Round Morroósa.

————, a circle Maroódair.

Round, all round Maroóee.

Rowing in a boat Coójee.

Rub, to Soósooing, or soósootee
                              oótooshung.

——, out Seéree oótooshoong, or
                              Soósootee; oóteetung, or
                              coónshoong.

——, not out Coónsoona.

Rubber, Indian Neéka.

Rum, or spirits Káraboo.

Run, to Háyay sit´choong[101].

Running Háyay.

Sail of a ship or boat Foo.

Sail, to, in a boat Hárashoong.

Salt Máshoo.

—— water Spookarása Meézee.

—— to the taste Spookarása

Salute, to, a person Kámeeoong.

Sand Sínna.

Say it, I can Ang.

————, I cannot Nárang[102].

Sea Námmee.

—, the, or ocean Oóshoo.

—, shore Háma, or Oómee.

— weed Moo[103].

—, high Oonámmee.

Seal of a watch Ing, or Fang.

Seam between two planks Nágo.

Scrape, to Sájoong.

Scratching Weégosa.

Screw, to Meégoorashoong[104].

Screw Jírree.

Scull of a boat Doo.

Scull, to, a boat Meégoorashoong.

See to, or look, (lit. to eye) Meéoong[105].

See, I cannot Meérang.

Seed Nigh.

Separate, to Wóckkayoong.

Seven Sit´chee(Loo-Choo); Nánnatsee
                                    (Japan).

Seventeen Sit´chee joo.

Seventy Sit´chee hácoo.

Servant Toómoo, or Eéree, or Sad´ge-ee.

Sew, to Náwyoong, or No-á-yoong.

Shade, or shady Kájee.

Shake, to Kátcheeming.

Shaking a thing Yoótoo yoótoo.

Shallow Asássa.

Sharp Aka, or chírraring?

Shave, to Soóyoong.

Shell Oósheemaw.

Shell fish (like a crab) A´mang.

Shield Timbáyee.

Ship Hoónee[106].

—— , large Hooboónee, or Wesára Hoónee.

—— , small Hoónee gua, or Coosára Hoónee.

—— goes away Hoónee eéchoong.

—— returns Moóchee eéchoong.

Shoes, or sandals Sábock, or Sabaugh.

Short Injása.

Shoulders Kútta.

Shrub, with leaves resembling a Sootítsee.
  palm tree, probably sago tree

Shut, to Meecheéoong.

Shut it Mechírree.

Skin Ka.

Skin, of a bullock Oóshee noo ka.

—— , of a man Choo noo ka.

Sick Yádong.

—— man Ic´kkeega yádong.

—— belly Wátta éddee.

Side, of a person Hárraga.

—— , of a thing Táttee.

Sigh, to Hoóee eéchee.

Silk Eéchoo.

Silver Jing.

110

Sing, to Oótashoong, or oótayooshoong,
or oótayoong.

Sister O'nigh.

Sit down, to Eéoong.

————, in a chair Eéchawng, or Eeree.

————, on the ground Eémeesháwdee, or Eédee.

————, or be seated Yoocoótee.

Six Roócoo (Loo-Choo); Moótsee
(Japan).

Sixteen Roócoojoo.

Sixty Rookpáckcoo.

Sleep, to Nínjoong.

Sleeping Níntee.

Slow Yoóna, or Yáwna.

Small Coósa.

Smell, to Kánnoong, or Kasháshoong.

Smell Kabbásha[107].

Smoke, to Foótchoong, or koótchoong.

Smoke Kínsee.

Smoking tobacco Tobácco foókee.

Smooth Nándooroosa.

Smooth down, to Nádeeyoong.

Snake Háboo.

Snake stings Háboo coótee.

Snatch, to Kátayoong.

Sneeze, to Hónna feéoong.

Snore, to Níntoong.

Snuff (lit. nose tobacco) Spáchee, or Hónna Tobácco.

Sole of the foot (lit. belly of the foot) Shánna wátta.

Son Ic'kkeega oóngua.

Song Oóta[108].

Sore from riding Náutee.

Sorry Natskásha.

Sour Seésa.

South Whfa or fa.

Speak, to Moónooyoong[109].

Spear to catch fish with Toóga oóyoong.

Spectacles (lit. eye-glass) Mee kágung.

Spider Coóba.

Spider's web Coóba mang.

Spit, to Simpáy-oong.

Spittle Simpáyee.

Spoon Káa.

Spy glass Toómee kágung.

Square Káckkoo.

————, of a stone mason Bánjaw gaúnnee.

Squeeze, to Mímmeejoong.

Stab, to Choong.

Stand up, to Tátteeoong.

Stand back to back Coósee noóchasa.

Stars Foóshee.

Stay on board ship Hoónee oótee.

Stem of a boat Oomoótee.

Stern of a boat Coóma toómo.

Stone Is´hee.

——— cutter's hammer Oong.

————, carved Káwroo[110].

Stop Mátee[111].

Straw Wárra.

Strike, to Réjeecoong.

String Ko-eéroo.

Strong Choósa.

———— wine Choozáckkee, or Sáckkeechoo.
Sucking Noódee[112].
Sugar Sáta.
———— cane Oójee.
————, to make Sáta skóyoong.
Sulky Hárradat´chee.
————, not Hárradat´chee soóna.
Sun Teéda.
Sunset Teéda ságayoong[113].
Sunshine Teéda téttee.
Sunrise Teéda ágayoong.
Swallowing Noónootoósha.
Sweet Amása.
———— wine A´mazac´kkee[114].
———— potatoes Moo, or Moóndee.
Swim, to Weéjoong.
Swimming Weéjee.
Sword Tat´chee.
   A flight of stone steps Keesíee.
   A single step Coodámmee.
   To stick a thing in the ground Táteeing.
Table, round Mádooee.
Tail of a bird Dzoo.
Take off the hat, to Hásseeoong.[115]
Tattoo marks on the right arm Oódeemaw.
———————————— on the left arm Toóga.
Tea cup Cháwung.
————, to break a Wy´oong.
—— pot Tácoo.
——, in an octagon bucket Tácoo cee.
——, the metal pot in the inside of Tácoo mee.
  the bucket
——, the cover of a Tácoo whfoóta.
——, the handle of a Tácoo tee.
——, the ears of the bucket of a Tácoo toódee.
Tear, to Yáyoong.
———— a thing in pieces Cheéreetawng.
Tears Náda.
Teeth Há (an aspirate).
————, to set on edge Ha gíshee gish.
Temple Meéa (Chinese).
———— yard Tírra.
Temples, human Koómeegung.
Ten Joo (Loo-Choo);
                          Too (Japan).
Thank you Ka foóshee.
That A´ddee.
There Ic´kkee.
Thigh Moómoo.
Thirteen Sanjoo.
Thirty Sangbácoo.
This Coódee.
Thousand Mang.
————————, ten O´koo.
Three Sang (Loo-Choo);
                    Meétesee (Japan).
Three sided figure Sang cac´kkoo.
Thread, sewing Eéchoo[116].
Thresh, to Oótchoong[117].
Throat Noódee[118].
Throw to, a stone at a mark Náging.
————————, away any thing Oóchung-ging.

Thumb Hoóee Eébee.
Tie to, a knot Coónjoong.
Tide Kádezee.
Tin Sheédookánnee.
Tired, or fatigued Amus´heenoo.
Tobacco Tobácco[119] (as in England).
———— pouch Coóshee sat´chee, or foósa.
To-day A´choo.
To-morrow A´cha.
Toe Shánna eébee (lit. foot
                                                finger).
Toe-nail Shánna thímmee.
Tomb Háka.
Tomb-stone Coóroo ishee.
Tongue Stcha.
Torn, part of any thing Yádee tung.
Touch, to Sáyoong, or sit´choong.
Town Meéattoo, or Métto.
Tray, or waiter Chírreedeh.
Tread, to Koóraming.
Tremble to, with cold Koórooyoong.
Tree Kee.
——, branch of a Eéda.
——, Banyan Gádesee mároo kee.
——, with red and white flowers Hoóyoo.
Tree, with large red flowers, which Dee-eégo-kee.
  are called *acka banna*
Trowsers Coo, or Hackkáma.
Turban worn by the lower order of the Sájee.
  natives
Turn round to Meégoyoong.
Two Nee (Loo-Choo); tátesee
                                                (Japan).
Twelve Neéjoo.
Twenty Hácoo.
———— one Hácoo it´cheejoo.
———— two Hácoo neéjoo.
———— three Hácoo sánjoo.
———— four Hácoo sheénjoo, or sheehácoo.
———— five Hácoo goónjoo, or goohacoo.
———— six Hácoo roócoojoo.
———— seven Hácoo sit´cheejoo.
———— eight Hácoo fat´cheejoo.
———— nine Hácoo coójoo.
Tyger Toóra.
Vase, or urn Jeéshee.
Veins Kájee.
Very well (speaking of health) Oogánjoo.
———— (well done, good) Eétshang.
Victual or dinner box Píntaw.
————, the drawers in it Joobáckkoo.
Ugly Ootooroósa.
Umbrella Shássee kássa.
Undress, to Ching hájeeing.
Untie, to, a knot Hoótoochoong.
Upper garment Eéshaw, or Hoónta.
Water Meézee, or Meésee.
————, hot A´tsee meézee, or átcheeroo.
————, cold Feésa meézee, or feézeeroo
                                                meézee.
————, salt Spookoorása meézee.
————, a large jar containing Tookoóee.

113

Water tub Meez-ofwhókee (cont. of meézee
                                and ofoowookee).
Walk, to At´choong.
——, or crawl as a butterfly Seégatong.
——, slow Yáwna eéchoong.
——, quick Háyee sit´choong.
Walking hand in hand, as the natives Teefeécha.
Wash, to A´rayoong.
——, or bathe Indeetáwoong.
——, clothes Ching árayoong.
Washing clothes Ching áratee.
Watch Kárahigh.
—— key Sásee noo quaw.
We, or a fourth person Yoótay.
Weather Tínsee, or tínchee.
————, fine Yetínsee[120], or tínchee.
————, foul or bad Yánna tínsee, or tínchee.
Web-footed bird Itchoóma.
————————, beak of a Coóchee (lit. mouth).
———————— head Makarájjee.
———————— leg Sha.
———————— two legs Shándee.
———————— tail Májoo.
———————— wing Hónnee.
Well (lit. water's skin) Meézee ka.
West Neéshee.
Wet Inneétee.
Wet, to I´ndeetáoong.
What do you call this? Noóndeega.
Wheel of a ship Cooroóma.
Whiskers Bínta.
Whisper, to Mónotitchoong.
Whistling Feéfee.
————, as a bird Hoósa.
White Sheeroósa.
Wick of a candle Skeecoótshee.
Will you give me Wang yee quírree[121].
Wind Kássee, or Kázzee.
—— to come in Kássee noóchoong.
—— to go out Kássee eéchoong.
——, little Kássee gua.
——, great Weésa kássee, or táychfoo[122].
Wind, to, up a watch Feénoyoong.
————, a string round the finger Káramachoong.
Winking Mee oóchee.
Wine Sáckkee.
—— glass Támma sáckka sit´chee.
—— kettle Dáckkeezitza.
——, sweet Amazack´kee, compounded of
                                amása and sackee.
——, strong Choozáckkee, or sáckkeechoo.
——, weak Eéawzáckkee, or sáckkee ya.
Wing of a bird Hánnay.
—— feathers of a bird Kee.
Wipe, to, the face Soósooyoong.
Wish, to, or bid good bye Wóckkayoong.
Wrist (lit. neck of the arm) Tee noo coóbee.
Write, to Kátchoong[123].
Writing-desk Sheékoo.
Wrong in writing characters Náwshoong.
Woman Innágo.
——, plain Ootooroósa innágo.

———, old Teeshoóee innágo.

———, handsome Choorása innágo.

———, young Wóckka innágo.

Wood of any kind Támoong.

Yawning A´coobee.

Year[124] Ning.

———, one It´chee ning.

Years, eighteen, of age Joo hat´chee.

———, fourteen Joó shee.

———, thirty Sánjoo.

———, twenty-five Neéjoo goo.

Yellow Cheéroo.

———, dark Kássa cheéroo, or áka cheéroo.

———, dirty or dingy Cheéroo díngee.

Yes Oo.

Yesterday Cheénoo.

Yoke, across the shoulders of porters Baw.

You (a second person) Ya (tay).

Young Wock´ka.

——— woman Wock´ka innágo.

Yours Coóra ya moong.

FOOTNOTES:

[Footnote 25: This sound is the same as the Italian *gn*, and will be found in the words *Gnafing*, signifying more; *Quangning*, a man of rank; and also in *Neesa*, bad, and *Nee*, two, which are most commonly pronounced as if a *g* were prefixed to the *n*.]

[Footnote 26: The *o* in this word is sounded as in the English word *Bode*.]

[Footnote 27: See sentence No. 101, Part II.]

[Footnote 28: This word also signifies milk, and the female breast.]

[Footnote 29: In speaking of books with reference to their number, they say *teetsee sheemootsee*, one book; *tatsee sheemootsee*, two books; but of a single book they only say *sheemootsee;* and we never found that they had any plural termination.]

[Footnote 30: See sentence No. 111.]

[Footnote 31: There is a great similarity between this word and that which signifies *to be alive*, (Itch-chawng).]

[Footnote 32: This word signifies both a ladder and a bridge.]

[Footnote 33: See Sentences Nos. 25 and 41.]

[Footnote 34: This word signifies both a cask and a candlestick.]

[Footnote 35: See Sentence No. 70.]

[Footnote 36: *Noo* seems to express *of*, or the *'s* used in the English language: as *Ooshee noo chee*, the cow's milk, or the milk of the cow; *Ooshee noo ka*, the bullock's skin, or the skin of the bullock;*Doochoo noo choe*, Loo-choo's people, or the people of Loo-choo; and will be found in a variety of other instances.]

[Footnote 37: See Sentences Nos. 18, 19, and 21.]

[Footnote 38: The compass was generally called *Kassee tooee*, which two words signify wind and a cock or fowl; but the landsmen called it *Karahigh*, which signifies a watch.]

[Footnote 39: This is probably *Oowhoko*, signifying a great many persons.]

[Footnote 40: The day at Loo-Choo is divided into six hours, as also the night. In counting a number of days they apply the numerals in a similar manner to that which will be found in a note on*Twitchee*, an hour; but they did not seem to have any names to denote the days of the week.]

[Footnote 41: This word is generally used by the master of the house when his guest announces his intended departure, by saying, *Cung, cung.*]

[Footnote 42: See Sentences Nos. 74 and 76.]

[Footnote 43: See Sentences Nos. 29, 32, 33, and 37.]

[Footnote 44: See Sentences Nos. 24 and 107.]

[Footnote 45: See Sentences Nos. 31, 36, and 27.]

[Footnote 46: See Numerals, Loo-Choo and Japan, Part II. after the Sentences.]

[Footnote 47: This word, which is composed of *addee*, this, and *coodee*, that, I am not positive of, and I have therefore affixed a query against it.]

[Footnote 48: This is a very difficult word to pronounce, and I am not certain of having conveyed its true sound.]

[Footnote 49: See Sentence No. 111.]

[Footnote 50: See Sentence No. 55.]

[Footnote 51: See Sentence No. 20.]

[Footnote 52: See note on Numerals.]

[Footnote 53: The nearest sound to that of *flail* which a native of Loo-Choo could utter was that of *Freyroo*; generally speaking they found great difficulty in pronouncing English words. The nearest sound to that of our *l* was *Airoo*, and to that of *vil* was *Bayroo*.]

[Footnote 54: See note on Numerals.]

[Footnote 55: See Sentences Nos. 45, 47, and 48.]

[Footnote 56: The intention of departing from a house is generally announced by *Cung, cung*.]

[Footnote 57: The hair of the natives is formed into a knot on the crown of the head, and fastened by two pins of silver or brass, the one ornamented by a flowered head, called *kamma-shishee*, and the other *ooshee-thushee*. That worn by the children is called *jeefa*.]

[Footnote 58: This word is used to denote a *tree* as well as a *hand*; this probably arises from the similarity; considering the *hand* as the trunk, and the fingers the branches of the *tree*.]

[Footnote 59: A piece of China crape, or very fine paper, is used as a handkerchief by the superior classes of the natives, and is generally worn in the bosom: the lower orders substitute a coarser kind of paper.]

[Footnote 60: A negative in frequent use.]

[Footnote 61: This word may be applied to being in want of water.]

[Footnote 62: See Sentence No. 2.]

[Footnote 63: A strong aspirate.]

[Footnote 64: See note on *I* or *me* (first person) next page.]

[Footnote 65: These two expressions were obtained by catching a butterfly and then letting it go.]

[Footnote 66: The *jeeshee*, or *vase*, is a stone jar in which the bones of the dead are deposited at the expiration of seven years after burial.]

[Footnote 67: The same word (*obee*) signifies both the hoop of a cask and the girdle worn round the waist; this probably originated in the girdle being substituted for the hoop, which appears to have been worn formerly.]

[Footnote 68: *Ma*, signifying a horse, is a Chinese word, and was probably introduced into Loo-Choo with that animal.]

[Footnote 69: The names of the hours will be found in the second part; the divisions of time will be found under their different heads of day, month, year, &c.]

[Footnote 70: While seeking to obtain from the natives the pronouns *I, you*, and *him*, I at first got *chooee, lay*, and *meechay*; but on further enquiry I found that these had not that meaning, they were superseded by *wang, ya*, and *aree*, for *I, you*, and *him*; but as I heard *chooee, lay*, and *meechay* repeated in enumerating persons, I have set them down as first, second, and third persons, that being the sense which they seem to bear. The word *chooee*, or *choo*, it would seem signifies man (homo) in a general sense.]

[Footnote 71: See Sentence No. 96.]

[Footnote 72: See Sentence No. 99.]

[Footnote 73: See Sentence No. 101.]

[Footnote 74: See Sentence No. 6.]

[Footnote 75: See note, "Holding a thing."]

[Footnote 76: See Sentences Nos. 81 and 82.]

[Footnote 77: See Sentences Nos. 38 to 44.]

[Footnote 78: Literally to sew clothes.]

[Footnote 79: Literally to work rope.]

[Footnote 80: *Skoyoong*, or *Sookooyoong*, signifies to bake.]

[Footnote 81: This word, which is composed of *ickkee* and *ya* (*ickkee* signifying *there*, and *ga*, which may possibly have been originally *ya, you*), appeared to me to bear a similar meaning to our *you, sir*, or *you, there*, as the natives invariably called out *ickkeega*, when wishing to attract the attention of any one.]

[Footnote 82: See note on the *kawroo*. The *kaw* is also burned when an offering of rice is made on the *kawroo*.]

[Footnote 83: The following are the names of the months or moons.

January Shaw gwautsee.

February Nee gwautsee (lit. 2d month).

March Sang gwautsee (lit. 3d).

April Shee gwautsee (lit. 4th).

May Goo gwautsee (lit. 5th).
June Roocoo gwautsee (lit. 6th).
July Sitchee gwautsee (lit. 7th).
August Fatchee gwautsee (lit. 8th).
September Coo gwautsee (lit. 9th).
October Joo gwautsee (lit. 10th).
November Shee moo stitchee, or joo itchee gwautsee.
December Shee wasee, or joo nee gwautsee.

The twentieth day of the tenth month (October), *Joo gwautsee, neejoo nitchee*, was, according to Loo-Choo time, the second day of the tenth month, *joo gwautsee, nee nitchee*.]

[Footnote 84: A strong aspirate on the first syllable.]

[Footnote 85: The negative is almost invariably placed after the word.]

[Footnote 86: See note on numerals.]

[Footnote 87: The sound of the *oong*, or *oomb*, is very difficult, and can only be approximated by closing the teeth firmly and compressing the sound of *oong*.]

[Footnote 88: See note on Numerals.]

[Footnote 89: See Sentences Nos. 49 to 53.]

[Footnote 90: *Sheenoostang* signifies to *cover over*, and possibly *ooroo* should have been written *eeroo*, which is *colour*; and this word, signifying *painting*, would then be literally *to cover over with colour*.]

[Footnote 91: This is literally the *belly of the hand*, or the *hand's belly*. For an explanation of the *noo* see observations on the Loo-Choo language at the beginning.]

[Footnote 92: This word seems to derive its origin from *ackka, burning*.]

[Footnote 93: This word, *Katcheemeeoong*, to pinch, appears to be formed of the words *Ka*, skin, *chee*, blood, and *meeoong*, to see; and may be translated to *see the blood through the skin*, or *in the skin*.]

[Footnote 94: This sound is not unlike that which the screwing about the scull of a boat on the pivot causes.]

[Footnote 95: The same word signifies a flower.]

[Footnote 96: *Feetchoong* signifies to pull, so that it may with more propriety be applied to the harp, or touching the strings of the violin with the fingers.]

[Footnote 97: A strong aspirate on the last syllable.]

[Footnote 98: See Sentence No. 105.]

[Footnote 99: Literally, to upset.]

[Footnote 100: For the sound of this word see note on the English word *no*.]

[Footnote 101: See Sentence No. 8.]

[Footnote 102: *Narang*, or *nang*, is used on most occasions as the negative.]

[Footnote 103: The same word signifies *sweet potatoes*.]

[Footnote 104: This word it will be observed signifies both *to screw* and *to scull;* this may originate in the screwing motion of the oar from side to side of the boat.]

[Footnote 105: See Sentences No. 38 to 44.]

[Footnote 106: The similarity in sound of this word to that of a character (*Hoonatee*) written on a piece of paper in the hats of the men employed working for the ships, has suggested the idea that the meaning of the character may have some reference to a ship.]

[Footnote 107: See Sentences Nos. 102 and 103.]

[Footnote 108: Words of Loo-Choo songs:
"Sasa sangcoomeh sangcoomeah kadee yooshee daw, tantoong tantoong tang."
A boat song: "Whee yo ee.—Whee yo ee." The steersman gave "Whee," and was followed by the other men with a repetition of "Whee yo ee."
Another boat song: "Quee yay hanno ha.—Quee yay hanno ha." To both these airs the rowers kept very good time.]

[Footnote 109: See Sentences Nos. 1 to 7.]

[Footnote 110: The *kawroo* is a small square stone excavated a little on the upper part, in which an offering of rice is made. On the face of this stone is carved a variety of characters denoting the rank, &c. of the person who makes the offering.]

[Footnote 111: See Sentences in Part II.]

[Footnote 112: See Sentences Nos. 29, 32, 33, and 37.]

[Footnote 113: See Sentences Nos. 108, 109, and 110.]

[Footnote 114: *Amazackkee* is a contraction of the words *amasa*, sweet, and *sackkee*, wine; the latter always changing *s* into *z* when preceded by any other word. See *wine, strong, weak*, &c.]

[Footnote 115: Tattoo marks will be found in Part II.]

[Footnote 116: *Eechoo*. This word is used to denote *thread*, silk_, and *ribbon*.]

[Footnote 117: *Ootchoong*, or *oochoong*, signifies *to work, to play*, and *to make*.]

[Footnote 118: Possibly this word implies the act of swallowing.]

[Footnote 119: The sound of this word is precisely the same as that of our *tobacco*. I have, therefore, spelt it in the same manner.]

[Footnote 120: See Sentence No. 109.]

[Footnote 121: See Sentences Nos. 45, 47, and 48.]

[Footnote 122: This is probably the *tae fung* (great wind of the Chinese, called by us *tyfoon*), a severe gale of wind in the China Sea.]

[Footnote 123: See Sentence No. 73.]

[Footnote 124: The year at Loo-Choo, according to Jeeroo's account, is divided into twelve months of thirty days each, making in all 360 days, and every sixth year one month is intercalated.]

NOTE.

In the following Sentences the English is given before the Loo-Choo. No Sentence has been inserted the meaning of which was not distinctly ascertained; but it happened frequently that the precise import of some words in a Sentence was not made out, and in order to enable the reader to judge to what extent this took place, a literal translation of the words in each Sentence is given in the last column; and where a word occurs, the meaning of which is doubtful, an asterisk is put in its place.

In the last column it will be observed that every verb having the termination *oong, ung*, &c. is translated as if it were the infinitive, although the sense, as denoted in the first column, points to another mood.

SENTENCES, ENGLISH AND LOO-CHOO.

Of Speaking.

No. *English. Loo-Choo. Literal Translation.*

1. I speak Moónooyoong I to speak.

2. I speak, you hear Moónooyoong, ya sit´choong, I speak, you to hear, or Chickkee or hearing.

3. I speak to you Ya, or ea moónooyoong, or You to speak, or I. wang. Ya too moónooyoong You * to speak.

4. I speak Chinese Wang Quántoong I Chinese to speak. moónooyoong

5. I cannot speak Chinese Wang Quántoong moónoorang I Chinese cannot speak.

6. I am learning to speak Wang Doóchoo cootoóba I Loo-Choo learning or Loo-Choo yoóshoong[125] studying to *.

7. Mádera speaks English I´ngere Mádera moónooyoong English Mádera to speak.

Of Going and Coming.

8. A man running to the Háyay tímma ic´kkeega Running boat man. boat

9. I am going on shore Wang amáki eéchoong I shore to go.

10. To-morrow I will return A´cha choó-oong To-morrow to come.

11. To come back again A´mma ka choong[126] * * to come.

12. I am going on board Timma ki eéchoong Boat * to go.

13. I came yesterday Cheénoo chung Yesterday came.

14. Go down there Amúnka ic´kkee * there.

15. Come up here Nooboótee coo Ascend here.

16. You go below Yá oódee meéshawdee You * *.

17. To go out of a place Yá ka saut eéchoong * * * to go.

18. To come into a place Yá ka saut choong * * * to come.

19. Tayin[127] returns Tayin[127] choo-oong The great man to come.

20. To go in a boat to Doóchoo timma eéchoong Loo-Choo boat to go Loo-Choo to carry fish eéo katámmeeoong fish to carry.

21. To go to sea in a Timma eéchoong oóshoo Boat to go sea fish to boat to catch fish eéo cheéoong catch

22. Where is Tayin gone Táyin makáyee ga ímjara Tayin * * *.

23. Tayin has gone to Táyin eéchoong hooboónee Tayin to go large ship the other ship to meéyoong Sheenoóma to see *. pay his respects

24. When all are drunk I´gnea weétee amáki All drunk shore * we shall be permitted moótotee yoótoosha *. to go on shore

118

25. I am going now, he Atookárra wang eéchoong By and by I to go, by will come presently atookárra eéchoong and by to go.

26. I am going on shore Wang amáki eéchoong I shore to go I to dinner moónookámoong eat.

27. I am going on board Wang hoónee ki eéchoong I ship * to go I to to dinner moónoo kámoong eat.

28. When the ships depart A´cha hoónee níttee Doóchoo To-morrow ship * to-morrow all the mang hoónee Loo-Choo thousand Loo-Choo people will oócooyoong ship *. pray

Of Eating and Drinking.

29. To drink wine Sac´kkee noómoong Wine to drink.

30. Sweet wine Amazac´kkee Sweet wine.

31. I eat Moónoo kámoong I to eat.

32. I never drink tea Cha noódee nárang Tea drinking never.

33. Tayin and you never Táyin ya sac´kkee noódee Tayin you wine drink drink wine nárang never.

34. The parting glass Wóckkarittee Departing.

35. It is good (to eat) Coódee mása This good (to eat).

36. It is bad, throw it Neésba is´kung Bad *. away

37. It is tea, to drink Meézee tájeeing cha noódee Water to boil tea drinking.

Of Looking and Seeing.

38. To look at the sun Teéda meéoong kágung Sun to see glass. through a glass

39. I look, or I see Moónoomeéoong I to see.

40. The English gentleman I´ngere táyin meésheeoong English great man to is looking look at.

41. Stop, you shall look Mátee*, atookárra ya Stop, by and by you presently meésheeoong to look at.

42. Clouds obscure the Koómoo teéda oósooóstang Clouds sun to cover sun over.

43. The branches of the Toómee kágung kee noo Spy-glass trees tree obstruct the káttakáshee meérang branches to hide. sight

44. If a Loo-Choo woman Doóchoo innágo I´ngere Loo-Choo woman English should see you she meéoong náchoong to see, to cry. will be alarmed

Of Giving.

45. Will you give me that Wang yee quírree I * giving.

46. Give me that pencil Hoódee moot´choo Pencil bring.

47. I gave him some paper A´ree nee queétang Him * giving.

48. By and by I will give Atookárra qua gnee queéoong By and by children * it to my children to give.

Of Opening and Shutting.

49. Shut this, or it Akíttee nínjoong Shutting to sleep.

50. Open this, or it Akíttee mírree, or Opening it. akátindee

51. Do you open this, Akátindee, or ya akírree Opening, or you or it opening.

52. Open this book Ya sheémootsee akírree You book opening.

53. Open your watch that Akátindee kárahigh meéoong Opening watch to see. I may look at it

Of Losing and Finding.

54. To lose a pencil Hoódee oótoochung Pencil to lose.

55. To find a pencil Hoódee toómatung Pencil to find.

Of Quantity.

56. Two small suns Tátsee teéda gua Two suns small.

57. A few boys Coósa wárrabee Few boys.

58. A few Men Ic´kkeekoósa Men few.

59. A great many men Ic´kkeerássa Men many.

60. A few books Sheémootsee sánsatche Books few.

61. A great many books Sheémootsee tóro Books many.

62. Six kinds of wine Moóeeyroo noo sáckkee * of wine.

Of Making.

63. Making a false step Koónsinda dákatchee * *.

64. Vases made at Napa Nápa jeéshee scoótee Napa vases made.

65. Sand spread on a level Sínna oóshoo sháee máshoo Sand sea * salt plain on which water tátchoong to make.

119

is sprinkled for
making salt

66. Sing a song Ya oóta yoóshoong You song to sing.

67. Jeeroo sings well, Jeéroo oóta yoóshoong Jeeroo song to sing * or with good taste
cheécheegoótoo * *.

Of Bringing and Carrying.

68. Bring your children Ya qua saúteecoo You children bring.

69. Bring fire here Fee toóteecoo Fire bring.

70. This vessel carries Hoónee jeéshee káttamittee Ship vases * Oonting.
vases to Oonting Oónting

71. Boy, bring fire to I´rree fee toóteecoo tobácco Boy fire bring,
light my pipe foókee tobacco smoke.

72. Bring a cup of water Cháwung náki meézee eéteecoo Teacup * water *
here here.

Of Writing and Sketching

73. To write a letter Jee kátchoong A character to write.

74. Tayin is sketching Táyin háshee noo Tayin bridge of to
the bridge eékatchoong sketch.

75. Tayin sketches very Táyin yoókatchee choorása Tayin * sketches
well handsome.

76. To sketch a Loo-Choo Doóchoo meéa eékatchoong Loo-Choo temple to
temple sketch.

Of Compliment.

77. Thank you Ká foóshee * * *.

78. How do you do Yoo ky´moong * * *.

79. Very well Oogánjoo * * *.

80. I am very sorry Oomoótee shangcoómeh * * *.

Of Living or Residing.

81. Tayin lives here Táyin simmájoo coo Tayin lives here.

82. A man living in the Ickkeegá simmá áwhfee A man living country.
country

83. I live on board the Wang hoónee gua ímmatong I ship small to live.
brigs

Of Burning and Scalding.

84. Fire will burn you Fee yáddee Fire burns.

85. Water will scald you Meésee yáddee Water burns.

86. Scalding oneself with Meézee fidgeroósa yoo Water hot * burns. hot water yáddee

Of Enquiry and Reply.

87. What is the name of Noóndeega coóra na What is this name. this

88. The name of this is Coóra ga na ya This * name *.

89. How many children Qui eecootiéga * * *.
have you

90. How old are you or Eecoótseega * * *.
they

91. I am fourteen years Joóshee Fourteen.
of age

92. I am eighteen years Joohatc´hee Eighteen.
of age

93. ——— twenty-five, &c. Neéjoogoo Twenty-five.

Miscellaneous.

94. To boil potatoes Mootájeeing Potatoes to boil.

95. I am very busy Yoo joónatan * * *.

96. The sting of a snake Háboo coótee sheénoong Snake sting to kill.
will kill

97. Sucking milk at the Chee noóma chee Milk * breast.
breast

98. A child drinking milk Chee noódee wárrabee Milk drinking child.
at the breast

99. A child kissing its Wárrabee úmma coóchee Child mother mouth
mother spoótee kissing.

100. A woman leaning Innágo kákatong eéki Woman to lean anchor.
on an anchor

101. A live shell-fish Amang it´chchawng Shell-fish to be alive will bite coóyoong to bite.

102. This flower has a Fánna mása kabásha Flower sweet smell. pleasant smell

103. This flower has no Fánna nang kabásha Flower no smell. smell

104. Loo-Choo women Doóchoo innágo fwhoóco Loo-choo woman great are not very ooórung many *. handsome

105. The sootitsee (sago Sootítsee wang tseéchoong Sootitsee I * *. tree) pricked me yátee

106. To plant potatoes Moo jee hoótee céyoong Potatoes ground * *.

107. Drunk, I vomit Weétee moónoo háchoong Drunk I vomit.

108. After sunset it is Teéda ságatee seedásha Sun setting cool. cool

109. When the sun Teéda téttee, koómoo nang, Sunshine, clouds none, shines, and there yaytínchee fine weather. are no clouds, it is fine weather

110. The sun sets at six Roócoo twit´chee teéda Six hours sun to set. o'clock ságayoong

111. The horse fell down, Ma táwrittee táyin noo Horse fell down, and the tayin eébee oótee tayin's finger broke. broke his finger

112. After seven years Sítchee ning, coótsee Seven years' bones we wash the bones arátee jeéshee ittee washing vase putting and put them into in. a vase

113. Without any flesh Shíshee ning Flesh none.

114. The people of Doóchoo noo choo sibíttee Loo-choo people Loo-Choo I shall yoótoosha remember * *. never forget

115. You will soon Sibíttee wása Remember bad. forget them

116. Twelve hours make Joo nee twit´chee, it´chee Ten two hours, one one day nit´chee day.

117. Thirty days make one Sánjoo nit´chee, it´chee Thirty days one month moon, or month gwaútsee

118. One year consists of It´chee ning, joo nee One year, ten two twelve months gwaútsee months.

FOOTNOTES:

[Footnote 125: *Yooshoong* probably signifies *to recite*, as it is used in requesting a person to sing as well as in this instance.]

[Footnote 126: Probably instead of *amma ka*, this should have been *amaki* (shore), which would makeit coming to the shore, which was the case.]

[Footnote 127: *Ta-jin*, in Chinese, signifies a *great man;* it is translated by Mr. Morrison *his excellency.*]

[Transcriber's Note: Japanese characters in the table below are denoted as such.]
NUMERALS.

English. Loo-Choo. Characters. Japan.

1 One It´chee [Japanese character] Teétsee, or te 1.
2 Two Nee, or gnee [Japanese character] Tátsee, or ta 2.
3 Three Sang [Japanese character] Meétsee, or mee 3.
4 Four Shee [Japanese character] Eéotsee[128], or yoo 4.
5 Five Goo, or go [Japanese character] I´ttitsee 5.
6 Six Roóko [Japanese character] Moótsee 6.
7 Seven St´chee [Japanese character] Nánnatsee 7.
8 Eight Fat´chee, or [Japanese character] Eeyátsee 8. kwat´chee
9 Nine Coo [Japanese character] Koónnitsee 9.
10 Ten Joo, or dzoo [Japanese character] Too 10.

Both sets of these numerals are in common use at Loo-Choo, though it would not perhaps be correct to apply them to the same word, as I never recollect having heard a native say "itchee sheemootsee," one book, or "teétsee twit´chee," one hour, but always "teétsee sheémootsee," one book, and "itchee twitchee," one hour. I at first imagined "teetsee, tatsee," &c. were ordinals, but I have since found from Captain Broughton's Voyage that they bear a great resemblance to the numerals of Japan, and as such I have inserted them.

The characters, of which the above are copies, were written by a native.

FOOTNOTES:

[Footnote 128: The *o* in this word is to be pronounced as the diphthong *oa* in boat.]

NAMES OF PERSONS.

The Kowung, or King - Sháng fwee.

The Pochin ta foo, or Prince - Shang pung-fwee.

The Chief of the Paychins who attended the ship - Oókooma Mowchowshoóa.

The second Paychin - Madáyra Sháyoon.

The third do. - I´ssacha Sándoo.

The fourth do. - Jeéma Tsí-se-eu.

His eldest son - Maátsee Tsí-chee.

His friend (an elderly man) - Oóhoomee Chínchawhee.

The fifth Paychin - I´ssecha Háckkeeboócoo.

The sixth do. - Jeéroo Jeéda.

The first Linguist - Mádera Káwsheeoong.

The second Linguist - A´nya Toónshoonfa.

His wife - Oóshee.

One of the junior Paychins - Yáma Too.

The teacher (an old man) - Yáckkabee Oómeejeéroo.

His eldest son - Yáckkabee Oómee-nee whaw.

A boy - O´seejee.

One of the principal attendants of the}
Pochin ta foo } - Mádam Báshee.

Another - Eévaroo.

NAMES OF PLACES.

Corea - Córay.

Pekin - Péking.

Fokien - Fótchien.

China - Quántoong.

Chusan - Choósan.

England - I´ngeree.

The island of Loo-Choo - Loo-Choo, or Doó-Choo.

The town of Napakiang - Nápa ummeátto.

The high distant islands seen from Napa - A´makírreema.

The Sugar Loaf Island - Eégoos eécoondee.

Japan - Níphon.

Canton - Cánton.

NAMES OF THE DAYS OF THE MOON FROM NEW TO FULL.

1. Chee tátchee.
2. Hádjee mee nítchee.
3. Hádjee mee san nit´chee.
4. Hádjee mee noo ka.
5. Hádjee mee goo nit´chee.
6. Hádjee mee roócoo nit´chee.
7. Hádjee mee sit´chee nit´chee.
8. Hádjee mee fatchee nit´chee.
9. Hádjee mee coo nit´chee.
10. Yoóka.
11. Joo it´chee nit´chee.
12. Joo nee nit´chee.
13. Joo san nit´chee.
14. Joo yoóka.
15. Joo goo nit´chee.

THE NINE ORDERS OF RANK OF PAYCHINS, OR CHIEFS, WHO ARE DISTINGUISHED BY THE COLOUR OF THEIR BONNETS, CALLED HATCHEE MATCHEE.

1st. Ching neéstchoo noo Hat´chee mat´chee { A pink ground with spots, circles, and diamonds, of black, yellow, blue, white, and green.

2nd. A´cadjee noo Hat´chee mat´chee { A pink ground with spots, &c. of red and yellow, blue and black.

3rd. O´jee noo Hat´chee mat´chee { A green ground with spots, &c. of red, yellow, blue, and black.

4th. Moóla sat´chee noo Hat´chee mat´chee { A pink or light purple ground, with spots of the same colour.

122

5th. Cheéroo dínjee noo Hat´chee { A dingy yellow ground, with spots of
mat´chee { the same colour.
6th. Cheéroo sy ya noo Hat´chee { A bright yellow ground without
mat´chee { spots.
7th. Chíddeeming noo Hat´chee { A red ground without spots.
mat´chee
8th. Akása noo Hat´chee mat´chee - A red ground without spots.
9th. O´sa noo Hat´chee mat´chee - A green ground without spots.
The attendants of the chiefs wear a red Hatchee matchee of a coarser texture.

TATTOO MARKS ON THE ARMS OF SOME OF THE NATIVES OF THE GREAT LOO-CHOO ISLAND.

1. 3.

Right arm. Right arm. Left arm.
This man had [Illustration: [Illustration: [Illustration:
not any mark Oódeemaw.] Oódeemaw.] toóga.]
on the left
arm.

2. 4.

Right arm. Right arm. Left arm.
[Illustration: [Illustration] [Illustration:
Coódee Oódemaw.] toóga.]
The four men, whose arms were marked in the above manner, were young and of the lower order, probably fishermen. It appeared to have been done by puncturing the skin, and staining it with Indian ink in the manner practised by our seamen.

The above marks are quite as large as the originals; they were on the inner part of the fore arm, close up to the elbow joint. Some were marked on both arms, others only on the right, but we did not observe any who had them only on the left arm.

NAMES OF THE HOURS.

One hour, or one o'clock It´chee twit´chee }
Two hours, or two Nee twit´chee }
Three Sang twit´chee } The day
Four Shee twit´chee }
Five Goo twit´chee }
Six Roócoo twit´chee }
Seven Sit´chee twit´chee }
Eight Fat´chee twit´chee }
Nine Coo twit´chee } The night.
Ten Joo twit´chee }
Eleven Joo it´chee twit´chee}
Twelve Joo nee twit´chee }
The day at Loo-Choo, i.e. between sunrise and sunset, is divided into six hours, as is also the night.

COMPARISON BETWEEN THE JAPANESE AND LOO-CHOO LANGUAGES.
NOTE.
The following comparisons are given, with the view of pointing out as nearly as circumstances will permit what resemblance there is between the languages of the islands of Loo-Choo, Niphon, or Japan, and Insu, lying in the Japan Sea, and which by some voyagers have been considered the same language.

In the first comparison, viz. that between the languages of Loo-Choo and Japan, the Japanese words are extracted from the translation of Thunberg's Voyage to Japan, printed in London 1795, 2d edit. vol. iii.

In the second, viz. that between Loo-Choo and Insu, the Insu words are taken from Broughton's Voyage.

A third comparison is given between the languages of Loo-Choo, Niphon, and Insu, together with the two sets of Numerals in use at Loo-Choo, the Japanese from Thunberg, and the Insu from Broughton.

It ought to be recollected that as Mr. Thunberg was a foreigner, and wrote in a different language from that in which the Loo-Choo words have been recorded, a difference of sound may be suspected between them when no material difference really exists between the two languages.

The letter u has been substituted in the spelling of the Japanese words for the v used by Thunberg.

COMPARISON BETWEEN THE JAPANESE AND LOO-CHOO LANGUAGES.

English. Japanese[129]. Loo-Choo.

All Mei Innea.
Anchor Ikari Eki.
Angry Fandatsuru Neetsa.
Answer, to Fento suru Aree ga aanyoong.
Arm Ude Teenoo.
Arrow Ja Eea.
Attendant Sairio Eeree.
Bad Warikakuse Neesha, or Wasa.
Bake, to Jaku Irree-chang.
Bare (naked) Haguru Harraka.
Bed Nedokuri Coocha.
Belly Stabara Watta.
Bend, to Oru Tammeeoong.
Bird Tori Hotoo.
Birdcage Tori no su Hotoo coo.
Bitter Nigaka Injassa.
Blood Tji, or Kjets Chee.
Blow, up the fire, to Fuku Footchoong.
Boat Temma Timma.
Boil, to Tagiru Tajeeing.
Bone Fone Cootsee.
Book Somots Sheemootsee.
Bow Jumi Yoomee.
Branch of a tree Jeda Kee.
Brass Sintju Cheejackkoo.
Breadth Jakohaba Habba.
Breast Mone Moonee.
Breathe, to Ikitsuku Itchooshoong.
Bridge Fae, hae Hashee.
Brother Kiodai Weekee.
Bucket Tango Tagoo.
Button Botan Kogannee.
Calf of the leg Stosone Koonda.
Candle Rosoku Daw.
Candlestick Rosoks tatti Soo-coo.
Cannon Issibia Isheebeea.
Carry away, to Mootsu Mootchee eechoong.
Cat Mio Mia.
Charcoal Sumi Chacheejing.
Cheeks Hogeta, fo Hoo.
Child Kodoma Warrabee.
Circle Maru Maroodair.
Castle, or tower Siro, so Eegooscoo.
Climb, to Nagoru Noobooyoong.
Cloth So king Ching.
Cock Otori Woo tooee.
Cold Samka kang Feesa.
Compass Fobari Karahigh.
Colour Iro Eeroo ceeroo.
Come, to Kuru Choong.
Cool Sususi Seedasha.
Copper Akaganni Acoogannee.
Count, to Kansju Oohawkoo-oong.
Cow Us Mee ooshee.
Creep, to Fau Hawyoong.
Cup, tea Tiawang Chawung.
Dark Mime Coorasing.
Daughter Musme, gogo Innago oongua.
Deep Fukai Fookassa.

124

Dig, to Foli Ooehoong.
Die Sinnoru sinu Nintoong.
Dice Saii Sheego roocoo.
Door To Hashirree.
Dog Inu Ing.
Drink Nomimono Noomoo.
Drink, to Nomu Noomoong.
Drunk, to be Namoji jeikfsari Weeoong.
Duck, tame Afiru Afeeroo.
Dry, to Karruru Karachoong.
Earth, the Tji dsi Jee.
Ear Mimi Mimmee.
East Figasi Fingassee.
Egg Tamago Cooga.
Elbow Ude, fisi Tenoo feejee.
Empty, to Akwuru Karashoong.
Exchange, to Kajuru Kayra (fans); to exchange
                         fans at Loo-Choo.
Face Tsera Steera.
Fall, to Tawareta Tawshoong.
Fan Oge Ojee.
Farewell Kingo, nigoserru Wockkatee.
Father Tete, toto Shoo.
Fat Kojuru Quaitee.
Feather Tori no fa Tooee noo hannee.
Fin, a fin Jokofiri fire Hannay.
Finger Jubi Eebee.
Find, to Midassu Toomatung.
Fire Fi, finoko Fee.
Fish Iwo, sakkana Eeo.
Fish Iwo tsuru Eeo kakeeoong.
Fishing net Ami Sheebee.
Flag, a Hato Hata.
Flower Fanna Fanna.
Fly, a Hai Hayeh.
Fly, to Toobu Toobeeoong.
Friend Ftoobai Eedooshee.
Foot Assi Shanna.
Firewood Takigi Tamoong.
Full Mits Meetchetee.
Girl Komusime Tackkee.
Girdle Skimmawas sansakagi Obee.
Give, to Fureru, jaru Queeoong.
Go down to Ururu, iru Ooritteo coo.
Go up to Aguru Noobooyoong.
Goat, he Jagi Woo feeja.
Gold Sin Ching.
Good Jukka Choorasa.
Good man Jukka fito Yookachoo.
Good for nothing Jonaka Maconarang.
Hair Kami Kurrazzee.
Hammer Kanatsutji Gooshung.
Hand Tee Kee.
Handkerchief Te no goi Teesadgee.
Hat Kasa Kassa.
Head Kubi Boosee.
Head-ache Attamanna, itama, Seebooroo yadong.
                    dutso
Heart Kokurro, sing Nacoo.
               singnoso
Hear, to Kikf Sitchoong, or skitchoong.
Heavens Ten Ting.

125

Heavy Omoka, omotaka Boosa.
Hen, a Mendori, metori Meetooee.
Hide, to Kaksu Meerang.
Hip Momo Gammacoo.
Hole, or cavity Anna Anna.
Horn Tsunno, kaku Stinnoo.
Horse Aki uma Ma.
Hot Atska Atteesa.
House Je Ya, or katchee.
Ink Sum, sumi Simmee.
Inkstand Susumi hake Simmee shee.
Iron Tets, furoganni Titzee.
Key Kagi Quaw.
Kill, to Korossu Sheenoung, or
                    Koorashoong.
Kiss Umakutji, or Sheemirree.
                Kwutjisu
Kiss, to Umakutji suru Coochee spootee.
Knife Haka Seego.
Knee Fisa, fisa no sarra Stinsee.
Kneel, to Fisatatsuru Shumma gitcheeoong.
Knot, a Fimmo Coonja cootchee.
Laugh, to Warau Worrayoong.
Learning, or studying Narau, Kicku Cootooba.
Letter, or character Moisi, tsi mousi Jee.
Lift to, a thing Motjiagaru Moochoong.
Light to, a pipe Fitobusu, fitomusu Sheeoong.
Lip Tsuba Seeba.
Liquor Sakki Sackkeedia, or
                    Samtchoo (Chinese).
Look to, or see Miru Meeoong, or meeing.
Looking-glass Kagami Kagung.
Long, or length Nagai Nagása.
Lose, to Song suru, makuru Ootoochung.
Live, to Inotji Simmatong.
Lacker, to Makie saru Nooyoong.
Man (homo) Momo Choo.
Man (vir) Otoko Ickkeega.
Mast Hobasi Hasseeda.
Mat Tattami Mooshooroo, or Hatung.
Match (fire-stick) Skedakki, skegi Kaw.
Measure, to Siakf, monosasa Gaujee hackkiyoong.
Mew, to (like a cat) Neko, naku Nachoong deeoong.
Milk Tji tji tji Chee.
Monkey Saru, salu Saroo.
Moon Tsuki Stchay.
——, full Mangets Oostitchee, or maroo.
Mother Fasa kasa Umma.
Mud Noro Dooroo.
Nail, finger Tsume, jassuru Thimmee.
Naked Hadaka Harraka.
Name Na Na.
Navel Fosso, feso Whoosoo.
Neck Kwabi, nodor Coobee.
Needle Fari Hayee skittee.
Night Josari, joru Yooroo.
Nipples Tjibusa Chee.
Nod, to Gatting suru Najeechoong.
North Kitta Cheeta.
Nose Fanna Honna.
Nostrils Fanna nosu Honnakee.
Offer, to Okuru, agurujasiagu- Ozagadee.

126

ru, nedoaskuru

Old Tassijori, furuje Teeshooee.

furuke

Open, to Akuru Akeeoong.

Overturn, to Tawaruru Kooroobashoong.

Paper Kami Kabee.

Pencil Fuda Hoodee.

Physician Isa Ishsha.

Pinch, to Nesumu Katcheemeeoong.

Pipe (tobacco) Kiseru Shirree.

Play to, with dice Sugoroko utsu Sheegoroocoo ochoong.

Plough Seri, seribetta, Sitchee.

tsuku tauts

Plough, to Togajassu Sitchoong.

Pour in, to Tsugu Irreeing.

Powder (gun) Jenso Eenshoo.

Pregnant Mimotji, farami Kassee jeetaung.

Press, to Siburu Sheetskeeoong.

Priest Boos Bodzee.

Push, to Sukikakaru Kooroobashoong.

Quarrel, to Ijou Titskoong.

Quick Faijo, faijaki Hayee.

Rain Ame Amee.

Rain, to Ame no fiuru Amee fooyoong.

Rainbow Nisi Noo, oojee.

Rat Nisumi Ack a-sa.

Read, to Jomu Yoomoong.

Rice Kome Coomee.

Rice, boiled Mes Umbang.

Ride, to, a horse Noru Manayoong.

Ring (finger) Ibiganni Eebee gannee.

Root Ne Wee-ee.

Rope Tsuna no na Chinna.

Round Mami Marroosa.

Row, to, in a boat Roosu Coojee.

Run, to Ajiubu Hayay sitchoong.

Sail Hoo Foo.

Salt Siwo Mashoo.

Salt water Siwo mis usiwo Spookarasa meezee.

Salute, to Resuru Kameeoong.

Sand Tsunna Sinna.

Scrape, to Kusagu Sajoong.

Screw Nesi Jirree.

Sea Ume Ooshoo.

Seal Fang hang ingjo Ing, or fang.

See, to Miru Meeoong.

Seed Tanna Ni.

Separate, to Saru Wockkayoong.

Serpent Kutjinawa hebi Haboo.

Sew, to No, noi Nawyoong, or noayoong.

Shallow Assai assaka Assassa.

Shave, to Soru Sooyoong.

Shell Kai Oosheemaw.

Ship Fune Hoonee.

Shoe Kwutsu Sabock.

Shoulders Kata Kutta.

Sick Itami mono, bioki Yadong.

mono, jamai mono

Silk Kinno Eechoo.

Silver Gin Jing.

Sing, to Utau Ootashoong, or ootayoong.

Sister (eldest) Musme are Oui.

127

Sleep Nur Nintee.
Sleep, to Nuru Ninjoong.
Slow Sisukamai, jojajora Yoona, yawna.
Small Ko, komaka Coosa.
Smell Nivi, niwoi Kabbasha.
Smell, to Kusamu Kannoung, kashashoong.
Smoke Honoo Kinsee.
Smoke, to Kemoli Footchoong.
Smoke tobacco, to Tabaco, nomu Tobacco, footchoong.
Sneeze, to Aksingu Honna feeoong.
Snore, to Ibikikaku Nintoong.
Snuff Fanna, tabak, kagi Spachee, honna, tob*
Sour Suika Seesa.
South Minami Whfa, or fa.
Speak, to Monoju, musmasu, Moonooyoong.
                    ju, moosuru
Spectacles Meganni, fanna, Meekagung.
                    meganni
Spider Kwumo Cooba.
Spittle Subakki Simpaee.
Spit, to Subakki, hawk Simpayoong.
Spoon Saisi Kaa.
Square Sikaku Kackkoo.
Stand up, to Okiru Tatteeoong.
Stars Fosi Fooshee.
Stone Isi iwa Ishee.
Strike, to Wutsu, utsu, tataku Rejeecoong.
Sugar Satto Sata.
Sun Fi, nitji Teeda.
Sunset Fi no iri Teeda sagayoong.
Sunrise Fino, de, fino, Teeda agayoong.
                    agaru
Swallow, to Nomikomu Noonootoosha.
Sweet Amaka, amai Amasa.
Swim, to Ojugu Weejoong.
Thigh Momo, solomomo Moomoo.
Thread Ito Eechoo.
Throw, to Naguru Naging.
Thumb Ojajubi, ojubi Hooee eebee.
Tiger Tora Toora.
Tin Susu Sheedookannee.
Tongue Sta, sita Stcha.
Tooth Jea Ha.
Touch, to Kamau, kakaru, Sayoong, or Sitchoong.
                    ateru
Tower To Eegooscoo.
Town Matji, sotomatji Mecatto, metto.
Tremble Fururu Koorooyoong.
Ugly Kisannai Ootooroosa.
Umbrella Fisasi Shassee kassa.
Vein Susi Kajee.
Wake, to Okiteoru Ooking.
Waken, to Okusu Oocatee.
Walk, to Ita Atchoong.
Warm Nakka, atska Attesa.
Wash Arau Arayoong.
Watch Tokei Karahigh.
Water Mis Meezee.
Water tub Furo Meezofwokee.
Weather, fine Jukka, fiuri, jui Yeetinchee, or tinsee.
                    teng
Weather, foul Warri fiuri Yannatinchee, or tinsee.

128

Well, a Jgawa Meezee ka.
West Nis Neeshee.
Wet Naroru Inneetee.
Wet, to Narassu Indeetaoong.
Wheel Kuruma Coorooma.
Wick of a candle Suku, saku Skee cootshee.
Wind Kase Kassee.
Wind up, to Sutsumu Feenoyoong.
Wing Toobu fanne Hannay.
Wink, to Manaku Meeoochee.
Wood Tagi Tamoong.
Write Kaku Katchoong.
Writing desk Fikidassi Sheekoo.
Year Fosi Ning.
Young Wakai Wockka.

FOOTNOTES:

[Footnote 129: From Thunberg's Voyage.]

NUMERALS.

Japan. Insu[130]. Loo-Choo.

1 Stozee Sheeneap Stitz Itchee Teetsee, tee.
2 Statze Too Statz Nee Tatsee, ta.
3 Mitzee Liep Mitz Sang Meetsee, mee.
4 Yeatze Eenep Yeatze Shee Eotsee, yoo.
5 Idotzee Asheak Itseitzy Goo Ittitsee.
6 Nitzee Ewan Nitz Roocoo Mootsee.
7 Nanatzee Arrawan Nanatzy Stehee Nannatsee.
8 Iosee Toopish Yeatz Fatchee Eyatsee.
9 Kikonitz Lepish Kokonitz Coo Koonnitsee.
10 Yoo Wanna Too Joo Too.

FOOTNOTES:

[Footnote 130: From Broughton's Voyage.]

COMPARISON BETWEEN THE LANGUAGES OF LOO-CHOO AND INSU. AN ISLAND IN THE JAPAN SEA.

English. Insu[131]. Loo-Choo.

Come here Arkee Cung coo.
To walk Appeass Atchoong.
To enquire the name of Tambene Noondeega.
 any thing
A ship Penzy, or Foonil. Hoonee.
A bow Koo Yoomee.
An arrow Ay Eea.
The beard Creak Feejee.
The teeth Meemack Ha.
A man Oikyo Ickkeega.
A woman Meanako Innago.
Fish net Ya Sheebee.
Tobacco pipe Tsheeree Shirree.
Water Wakha Meezee.
To drink Horopsee Noomoong.
A book Shoomootza Sheemootsee.
The finger Yewbee Eebee.
The thumb O yewbee Hoee eebee.
The thigh Momo Moomoo.
The arm Oondee Teenoo.
The middle finger Nagayewbee Nackkaeebee.
Paper Kame Kabee.
A dog Enoo Ing.
A cat Necko Mia.
A child Vasasso Warrabee.
The foot Assee Shanna.
The chin Olongyse Ootooga.
The ear Meemee Mimmee.

129

Yes O Oo.
No Ny Oongba.
Hair Kamu Kurrazzee.
A boat Timma Timma.
Tea Tcha Cha.
Sugar Sado Sata.
Tobacco Tabacco Tobacco.

FOOTNOTES:
[Footnote 131: From Broughton's Voyage.]

COMPARISON BETWEEN THE LANGUAGES OF LOO-CHOO, JAPAN, AND INSU.

English. Japanese[132]. Loo-Choo. Insu[133].

To walk Ita Atchoong Appeass.
A ship Fune Hoonee Penzy, or foonil.
A bow Jumi Yoomee Koo.
An arrow Ja Eea Ay.
The finger Jubi Eebee Askippi, yewbee.
The teeth Ha Ha Meemack.
A man Otoko Ickkeega Oikyo.
A fish net Ami Sheebee Ya.
A knife Haka Seego Magiddee.
An oar Ro Wayacoo Kanzee.
Water Mis Meezee Wakha.
To drink Nomu Noomoong Horopsee.
A book Somots Sheemootsee Shomotza.
The thumb Ojajubi, ojubi Hooee eebee O yewbee.
The thigh Momo, soto momo Moomoo Momo.
The arm Ude Teenoo Oondee.
Paper Kami Kabee Kame.
A dog Inu Ing Enoo.
A cat Mio, neko Mia Necko.
A child Kodoma Warrabee Vassasso.
The lips Tsuba Seeba Koodge.
The foot Assi Shanna Assee.
The ear Mimi Mimmee Meemee.
The hair Kami Kurrazzee Karnu.
A boat Temma Timma Timma.
Tea Tsjaa Cha Tcha.
Sugar Satto Sata Sado.
Tobacco Tabako Tobacco Tabacco.

FOOTNOTES:
[Footnote 132: From Thunberg's Voyage.]
[Footnote 133: From Broughton's Voyage.]

WORDS OBTAINED FROM THE INHABITANTS OF THE WEST COAST OF COREA.

English. Corean.

No Poodong.
Water Bool.
A pipe Dewton.
Hair Bodee.
Eyes Doon.
Mouth Jeep.
Nose Ko.
Hand So-an.
Beard Shee-om.
Tongue Chay.
Ear Quee.
Teeth Jee.
Tree[134] Phang na moo.
Grass[134] Phee.
Good[134] Hota.
Earth[134] K,hool.

Knife[134] Khul.
Jacket Chouksa.
Trowsers Choongay.
Shoe Po schien.
Stockings, or boots Hung inn.
Tobacco pouch Samb-jee.
Rice (food) Pa-ap.
Fan Pootsa.
Stove Tok.
White hat Pan-a-ee.
Black hat Kat.
A cock Tac.

FOOTNOTES:

[Footnote 134: These five words have the *h* so strongly aspirated that it was rarely we could pronounce them to the satisfaction of the natives.

Their language, upon the whole, is not unpleasing, and it has none of the harsh Chinese sounds. The natives have a remarkable facility in imitating our sounds, and they in general speak in a very loud tone of voice.]

CPSIA information can be obtained at www.ICGtesting.com
Printed in the USA
BVOW06s1648290416

446122BV00029B/645/P